# Killer Cops
## An Encyclopedia
## of
## Lawless Lawmen
### *by Michael Newton*

D1519904

**Loompanics Unlimited**
**Port Townsend, Washington**

*This book is sold for informational purposes only. Neither the author nor the publisher will be held accountable for the use or misuse of the information contained in this book.*

# Killer Cops
**An Encyclopedia of Lawless Lawmen**
© 1997 by Michael Newton

**Published by:**
Loompanics Unlimited
PO Box 1197
Port Townsend, WA 98368
Loompanics Unlimited is a division of Loompanics Enterprises, Inc.
1-360-385-2230

Cover by King Velveeda

**ISBN 1-55950-171-5**
**Library of Congress Card Catalog 97-80366**

# Contents

# Dedication

*For Harry Callahan and Al Shockley.*

# Author's Note

The text of *Killer Cops* is limited in scope to American lawmen. This restriction was adopted for purely practical reasons, since expansion to a global survey would have made the work at hand unmanageable. Such a comprehensive volume would, of necessity, have stretched to millions of pages — including histories of Nazi Germany and fascist Italy, South Africa, Tsarist Russia and the Soviet Union, sundry Communist regimes, Arab sheikdoms and Third World dictatorships. It would, in effect, fill a library, rather than a single book. Within America itself, the survey is restricted to the 19th and 20th centuries, again for practical reasons — namely, the availability of source material. Some latitude has been enjoyed with cases from the 19th century, when murderous lawmen were more likely to escape legal punishment (and because the subjects are deceased, hence unable to sue for libel). With one exception, wherein the officer admitted his crime but escaped punishment with an insanity plea, 20th-century cases have been selected on the basis of (a) felony convictions related to deliberate, malicious homicides and/or (b) public identification of particular officers as prime murder suspects in the statements of prosecutors and investigating officers. Several cases resulting in manslaughter convictions are omitted because they resulted from accidental deaths (as in drunk driving) or from "marginal" line-of-duty killings (as the shooting of a suspect who is later found to be unarmed). Names in **bold type** indicate subjects with their own discrete entries elsewhere in the text. Special thanks for contributions to the work in hand are owed to Dave Frasier at Indiana University, Rod Poteete in Las Vegas, and Sondra London.

# Foreword
## by Sondra London

In June of 1990, Loompanics author Jim Hogshire wrote an article on serial killers for an Indianapolis paper which profiled killer cop G.J. Schaefer, the serial killer I had dated as a teenager. It was through Hogshire's article that I first became aware of Michael Newton.

"Anything outrageous or shocking, I want to know about it," was the pull-out quote Hogshire chose to emphasize Newton's interest in the macabre. That was the first time I read the name of the author who has fast become one of the most significant crime encyclopedists of modern times.

Like anyone with a consuming professional interest in criminal history, I keep Newton's seminal work, *Hunting Humans: An Encyclopedia of Modern Serial Killers* (Loompanics, 1990), on my top shelf, and refer to it often. I have learned to rely on any book by Michael Newton; the data he provides is unfailingly comprehensive and accurate.

All too often, so-called "true" crime books comprise little more than sloppy rehashes of second-hand tales from unreliable witnesses, combined with official disinformation, gratuitous speculation, and embellishment upon insufficient data. A plague of this sort of embarrassment has recently resulted in an exodus of qualified authors from the field. Among the stalwarts adhering to high standards stands the redoubtable Michael Newton.

Meticulous about his research, he manages to retain an inexhaustable store of knowledge. Dozens of times I have called Mike needing arcane datum on some psychopathic phenomenon or other, and without fail he has been able to immediately provide the information I required, right off the top of his head.

Having published 130 books to date, Newton is nothing if not prolific. While prolific is not the same as provocative, persuasive, or praiseworthy, fortunately for the reader of this volume he is all this and more.

The reader will not only be informed, but entertained by this compendium of profiles of these oxymoronic creatures, these rogue cops who violate the spirit as well as the letter of the law to the utmost extent, by taking the very lives they have sworn to protect and defend.

From swaggering gunslingers to unrepentant racists, languid lady-killers to crooked con-hustlers, *muy macho* men to killer drag queens — the names and dates, the facts and figures of their felonious escapades are all here. The usual motives (money and women, drugs and guns, sick kicks and good old-fashioned sport-slaying) all provided their impetus for these paragons of rectitude, turning them into what surely must be our worst nightmare: the killer cop.

Newton's trademark mordant sense of humor comes through in his deadpan juxtapositions of the most implacably sordid circumstances with the trifling, chilling, and often absurd comments offered by the errant lawmen as their dark and deadly deeds came to light.

"Instead of nine, I wish I could be up here for 99," boasted one miscreant on the witness stand, who smugly concluded, "Somebody had to kill these people."

But not every deadly detective was so nonchalant about his crimes. "I just killed three people!" whispered one to his shift supervisor over the phone. In a spasm of contrition, he begged, "Please catch me before I kill more." Then, putting an enigmatic spin on his plea, he taunted gleefully, "I'm going to kill more tonight, too!"

Others seemed to reveal a sense of entitlement in their comments. When a Texas Ranger by the unlikely name of Bass Outlaw was caught red-handed in the fatal act by a fellow lawman who asked why he did it, he snarled, "Do you want some, too?" and shot his comrade in the head. After surrendering, he died screaming, "Oh God! Where are my friends?" One has to wonder at the malignant twist of fate that led this Outlaw who was sworn to uphold the law to fulfill the promise of his surname.

The obscure cases Newton presents here demonstrate his indefatigable research into the dark corners of criminal history. With the more well-known cases, he reveals a factual side of a story that may have been virtually obscured by the Hollywood myth-making machinery. An outstanding case in point is Newton's revisionist history of the legendary Wyatt Earp, a gunslinging gambler billed as "famous in the cheerful business of depopulating the county" around Dodge City in the 1870s.

From Newton we learn that in fact the infamous gunfight at the O.K. Corral did not even *occur* at the O.K. Corral, but rather in an alley next to a photographic studio run by a gentleman with the colorful name of Camillus Fly; that Wyatt Earp and Bat Masterson were brawlers known as the "Fighting Pimps"; and that Earp spent his final days haunting Hollywood soundlots, befriending cowboy stars such as Tom Mix and William S. Hart, and trying to interest someone in his life and legend.

More up-to-date are the likes of Manny Pardo. He was a bad cop from the beginning, falsifying documentation of over 100 traffic violations in his first year with the Florida Highway Patrol. Six years later, after being fired from another law enforcement position, he was connected to nine cocaine-related slayings in five months, and sent to death row, where he distinguished himself by conning supporters through the mail and ripping off money from women he claimed to love.

One of Pardo's self-described friends wrote to *The Orlando Sentinel Tribune*, pointing out that "each of his (Pardo's) victims was a thoroughly investigated, tried, convicted, and executed (by him) drug dealer whom Pardo had failed to get off the streets via the normal criminal justice system," concluding that instead of condemnation, this killer cop deserved a commendation!

In 1996, when several deceived women complained about this death row inmate being allowed to prey on them, a spokesperson for the Florida Department of Corrections responded that Manny

Pardo had broken no regulations with his pitiful but productive pleas to send money, observing that "Florida statutes have ruled it illegal to deny inmates that privilege, because doing so would deny them access to the outside world."

And so, as Newton observes, "With others who have killed repeatedly across the Sunshine State, he (Pardo) takes his ease with pen in hand and plays the waiting game."

G.J. Schaefer was another killer cop who whiled away his time with pen in hand at Florida State Prison.

From 1989 to 1993, the former boyfriend who had become a hardened criminal sent me thousands of pages of extraordinary prose. Part of that output was published early on, but while Schaefer was penning the homicidal scenarios he called "killer fiction," he was also sending me explicit murder confessions — bound up with death threats, were I to reveal them to law enforcement. At the same time Schaefer attempted to blame me for all the killings he had done, because 25 years earlier when he told me about his homicidal urges, I had left him instead of "helping" him.

Throughout his entire life, Schaefer embodied extreme contradictions. Besides being a cop and a killer, he was also an inveterate snitch. The combination makes a lethal mix, as he found out in the end.

In 1990, Joel Norris, the late author of *Serial Killers: The Growing Menace*, expressed an interest in co-authoring a book about Schaefer with me. Schaefer was puzzled about the nickname Norris had given him, "The Sex Beast," protesting that his were not sex crimes and that the press had never called him that.

When pressed, Norris could not cite a source to justify claiming that this was Schaefer's tag. Mike Newton observed from the sidelines that it was Melvin Rees who had been known as The Sex Beast, and suggested that Norris had juxtaposed his serial killers. Schaefer gave Newton points for discovering the secret of the spurious sobriquet, but remained as skeptical about him as he had been about Norris.

In July of 1990, after reading Jim Hogshire's article, Schaefer wrote, "Interesting story about Newton. I can't wait to see what sort of lies he printed about me in his book. The Joel Norris lies were pretty good. Encyclopedias are supposed to be real factual, so Newton's lies will be even better, ultimately, than those of Norris." Ten days later, after reading Newton's entry about him in *Hunting Humans,* Schaefer conceded, "Newton seemed sane and fair minded."

In mid-January of 1992, Schaefer was considering allowing me to collaborate with Newton on what he called his True Story, or "TS." "MIKE NEWTON: I had a letter from him. Answered it," he wrote. "I think he is qualified to run with the TS so I'm tentatively agreeable."

But a bare two weeks later, Schaefer realized that Newton was not buying into either his "framed ex-cop" alibi or his "misunderstood author" persona. Like myself, Newton believed Schaefer was every bit the classic serial killer he appeared to be.

Then the other side of Schaefer's pernicious personality began to surface. "Nobody is gonna... print that I'm a [serial killer]... without getting sued by me. That includes... Norris, Newton, you or anyone else."

Schaefer went on to issue veiled threats, suggesting that Mike Newton "... drop it, or he can learn first hand what a vicious, single minded litigator I can be because I'll not only sue him, I'll have him arrested on a formal criminal complaint..."

By April of 1992, the serial litigator had made it quite clear that he would not cooperate. "Please contact Mike Newton and have him return to you all the material you've sent him concerning myself and my case," he wrote in one of his more lucid moments.

By the end of 1993, Schaefer's letters to me had deteriorated almost exclusively to threats, and I'd had the prison put a block on any mail from him addressed to me. Not to be deterred, Schaefer routed his noxious ravings to Paul Woods, publisher of *Knockin' on Joe,* a British anthology of prison writings containing Schaefer's "Starke Stories":

> *I am a former street cop who is in open population in perhaps America's most repressive hellhole. I am not in a protective confinement cell: I walk the yard like a man. My closest associate in this slimepit is an Anointed Fourth Prince of the Hand of Death who was a contract killer for the Mafia... All I need to do is ask this gentleman to have SL and her kid murdered and it would be done. SL is alive at this moment because I choose to allow it.... She is vile beyond contempt... a thief and a liar. I've already sued Robert Ressler... I am suing all persons... who have libeled me. Suits are already filed against... Michael Newton, Loompanics, Robert Ressler, Joel Norris and others.*

All Schaefer's lawsuits were dismissed, because as a friend of the court, I submitted into evidence his handwritten confessions on behalf of a list of defendants that reads like a *Who's Who of True Crime*.

In *Schaefer v. Michael Newton* the court ruled that Schaefer is "a serial killer undoubtedly linked to numerous murders" and in *Schaefer v. Colin Wilson*, Schaefer was declared "libel-proof under the law."

In December of 1995, Schaefer was hacked to death in his prison cell. Vincent Rivera, who stands accused of the slaying, denies any culpability. The official version of the motivation for Schaefer's slaying is that he used up all the hot water in the dispenser, but inside sources suggest that it was Schaefer's twisted identity as killer cop and serial snitch that did him in at last.

# Introduction

Who will watch the watchman? Who polices the police?

We literally trust them with our lives from day to day. They have the power to detain, arrest, interrogate, or even kill, if circumstances justify the use of deadly force. Most times, when blood is spilled and lives are lost, investigators — typically selected from the same police department where the shooter draws his paycheck — find the killing to be "justified." In cases where the suspect proves to be unarmed, they speak of stress, poor visibility, and "threatening" behavior on the part of the deceased.

In 1992, the last year with statistics available, American police killed some 415 persons, coast to coast; there is no accurate report of suspects shot and wounded. We may assume that in most cases, where police were physically assaulted or recovered weapons at the scene, those deaths were justified as self-defense. Some instances — a teenage car thief shot while running from a stolen vehicle, the "gunman" who turns out to be unarmed — spark protest in minority communities, but few result in charges being filed. Before the 1980s, it was practically impossible for prosecutors to pursue a case against police who killed a suspect under any circumstances, and the rare attempts most often ended in acquittal. Times are changing, slowly, but the fact remains that officers who kill without due cause are still more likely to receive a commendation than a prison sentence.

We Americans enjoy a strange love-hate relationship with our police. On one hand, cops make up a "thin blue line" that marks the boundary between a civilized society and chaos; on the other, they are "fascist pigs," quick-trigger bullies hired specifically to keep the lid on an imperfect melting pot. We love the cop who talks a jumper down or rescues children from a burning tenement... until he pulls us over on the street and writes that ticket out for driving 60 miles an hour in a 45-mile zone.

From Jack Webb's simple-minded *Adam-12* and *Dragnet* to the controversial *NYPD Blue*, that double standard has been nurtured by the media. We cheer when Dirty Harry tortures villains on the silver screen, but cringe when L.A.'s finest use their clubs on Rodney King. At worst, in movies like *Bad Lieutenant, Internal Affairs*, and *Maniac Cop*, rogue policemen are promoted from their classic role as spoilsports to the mythic status of homicidal bogeyman.

In fact, the truth is we like our lawmen rough and ready with their fists and guns, as long as they are beating up or shooting someone who apparently deserves it. The frontier mystique is with us still, sometimes inflating reputations, oftentimes excusing violence that deserves a closer look — or prosecution as a felony. Frontier marshal Bat Masterson killed only one desperado in a stand-up fight, but his dime-novel exploits ran the score up to 20 or more, making him a legend in his own time. "Untouchable" Eliot Ness has killed dozens of gangsters on television and the silver screen, but his real-life model never fired a shot in anger at a living soul, in Chicago or anywhere else. On the flip side of that mythical coin, there *have* been lawmen who were bona fide prolific killers. Captain Frank Hamer, best known for his ambush of Bonnie Parker and Clyde Barrow in 1934, is said to have killed 40 or 50 gunmen during his career with the Texas Rangers, and Prohibition agent Clarence Pickering admitted gunning down 42 rum runners along the Canadian border in the 1920s.

Enforcing America's laws is admittedly risky business: in two centuries, from 1794 through 1993, an estimated 30,387 peace officers were killed in the line of duty. Over the same period, many times that number of civilians were shot, beaten, or otherwise fatally subdued in the name of law and order. (Records from only seven cities — Birmingham, Detroit, Indianapolis, Kansas City, Oakland, Portland, and Washington, DC — list 4,649 persons killed by police between 1960 and 1974, for an average of 332 killings per year.) And all too often, it seems, fictional portrayals of a "bad cop" have the ring of truth.

Early law enforcement in America demanded rugged men who were prepared to use their six-guns at the drop of a sombrero, facing down the worst of highwaymen and rustlers, cardsharps, thieves, scalp hunters, and the like. Unfortunately for the citizens they served, a disturbing number of frontier lawmen were also criminals themselves, inclined to rob a bank or stagecoach when the opportunity arose, often moonlighting as pimps and gamblers, never shy of settling a score by shooting unarmed adversaries in the back. Some wound up on the gallows for their crimes or were dispatched by local vigilance committees, others met their match to faster guns, but some — like **Wyatt Earp** — lived out their lives in peace, rewriting history to cast themselves as heroes of the lawless West.

Aside from criminal activity and private quarrels, racism and right-wing politics have prompted no end of homicidal police violence. Historically, from Reconstruction to the 1970s, American police have flocked to join the Ku Klux Klan and other groups devoted to the preservation of a "white man's country." Time and time again, police chiefs, sheriffs, and their officers have lent a hand in brutal lynchings, riots, floggings, and assassinations. In 1935, the police chief of Tampa, Florida, and several of his men — all members of the KKK — were charged with murder in the torture slaying of union organizer Joseph Shoemaker. All were acquitted, but the tide had turned three decades later, when Mississippi sheriff's deputy **Cecil Price** went to prison for his role in the murder of three civil rights workers. Far to the north, in Chicago, a pair of Ku Klux kops were jailed in 1968 for plotting to assassinate the city's mayor with a bazooka. In New York, around the same time, state police were among the latter-day Minutemen who planned to raid a hippie commune and slaughter its occupants.

Our nation's labor wars have often seen policemen drafted into service on the side of management, against the "radicals" and "revolutionaries" who went out on strike to win a decent wage. In many instances, they served the robber barons as official firing squads. From California's citrus ranches to the eastern coal fields and the Dixie cotton patches, police joined ranks with Pinkerton detectives and militia to enforce the status quo at any cost in blood and human suffering. Hundreds were slain in the half-century between Chicago's Haymarket riot, in 1886, and the 1937 Memorial Day massacre, wherein Windy City patrolmen opened fire on a peaceable union parade, killing ten unarmed marchers. On the rare occasions when a mercenary trigger man was charged with murder, juries bought and paid for by the rulers of the company town were certain to acquit.

For some corrupt policemen, homicide was strictly business. In New York, prior to World War I, Lieutenant **Charles Becker** ordered the murder of a gambler who threatened to blow the whistle on police corruption. Thirty-six years later, with another Mafia investigation underway, syndicate informer Abe Reles "jumped or fell" from the window of his sixth-floor room at Coney Island's Half Moon Hotel. The officers assigned to guard him passed his death off as a "prank" or suicide, and so the case was closed. Another 20 years would pass before retired mobster Lucky Luciano aired the truth: detectives on the guard detail received a $50,000 payoff to ensure that Reles testified at no more trials.

*Killer Cops* is not concerned with trigger-happy "cowboys" who pursue their duties with excessive zeal; it does not second-guess the officers whose handling of violent suspects leads to "accidental" deaths in custody. Instead, it lifts a different stone to scrutinize America's worst nightmare: sworn protectors of the law who use their badges as hunting licenses, killing on a whim for profit, sex, or personal revenge. No stretch of the imagination can describe their crimes — including torture, rape, dismemberment, and robbery — as justified. The officers depicted in these pages did not kill in panic, fearing for their lives, or by mistaking unarmed fugitives for deadly triggermen. Instead, they stalked "civilians" with the cunning skill of big-game hunters, using every trick at their disposal to protect themselves and cover up their crimes.

Despite their status as police, our subjects run the gamut of illegal, aberrant behavior. Several murdered total strangers in pursuit of sex, and some — by personal admission or from evidence produced in court — fit the recognized definition of sadistic serial killers. Others were inspired to kill by racial prejudice, while some were strictly mercenary, executing contract murders or bizarre insurance schemes. Corruption lured several officers to prey on criminals by stealing cash or drugs, assassinating anyone who jeopardized their plans. For others, jealousy or love affairs gone sour lit the deadly fuse of violence. No rank or agency has been immune from shame in this regard. Our cases span the continent and law enforcement's social scale, from small-town police departments to the hallowed FBI. Patrolmen stand convicted side-by-side with sergeants and lieutenants, chiefs and county sheriffs.

Jack Webb, portraying LAPD's Sergeant Joe Friday, once advised his TV audience that there would always be a few bad apples on the force "because we have to recruit from the human race." The cases singled out for *Killer Cops* reiterate that point, without indicting the police en masse. They illustrate that while abusers may be few and far between, and are bizarre exceptions to the rule, a better job can still be done at screening new police recruits and supervising veteran officers. In these times, when a fear of violent crime ranks high on every list of major problems in America, we must be ever-conscious of the public servants who defile their promise "to protect and serve."

# Alvord, Burt

The son of a traveling judge, born in 1866, Burt Alvord was 15 years old and living in Tombstone, Arizona, at the time of the infamous gunfight at the O.K. Corral. Though still a child, he recognized the underlying motive for the battle and the string of homicides that followed — namely, control of the county sheriff's office, which meant control of local vice and the collateral duty of collecting taxes, which might wind up in the sheriff's pocket instead of the local treasury. Five years later, in 1886, Alvord took his first step toward that coveted post, becoming chief deputy to newly elected Sheriff John Slaughter, in Cochise County.

**Burt Alvord**
*Courtesy of Denver Public Library,*
*Western History Division.*

At first, Alvord seemed intent on building up a reputation as a dedicated lawman, running down rustlers and thieves, but he soon turned to crime on the side. Sheriff Slaughter grew suspicious, but he had no evidence that would support indictments, and Alvord took over the sheriff's office when Slaughter retired in 1890. A few years later, Alvord switched to full-time rustling, with his headquarters in Mexico, but he returned to "law enforcement" by 1899, serving as a constable in Wilcox, Arizona. Local residents did not seem to mind his record as a gunman, including several known murders, and they were presumably unaware of Constable Alvord's latest sideline — at least, for a while.

Alvord was barely settled in Wilcox, when he forged an alliance with another corrupt lawman, **Billie Stiles**, to begin robbing trains. The gang was captured as a group after a stickup near Cochise, in September 1900, but Stiles orchestrated a jail-break, and they were soon back in business. Alvord and Stiles were jailed again in 1903, and once again they managed to escape. Tiring of life on the run, Alvord contrived to fake their deaths, sending caskets filled with their alleged remains back to Tombstone, but authorities saw through the trick and continued their search.

In 1904, a flying squad of Arizona Rangers followed Alvord into Mexico and cornered him at a place known as Nigger Head Gap. A brief shoot-out left Alvord wounded, and he was returned to Arizona for trial, serving two years in prison on various charges. Nothing certain is known of his life following parole: Alvord was reportedly sighted in Jamaica and sundry towns in Latin America before 1910, when the death of an obscure laborer on the Panama Canal wrote *finis* to a strange and wasted life.

## Anderson, James S.

A retired New York City policeman, James Anderson was known for his explosive temper on the home front, frequently engaging in domestic battles with his wife Sheilah. It was the second marriage for both, and both had children from prior unions, a fact which only served to aggravate their frequent quarrels. Booze helped, too, and it was sometimes difficult to tell which of them was the loudest or the most abusive. When it came to violence, though, James won the prize hands down. On one occasion, in New York, a friend of Sheilah Anderson's, Ron Blount, ordered James from his home over the officer's "threatening and abusive behavior" toward Sheilah. Later, when the couple was residing in Coral Gables, Florida, James brandished a butcher knife at Sheilah and her children, slashing up a waterbed and some of Sheilah's clothes. Later still, in New Hampshire, Sheilah petitioned a Plymouth judge for a restraining order against her husband, complaining that James "had been drinking and being abusive to her for two days." In the course of that rampage, he had tipped a bed over while Sheilah was in it, hurled furniture around their home, and set napkins on fire, threatening to burn down the house if she would not leave.

Sheilah Anderson had been missing for three days when her children, Christopher and Heather Grody, reported her missing from the couple's Alexandria, New Hampshire, home on June 15, 1993. James initially told investigators that Sheilah had gone shopping with a woman named Dianne — last name unknown — and had never returned. The story rang hollow, but in the absence of solid evidence, no charges could be filed. A short time later, following a bungled suicide attempt, James was held for observation at the state hospital, in Laconia. He was still there on July 2nd, when police corporal William Magee accompanied Heather and Sheilah's mother, Phyllis Reid, to the empty house. Their mission was to get some clothes for James, but it took a very different turn when Heather found a half-burned sneaker lying near the house. A few yards further on, Corporal Magee found evidence of a recent fire, including an ankle bracelet and fragments of bone he believed to be human. Medical examiner James Kaplan was summoned, confirming the find, and Magee then called in for a search warrant. A full-scale search began the next day, and while the charred remains were incomplete, most of the bone fragments burned beyond any scientific testing, a DNA match was established using one bone that apparently had been extracted from the burn pit by the family dog. Another fifteen months would pass before an open garbage bag, containing Sheilah's head and torso, was discovered in the woods nearby, identity confirmed from dental records. Those pitiful remains were also charred, and there was evidence of brutal beating: a hole in Sheilah's skull, together with a broken nose, a fractured jaw, and several shattered teeth.

James Anderson, meanwhile, was busy changing his story. Once the first lie was exposed, discounting Sheilah's shopping trip, he told detectives that she had committed suicide with a deliberate overdose of drugs. State Police Sergeant James Kelleher threw the suspect a curve ball, stating falsely that examination of the bones disproved the O.D. story, whereupon James changed his tune again. Sheilah indeed committed suicide, he said, but she had actually slit her wrists. At that point, something had come over him — the booze, perhaps — and he had burned her body, rather than simply picking up the telephone to report her death.

It was a flimsy tale at best, and Anderson was charged with murder in October 1994, his trial delayed for over a year by legal maneuvering. Defense attorneys Darcie Spence and Andrew Schulman tried to have the evidence, including Sheilah's bones, excluded on the grounds that Corporal Magee did not possess a warrant when he made the first discovery. In Sheilah's absence, they maintained, only the murderer himself could give permission for a warrantless search of the property, but prosecutors defeated that motion by pointing out that Phyllis Reid shared title to the house, having advanced the couple $69,000 for the original purchase. Next, the defense team tried to have Anderson's various contradictory statements stricken from the record, but James had repeatedly waived his right to silence in the presence of multiple witnesses. More to the point, he had also written a letter from jail, to one of his daughters, confessing the crime. It read in part:

> *Every night I had to hear from her "What are you go-*
> *ing to do?" Finally, on June 12, she started again, and I*
> *told her give me a night off. I do not want to hear this crap*
> *tonight, and she said to me, "Why should you care, your*
> *three daughters are a bunch of whores and uneducated."*
>
> *I went and got my switchblade and stabbed her in the*
> *stomach and said, "That is for calling my Julie a whore."*
> *Then I stabbed her again in the stomach and said, "That is*
> *for calling my Elizabeth a whore," and then I stabbed her*
> *again in the stomach and said, "That is for calling my*

*Dana a whore," and then I stabbed her in the chest and said, "You will never call my daughters whores again."*

Soon after writing that letter, on Christmas Eve 1995, Anderson and two other inmates assaulted corrections officer Ed Peterson in the Grafton County jail. The three were on their way to breakfast when prisoners Joseph Poitras and Henri Tallard grabbed Peterson's arms, Anderson kicking him in the ribs, stabbing his face with a ball-point pen, smashing a two-way radio over his head, and dragging Peterson along the floor with an electric cord wrapped around his neck. The guard suffered head lacerations, fractured ribs, and a bruised kidney before backup arrived to subdue the would-be escapees.

Three weeks after that incident, on January 16, 1996, James Anderson appeared in court and pled guilty to first-degree murder in Sheilah's death. Acting against the advice of his lawyers, Anderson said that he wanted "to get on with my life. It's been going on for two and a half years. I can't see going through a trial. I'm guilty." He admitted stabbing Sheilah four times, at the climax of another drunken argument, but denied beating her first or dismembering her remains. The details hardly mattered at that point, and Judge Peter Smith immediately sentenced Anderson to life imprisonment without parole. Six months later, he was back in court with another guilty plea for the Christmas Eve incident, admitting to assault, kidnapping, conspiracy, and attempted escape. Anderson drew a sentence of ten to 30 years for the assault, with an additional 7½ to 15 years on the other three counts. Informed that the new sentence would run consecutively with his life term, Anderson told the court, "It's okay."

# Baird, Carl

Carl Baird had been the chief of police in tiny Walpole, New Hampshire, for less than two years when he suddenly left his post on Thursday, February 10, 1994. The move was sudden, and local wags could not agree on whether he had resigned or been fired by the town's board of selectmen. The matter was still being debated on Saturday, February 12, when the 41-year-old ex-chief entered Walpole's town hall for the last time. Confronting one of the selectmen, 51-year-old Roger Santaw, Baird drew a pistol and pumped several shots into Santaw's chest, killing him where he stood.

Baird fled immediately, racing to his car and leaving Walpole, driving west across the state line to Vermont, stopping only when he reached Danby, some 35 miles away. Vermont authorities found him there, slumped in the seat of his vehicle, dead from a single self-inflicted gunshot to the head. In the aftermath of the tragedy, locals agreed that Baird and Santaw had been adversaries for some time, their conflict resulting in Baird's ouster from office, "but it was not known what the feud was about." In retrospect, Baird was described by those who knew him in life as "a quiet person who never showed much emotion" — that is, until the day when his buried rage erupted into lethal violence.

# Batsel, James: See McKenna, Mark

# Baughman, John Earl

On the night of July 26, 1970, a motorist reported sighting a body sprawled beside a gravel road, on the outskirts of Flossmoor, Illinois. Police responded to the rural lover's lane and found one of their own, Sergeant Dean F. Spence, stretched out dead on the ground. The 32-year-old officer was clad in a T-shirt and athletic shorts; he had been shot four times, in the face, chest, and right forearm. Discovery of his car nearby, with Spence's wallet in the glove compartment and the police radio disconnected, keys still in the ignition, seemed to rule out robbery in the case. There was no blood or sign of struggle in the victim's car, which led investigators to surmise that he was removed from his vehicle at gunpoint and afterward shot where his body was found.

Sgt. Edward Mayer, with the Will County sheriff's office, described Dean Spence as "a well-liked guy" who spent his free time coaching Little League and counseling youngsters in trouble. Janet Spence, employed as a waitress in a local pizzeria, had been working the night her husband was killed. She denied any knowledge of how or why Dean was murdered, but another woman in the area was not so reticent.

Agents from the Illinois Bureau of Investigation made a point of questioning the victim's friends. One such friend was John Baughman, a railroad detective who had once worked with Spence on the Homewood Police Department. Baughman also denied any knowledge of the killing, but his wife, Gertrude Baughman, told a very different story. In fact, she told investigators, she had been involved in a romantic affair with Dean Spence, and had recently confessed all to her husband. "John went to Dean and told him to back off," she said. "He later told me that Dean had ignored him. That's when John told me he shot Dean."

State police came calling on the Baughmans at home, on August 13th, and Gertrude repeated the story in front of her husband. John broke down in tears and admitted the shooting, whereupon he was driven to Joliet and lodged in the Will County jail. By that time, detectives had checked out his background and knew that Baughman had been fired from the Homewood P.D. after he was accused of burglarizing a local gas station. The formal charges included theft and official misconduct, resulting in immediate dismissal and a sentence of one year's supervised probation.

Confession to a murder should have been the end for John Baughman, but it didn't quite work out that way. By September 10th, when a grand jury met to consider his case, Baughman had retained an attorney and recanted his statement. Prosecutor Louis Bertani wanted more than oral statements from Baughman and his wife — the latter report mere hearsay, in any case — and the grand jury agreed, declining to charge Baughman without solid physical evidence.

The ex-cop and admitted killer returned to his wife and three children, apparently unfazed by his near-miss with justice. He was soon back at work on his job as a railroad detective, repairing clocks in his spare time, and life proceeded normally, from all appearances, for the next 14 years. Then, on a Saturday morning in April 1984, firefighters were summoned to the Baughman home in Matteson, Illinois, where they found Gertrude Baughman lying dead, severely burned, on the floor of the garage.

John Baughman, now a widower, was ready with an explanation of her death. The couple had been getting ready for a camping trip, he said, when Gertrude carelessly spilled a can of gasoline, which was ignited by a portable stove, setting fire to her clothing. Baughman had tried to extinguish the flames, but in vain. Autopsy results contradicted his story, however, Dr. Edmund Donaghue reporting that there was no soot in Gertrude's lungs, proof positive that she was dead before she burned. Furthermore, the medical examiner reported, severe bruising around Gertrude's throat indicated that she had been strangled first, then set afire when she was dead.

Baughman *was* indicted this time, on a charge of first-degree murder, and his trial convened in September 1985. Prosecutors suggested greed and revenge as twin motives, noting that Gertrude Baughman was heavily insured, suggesting that John still seethed with resentment over Gertrude's testimony against him in the 1970 Spence murder. A pathologist employed by the defense contradicted Dr. Donaghue in court, stating categorically that Gertrude was alive when she burned, informing the jury that any statement to the contrary would be "inadequate." Baughman, testifying in his own behalf, wept on the witness stand, denying any role in his wife's death. The damage to her neck was suffered, he maintained, as he grappled with her on the floor of the garage, trying to beat out the flames in her clothing.

Baughman's trial lasted four days, and jurors deliberated four hours before acquitting him on September 13, 1985. Six years later, at age 49, he remarried and found apparent bliss with Velerie Joyce Baughman, an attractive, twice-divorced blond with children of her own. The marriage seemed to be a happy one, and by the spring of 1995, the Baughmans were in Antigua, embarking on a second honeymoon.

They checked into the Royal Antigua Hotel on May 12, and Baughman left a note beneath his wife's pillow a few nights later. It read: "Velerie, this has been the best, most romantic vacation. I love you so much and each day I thank God I found you." On May 22, their last night at the Royal Antigua before moving on, John led Velerie up to the roof of the eight-story hotel to "enjoy the breeze." Moments later, Velerie Baughman plunged to her death, dropping 99 feet to strike the pavement with such force, a pathologist later testified, that "she suffered dozens of fractures. Most of her internal organs were split."

Unknown to John Baughman, island resident Philbert Jackson witnessed the fall through binoculars, afterward telling police that Velerie was "facing the hotel" as she fell to her death, and that "her body was bent in the shape of a V, with her legs pointing upwards." Scanning the roof, Jackson saw a man staring down at the corpse. "He was just standing there," Jackson said. "After I yelled, he reacted to the woman falling. He put his hand to his head and started pacing back and forth." Moments later, Baughman was at his wife's side, having raced down the fire escape to cradle her broken corpse in his arms.

Antiguan authorities wasted no time in charging Baughman with murder, but he ran true to form, blaming Velerie's death on a clumsy accident. "We went up there for the breeze," he told police, "as there is always a breeze up there. I had a love note in my pocket. I took it out and was handing it to her and it dropped to the floor. We both went to pick it up, and she either stepped on her slipper or she stubbed her toe, and she stumbled forward. Then I heard her say, 'Honey,' and she stumbled over the top. She just did not catch her balance."

Baughman produced the note as evidence; British authorities countered with a $200,000 insurance policy on Velerie's life, purchased the previous year. Baughman's second murder trial opened in Antigua on March 25, 1996, with High Court Justice Albert Redhead barring any testimony on prior charges as prejudicial. Velerie's son from a previous marriage, attorney Victor Des Laurier, was called as a witness to describe his mother's morbid fear of heights. Hotel manager Avon Simon noted the curious circumstance that defendant Baughman had changed the reservations for the last leg of his vacation to a single booking, shortly before his wife's fall. Two civil engineers took the stand, describing Velerie's fall as an impossible accident based on velocity and the distance of her body's impact from the building, proof that she had been violently "propelled" from the roof.

On April 4, 1996, jurors deliberated less than three hours before returning to convict John Baughman of first-degree murder. He was sentenced to hang, his days numbered by Antiguan statutes that limit criminal appeals to a maximum five years' duration. Back in Illinois, IBI detective David Hamm was satisfied with the result. "Twice before he got away with murder," Hamm declared. "I think he thought he was immune from Lady Justice, but he was wrong."

## Becker, Charles

Charles Becker was once described as "the crookedest cop who ever stood behind a shield" — no small achievement in New York City in the period of Tammany Hall, when civic corruption was an open secret and gangsters cooperated freely with municipal government to keep profits flowing from gambling and prostitution. So infamous was Becker, in fact, that he was featured in a novel and later inspired the first American gangster movie, but his reputation would not save him in the end.

Becker was still a uniformed patrolman, in the 1890s, when novelist Stephen Crane saw him brutally beating a young prostitute, furious at the girl for allegedly withholding Becker's normal payoff. The scene was immortalized in Crane's novel *Maggie: A Girl of the Streets*, but Becker had already moved on to bigger and better things. A protégé of Tammany leader Tim Sullivan, Becker was promoted to lieutenant in 1911, when bumbling machine politician Rhinelander Waldo became New York's latest police commissioner. Assigned as Waldo's aide, Becker was also placed in charge of NYPD's Special Squad Number One, overseeing the smooth flow of graft from criminal activities along Broadway, in the Tenderloin, and Hell's Kitchen districts. Becker kept an estimated 25¢ on the dollar for himself, while the rest found its way into deep pockets and political coffers around City Hall. Pimps and gamblers who paid up were protected; those who balked came in for raids and beatings from the men of New York's Finest, under Becker's watchful eye.

One gambler who paid his way, initially without complaint, was Herman ("Beansie") Rosenthal, proprietor of The Hesper, a joint on West 45th Street. Things ran smoothly while Becker received a flat 50% of the Hesper profits, but greed got the best of him in 1912, and he demanded a larger cut. Rosenthal balked at giving up more than half his income to a crooked cop, and Becker responded with a raid that left the club in ruins. Taking the harassment a step further, Becker also placed a man on guard outside the club around the clock — and, incredibly, stationed another patrolman *inside* Rosenthal's apartment, where he was visible 24 hours a day. The intrusion drove Rosenthal's wife to a nervous breakdown, and Beansie went looking for revenge.

His chosen method was exposure — first to newsman Herbert Bayard Swope, with the *New York World*, and then to Manhattan District Attorney Charles Whitman. Fearing possible indictment, Becker had a word with mobster "Big Jack" Zelig, and Rosenthal's fate was sealed. Four gunmen were assigned to execute the contract: Harry ("Gyp the Blood") Horowitz, Louis ("Lefty Louie") Rosenberg, "Dago" Frank Cirofici, and Jacob ("Whitey Lewis") Siedenschner. They caught up with Beansie in the predawn hours of July 16, 1912, riddling him with bullets as he emerged from the Hotel Metropole, on West 43rd.

An investigation was ordered, and Lieutenant Becker was placed in charge of the case. There was a witness to the shooting, but Becker took him into custody, hiding him out in the lockup at a remote station house, while detectives were ordered to "lose" the license number of the murder car. D.A. Whitman was spinning his wheels in frustration, until a tip led him to the witness, and his own investigators retrieved the witness after a scuffle with Becker's police. With license number in hand, the suspect vehicle was soon traced to an underworld character, "Billiard Ball" Jack Rose (so called because of his shiny bald head). Rose sat in jail for ten days without talking, until it became apparent that Becker was reneging on his promise to protect those involved in the Rosenthal murder. Finally, he named the shooters, and they began talking in an ultimately futile effort to save themselves from the electric chair. It was too late to finger Jack Zelig, gunned down by a rival mobster on October 5, 1912, but Charles Becker was indicted for planning and ordering the hit.

Convicted at his first trial, Becker saw the verdict overturned on appeal, his lawyers insisting that prosecution witnesses had perjured themselves, swayed by promised rewards from the district attorney. Be that as it may, he was convicted a second time and sentenced to die in Sing Sing's electric chair. Becker's only hope now lay in executive clemency, but with Charles Whitman newly elected as governor, that hope likewise vanished. Becker went to the chair on July 7, 1915, requiring several jolts of power to finish the job in one of Sing Sing's sloppiest executions on record. Afterward, his loyal wife commissioned a silver plate for the lid of his coffin. It read:

CHARLES BECKER
MURDERED JULY 7, 1915
BY GOVERNOR WHITMAN

The plaque was removed under threat of prosecution for criminal libel, but some defenders still champion Becker's cause to this day, describing him as the innocent victim of a frame-up, motivated by anger at Becker's "vigorous work" in suppressing organized gambling. Sing Sing warden Thomas Osborne is said to have believed Becker innocent, but history records the archetypal bad lieutenant as a thief and murderer. In 1912, D.W. Griffith used the Rosenthal murder case as inspiration for his pioneering gangster film, *The Musketeers of Pig Alley.*

# Boyland, Sherman M.

On the night of June 24, 1989, Shelby County sheriff's deputies were conducting a "jump-and-grab" drug sting in Memphis, Tennessee. Instead of using undercover officers to purchase drugs from dealers on the street, these officers were running a "reverse sting," offering cocaine for sale themselves, arresting customers who bought the drugs before they had a chance to sample the product.

One who took advantage of the service was Memphis barber Michael Gates, a passenger in a car that pulled up to the bogus drug dealers and purchased a small amount of cocaine. Before the deputies could "jump-and-grab" him, though, the vehicle sped away, and a high-speed chase began. Gates bailed out of the car when it slowed at a railroad crossing, and two officers ran him to earth, one sitting on his back while the other attempted to handcuff his wrists, Gates allegedly resisting violently. Moments later, more deputies arrived on the scene, Sherman Boyland among them.

It is difficult to say with any certainty what happened next. Officers at the scene initially refused to cooperate with federal investigators, five of them agreeing to testify only when they were threatened with perjury charges. According to their final statements, Deputy Boyland knelt before Gates while others were cuffing his wrists, choking Gates with one hand and punching him repeatedly with the other. Several officers allegedly "admonished Boyland to stop," all without result, until one or more finally grabbed him and "just ripped him away" from the prisoner. Sadly, their effort was too little and too late. Gates was transported to a nearby hospital, but he never made it, pronounced dead en route.

Boyland and company, meanwhile, were still running their "jump-and-grab" sting on the street, unaware that Gates had died. A short time after he was driven from the scene, another car approached the officers, this one occupied by Arthur Robinson and Lahara Rose. More drugs were sold, and the suspects were arrested. Deputy Boyland assaulted both of them, before and after they were handcuffed, desisting only when Officer Todd Cash physically dragged him away from Art Robinson. Even then, still raging, Boyland tried to resume the attack, but was restrained by his comrades.

News of Michael Gates's death raised an outcry in the Memphis black community, and Sheriff Jack Owens suspended 17 deputies pending investigation of the case, later returning the officers to administrative duty. On April 25, 1990, a federal grand jury indicted Deputies Boyland, Overton Wright, and Jacqueline Hollowell on charges of violating Gates's civil rights; Boyland alone faced charges of causing Gates's death, plus additional counts concerning victims Rose and Robinson. If convicted on all counts, he faced life imprisonment and fines exceeding $250,000.

The trial was delayed for nearly a year, but Boyland was finally convicted in federal court, on March 22, 1991, on multiple counts involving all three victims. His co-defendants were cleared across the board, leaving Boyland alone to receive a sentence of 71 months in prison. U.S. Attorney General Dick Thornburgh noted with apparent satisfaction that Boyland was the forty-sixth American policeman convicted on charges of violently abusing authority in the past three years. The conviction was affirmed on appeal, and the U.S. Supreme Court denied Boyland's plea for a writ of certiorari in June 1993, thereby closing the book on his case.

# Bradford, Glenn Patrick

Firefighters in Evansville, Indiana, expected nothing out of the ordinary on August 2, 1992, when they answered an alarm at the home of Tamara Lohr. Once inside the house, however, they found the 24-year-old corrections officer dead in her bedroom. Autopsy results showed that Lohr had been stabbed 21 times in the face, neck and back, before her house was set afire with gasoline. A gas can was also found in the bedroom, completing the scenario of arson used to camouflage a murder scene.

On Monday, August 3rd, Police Chief Art Gann announced that 30-year-old Patrolman Glenn Bradford, with four years on the force, was one of several suspects in the case. It had been Bradford who reported the fire, shortly after 6:30 a.m. on Sunday, and investigators now disclosed that Bradford "had a relationship" with Lohr, spanning some four years prior to her death. Friends and neighbors of the murdered woman told reporters that Bradford frequently stopped by Lohr's house, either while on duty or immediately following his overnight shift. Bradford's wife was likewise questioned as a suspect, but was quickly released. On September 10, Bradford was formally charged with first-degree murder and arson. He pled not guilty the following day, and was transferred to another jail in neighboring Posey County, with trial set for being on January 25, 1993.

In custody, Bradford denied any role in Lohr's death, while defense attorney Terry Noffsinger blamed his client's indictment on negligent police work which had deliberately ignored other viable suspects. Homicide detectives replied that Bradford and Lohr had been caught up in the midst of a tempestuous affair, with Lohr furious that Bradford refused to leave his wife, Dawn Bradford, twice confronting Lohr in an effort to break up the relationship. "Mean mail" had been exchanged between Bradford and Lohr on the police computer system, including threats from Lohr to show off photos of herself with Bradford if his wife confronted Lohr again, but Bradford, by his own admission, had erased the computer messages a short time before Lohr was killed. Sgt. Ted Mattingly, with the Evansville Police Department, told newsmen that dispatchers were unclear on Bradford's whereabouts for a critical hour, between 11:05 p.m. and 12:01 a.m. on the night of the murder, but Lohr's neighbors reported a squad car at her house around 11 o'clock on the night of August 1.

Three days before Christmas 1992, Circuit Judge Richard Young denied attorney Noffsinger's motion for a change of venue from Vanderburgh County, but he did push the trial date back to May 3rd, and it was subsequently stalled for yet another month. When testimony finally began in the first week of June, Noffsinger tried to suggest alternate suspects, targeting a jailer fired for striking an inmate in 1991, along with a man arrested for peeping in Lohr's neighborhood, two weeks before she died. Prosecutor Stan Levco rested his case on June 8th, after playing tapes of contradictory statements made by Bradford on August 2nd and 5th. In one statement, the patrolman denied ever seeing a gasoline can at Lohr's home; three days later, he recalled that she had shown it to him and "seemed proud of it." Bradford also denied any friction in his relationship with Lohr, then later admitted clashes between Lohr and his wife, admitting he had described the four-year affair as "somewhat more peaceful than it actually was."

Jurors deliberated more than 15 hours on June 18, 1993, before convicting Glenn Bradford of murder and arson. At the penalty phase of his trial, Dawn Bradford asked Judge Young for leniency, describing her husband as "a very good father and a wonderful person." Lohr's mother, for her part, told the court, "He caused her a painful death, and I think he should be sentenced to the maximum." Judge Young agreed, and on July 14, he threw the book at Bradford, 60 years for murder and 20 years for arson, the sentences to run consecutively. Bradford looked stunned, but bitterness was evident in his ten-minute speech to the court. "I cannot sit here today and tell you I feel remorse for the killing of Tamara Lohr," he said, "because I had nothing to do with it." He did, however, "feel remorse for participating in this legal system and not seeing it for its potential dangers. I was blinded for all those years by my idealism."

Judge Young was unmoved by the self-serving speech as he passed sentence. "The single most aggravating factor," he said of Bradford, "is that at the time he was committing this crime, he was charged with the responsibility of protecting the people of Vanderburgh County from crime."

It should have been the end, but Bradford remained stubborn in custody, still denying his guilt, seeking counsel as a pauper to pursue his appeals. On the outside, brother Joe Bradford and a crew of sympathetic volunteers distributed leaflets claiming that Glenn had been framed by Prosecutor Levco. BRADFORD IS INNOCENT, the pamphlets declared. WHO WILL BE LEVCO'S

NEXT VICTIM? Joe Bradford declared that he was pursuing "several suspects," hoping to focus on one within a year, but the rest is silence, leaving Glenn to serve his sentence for a murder he insists that he did not commit.

Bradford appealed his conviction, alleging (among other grounds) that hearsay evidence was improperly admitted as evidence in his trial, and that newly discovered evidence supporting an alibi entitled him to a retrial. In December 1996, the Indiana Supreme Court unanimously rejected those claims and affirmed Bradford's conviction.

## Budzyn, Walter and Nevers, Larry

Thirty-five-year-old Malice Wayne Green was in no shape to drive on the night of Thursday, November 5, 1992. Later blood tests would show that he was high on both alcohol and cocaine, when he got behind the steering wheel, but he might still have made it home, with any luck. In the final analysis, it was geography that got him killed.

Detroit P.D. detectives Walter Budzyn and Larry Nevers were staking out a West Side crack house, looking for an armed robbery suspect, when Green pulled up to the curb in front. The officers approached him and identified themselves, requesting Green's driver's license. As later retold by surviving participants, Green reached for his glove compartment, apparently with something clenched in his fist. Budzyn and Nevers assumed that the "something" was drugs, ordering Green to open his hand. He refused, and a struggle ensued, five other policemen rolling up while the fight was in progress. Neighborhood witnesses — many of them crack addicts with no love for police — would later describe Green being pummeled by multiple assailants, kicked in the head at least once, and slammed repeatedly over the skull with heavy steel flashlights. The autopsy report revealed at least fourteen distinct and separate heavy blows against the dead man's skull.

The cry went up at once, throughout Detroit, that racist cops had murdered Malice Green for no good reason other than the color of his skin. Such accusations are routine, whenever blacks and white police clash on the streets these days, but in the Green case, there appeared to be substantial evidence which indicated that the charge was true. On November 16, 1992, four of the five officers present at Green's death were indicted on various criminal charges: Budzyn and Nevers were charged with second-degree murder; 33-year-old Robert Lessnau faced charges of assault with intent to do great bodily harm; and Sgt. Freddie Douglas (the only black officer involved) was hit with dual charges of involuntary manslaughter and willful neglect of duty (for not stopping the assault on Green). Exactly one month later, the four officers were dismissed from the Detroit P.D., in a move which Dewey Stokes, national president of the Fraternal Order of Police, described to the press as "a little harsh," Mayor Coleman Young apparently declaring publicly that Malice Green had been "literally murdered by police."

Three of the four indicted officers went to trial before Judge George Crockett in Detroit, on June 18, 1993. The arrangements were unusual, to say the least: two separate juries, one each for 42-year-old Budzyn and 52-year-old Nevers, while Officer Lessnau waived his right to a jury entirely, leaving Judge Crockett to decide his fate. (Sgt. Douglas had managed to separate his case from the others; on December 23, the charge of involuntary manslaughter was dismissed, leaving Douglas to stand trial for willful neglect at some future, unspecified date.)

Defense attorneys for the three accused officers stuck with the theory, already damaged during a December 1992 preliminary hearing, that Malice Green had not been beaten to death at all, but rather had died from the combined effects of alcohol and cocaine, producing heart failure. Assistant prosecutor Doug Baker, meanwhile, told the jury that Green's death was a clear-cut case of homicide: "It was simply the exercise of raw power over one human being by others." The trial stretched over 13 weeks, including 50 witnesses and more than 200 exhibits. At one point, in mid-July, Oakland County medical examiner Ljubisc Dragovic seemed to support the defense, with testimony that blows to the head alone had not caused Green's death; rather, Dr. Dragovic said, a combination of the beating, plus alcohol and cocaine in the victim's blood had combined to produce a fatal seizure.

If defense attorneys were cheered by the testimony, there was little else about their case to inspire confidence. Larry Nevers admitted striking Green "four or five times" with his flashlight, but insisted Green had been trying to grab Nevers' pistol. County paramedics, meanwhile, confirmed the beating, but had seen no move by Green in the direction of any cop's gun. Walter Budzyn, for his part, denied striking Green with his flashlight at all, testimony contradicted by a series of civilian witnesses at the scene. Defense attorneys pointed out that most of those were past or present crack addicts, but that response seemed to have little impact on the twin, mostly black juries.

Both panels retired to consider their verdicts on Friday, August 13. Ten days later, they were back with verdicts, convicting both Budzyn and Nevers of murder in the second degree. Judge Crockett, meanwhile, had found the evidence against Officer Lessnau inconclusive, acquitting him on the assault charge. While Lessnau got on with his life, filing civil lawsuits against the Detroit P.D. and various prosecution witnesses, Budzyn and Nevers were back in court for sentencing on October 12. Judge Crockett told Budzyn, "I don't believe in the common usage of the term that you are an ordinary murderer... (but) what you did was excessive in the extreme." That excess earned Budzyn a prison term of eight to 18 years, with parole possible in six and a half. There were no kind words for Larry Nevers from the bench, as he received a sentence of 12 to 25 years, with parole available in something under ten.

Mindful of threats on their lives from black inmates and gangs, Budzyn and Nevers were sent to serve their time at a federal minimum-security lockup in Fort Worth, Texas. Even there, however, while sharing a room, the killer cops were still nervous. A January 1993 newsletter, prepared by Nevers for his supporters on the outside, reported that he and Budzyn had befriended two other inmates, who would henceforth serve as "bodyguards" against potential attacks. According to Nevers, one of the "guards" was a convicted bank robber, while the other had been sentenced for dealing drugs and illegal weapons. Michigan's appellate court denied the officers a new trial in 1995, and the state supreme court followed suit a year later.

Ex-Sergeant Douglas, meanwhile, went to trial on the misdemeanor negligence charge in June 1994. A jury deliberated for just over one hour, before convicting him on July 1, and Douglas was freed on bond pending an appeal which upheld the conviction. Nonetheless, in March 1995, Douglas was reinstated to his former job with back pay, after a police trial board effectively overruled the previous jury verdict, finding no evidence that Douglas actually witnessed the beating of Green by Budzyn and Nevers.

On July 31, 1997, the Michigan Supreme Court overturned Budzyn's conviction and ordered a new trial, on grounds that the mostly black jury may have been inflamed by a group viewing of the movie *Malcolm X*, while the trial was in progress. The film included newsreel footage of Los Angeles policemen beating Rodney King, while a voice-over from Malcolm X described the white race as "the greatest murderer on Earth." The state's high court allowed Larry Nevers' conviction to stand, however, on grounds that evidence of his guilt was overwhelming, and thus outweighed whatever impact a movie might have had on his jury.

## Carlen, Keith

In 1991, after 21 years on the job with California's Oakland Police Department, 44-year-old Keith Carlen was a runner-up in the local police union's vote for "Officer of the Year." He didn't win, but that was almost secondary. Simply being nominated was a testament to Carlen's performance in uniform, the high esteem in which he was held by his superiors and fellow officers. And it had been no easy haul, considering his handicap. 12 years earlier, in 1979, Carlen had crashed his motorcycle on a freeway ramp, spending weeks in a coma before he returned to the world of the living. Back at work, Oakland's brass urged him to take a disability retirement, but Carlen refused. Instead, he took a desk job, then moved on to an easy walking beat in downtown Oakland, his superiors insisting that they "went out of their way to accommodate him."

Some thought it worked, Sergeant Dave Ellis recalling that "To know him, you wouldn't have thought he had a care in the world." Others had a different view, one ex-cop observing that "It was quite obvious he had suffered some neural side effects from the accident. It was similar to someone who has suffered a stroke, with a few speech impediments, and he seemed to be a little more touchy. He had flare-ups." Most often, when Carlen "flared up," it was regarding problems in his marriage. More specifically, he griped about his wife, 46-year-old Carol Ann, and her spending habits. Carol Ann Carlen "liked to travel, liked to spend money," as one friend remembers, while Keith grew increasingly angry over their mounting expenses. At the same time, Carlen neglected his home life. "He was doing association work so much," one patrolman says, "it was almost to a fault. It interfered with their relationship." Still, others thought that Keith and Carol Ann seemed happy in their new $350,000 bayside home, planning a European vacation for 1992.

They never made it.

At 11 p.m. on April 13, 1992, Carlen reported his wife missing. Last seen when she left her job at Bechtel Enterprises, in San Francisco, Carol Ann had reportedly phoned home around 6:30 p.m. to tell Keith that she was having dinner with a female friend of 20 years. Eight hours after Carlen filed his missing report, around 7:15 a.m. on April 14, Carol Ann's 1988 Honda sedan was found in a gang-infested Oakland neighborhood, parked among semi-trailers at a warehouse loading dock. The word "WAR" had been spray-painted in bright orange, across the driver's door. Police found Carol Ann in the trunk, reporting that she had been strangled, with no evidence of sexual assault. Her purse was in the car, cash undisturbed; the car, from all appearances, had not been broken into.

Carlen was sent home immediately on bereavement leave, detectives proclaiming as late as April 15 that he was not a suspect in his wife's murder. Still, something was clearly out of place. Carol Ann was found attired in sweat clothes, with no underwear, and friends said she would never drive alone from her home, on Bay Farm Island, into crime-ridden Oakland. The clincher came when detectives compared the "WAR" graffiti on her car to microscopic flecks of paint on Carlen's clothes and shoes.

They had their man.

On April 17, department spokesmen reversed their earlier pronouncement, announcing that Keith Carlen had confessed to murdering his wife. He had planned the killing, Carlen said, while driving home from work, around 6 p.m. on April 13. The motive was money, Carlen opting for homicide as a means to curb his wife's spending. He had parked his pickup at a pharmacy in Alameda, taken a taxi home, and confronted Carol Ann in the kitchen of their home. They had quarreled, Carlen strangling her with a scarf from a basket of freshly washed laundry, after which he placed her body in the Honda's trunk and drove to Oakland, disguised in a wig and false mustache that he had purchased two weeks earlier. Initially, Carlen had planned to leave the car outside a restaurant, thus validating his report of Carol Ann's night out with her friend, but he had changed his mind and left it at the warehouse, spray-painting "WAR" on one side to point a finger of suspicion at local gangs, before walking back to his truck. From there, Carlen had driven back to the Oakland police station, where he worked at the computer until 8:45 p.m., making sure that he was seen by several friends to fortify his alibi. While driving home, he ditched the wig, mustache, scarf, spray-paint and gloves.

Detailed confession notwithstanding, Carlen pled not guilty at his arraignment on April 17, in Oakland's municipal court. Defense attorney Lincoln Mintz cited Carlen's 13-year-old head injury as a contributing factor in the case. "He knows he has killed the woman he loved," Mintz declared, "but he had no more intention of killing his wife than he did of taking a rocket ship to the moon. No one is going to be able to punish Keith Carlen more than he is punishing himself right now."

At Oakland PD, Captain Jim Hahn disagreed. The purchase of wig and mustache offered clear evidence of premeditation, two weeks before the killing, and Hahn blamed the murder on a straightforward, if extreme, case of "domestic incompatibility." "Specifically," Hahn told the press, "he was upset she would be allowed to buy things and charge things. Every time he attempted to buy something for his own personal use, it ended up in a rather heated argument. He was berated for purchasing anything of his own." Assistant District Attorney Nancy O'Malley rejected Carlen's bid for a plea-bargain on reduced manslaughter charges. "The evidence doesn't support manslaughter," she said. "It supports murder, and I'll be asking a jury for a first-degree murder conviction."

Originally scheduled for January 1993, Carlen's trial was delayed until December 1994 by various legal maneuvers. Attorney Mintz still insisted that his client was guilty of no more than voluntary manslaughter, based upon his alleged mental disability stemming from the 1979 motorcycle accident. Years of marital stress, Mintz told the jury, had "accumulated to the point where he couldn't handle it anymore." Prosecutor Terese Drabec countered by describing Carol Ann's slaying as ruthless and premeditated, a "classic case of first-degree murder." She ridiculed the defense claim of diminished capacity, reminding jurors that "You don't get to kill someone just because you can't express your feelings."

On Thursday, December 15, jurors deliberated three hours before convicting Carlen of first-degree murder. Carlen responded by firing his lawyer, charging that Mintz had failed to call expert witnesses in support of Carlen's mental disability, and replaced him with new counsel Ted Cassman. Motions for a new trial dragged on into 1995, with a closed-door hearing before Judge Philip Sarkisian on August 18. Two months later, the new-trial motion was finally rejected, and Carlen was sentenced on October 25th, drawing a prison term of 25 years to life. A California state appeals court upheld his conviction on November 22, 1996.

# Coleman, Tom Lemuel

A native of "Bloody Lowndes" County, Alabama, Tom Coleman was born November 26, 1910, the son of a one-time state legislator who later served six years as county sheriff. The only noteworthy event of Sheriff Jesse Coleman's administration was the broad-daylight lynching of a black man named Will Jones in 1914. Sheriff Coleman not only failed to solve the crime, in an area where the unmasked lynchers were well known to all, but he also stubbornly refused to cooperate with state investigators on the case, despite personal pressure from the governor. That kind of loyalty to white tradition was rewarded in Lowndes County, and upon his retirement from law enforcement, Jesse was swiftly elected superintendent of the county's segregated schools, a post he held until he retired (and was succeeded by his daughter) in 1939.

Despite his father's position with the board of education, Tom Coleman was a poor student, frequently in trouble for disrupting classes, and he barely graduated high school. A certain aptitude in math would serve him in later life, but otherwise, his teachers were glad to see the last of him when he left Hayneville after graduation, working at a series of odd jobs around the state. Home again in 1933, Tom offered no objection when his influential father landed him a menial job with the state highway department, holding stakes for survey crews. Four years later, he married the 18-year-old daughter of a minister who doubled as school superintendent in a neighboring county, and they settled down to raise a family.

Not that Tom Coleman could ever be described as "settled," in the conventional sense. A hard-drinking man who often drove drunk but somehow managed to evade the police, he was known for his violent temper and pathological racism — traits, indeed, which hardly made him stand out in a county where Ku Klux Klansmen sported bumper stickers on their autos reading OPEN SEASON. In the 1940s and '50s, Coleman moved up through the ranks of the highway department, reaching the pinnacle of his career as a resident engineer whose job included supervision of convict road crews. Two children and a friendly draft board spared him from the rigors of combat in World War II, but Coleman cherished a fondness for guns all the same, wearing a pistol on the job and carrying a loaded shotgun in his car.

On the evening of August 21, 1959, one of the inmates at the Greenville prison camp got out of hand, causing a loud disturbance in the recreation hall. The convict in question was Richard Lee Jones, a 27-year-old illiterate black man, and while such problems are routinely solved with clubs in Southern prisons, guards at Greenville, for some unknown reason, decided to summon Tom Coleman. The engineer arrived with his trusty shotgun and found Jones still in the rec hall, armed with a broken soda bottle and a guard's billy club. Moments later, Jones was dead, cut down by a blast of buckshot at close range, and the official "inquest," held on the spot before the body was removed, promptly cleared Coleman on grounds of self-defense.

The shooting, and his work with inmate road crews, gave Coleman opportunities to meet and befriend many lawmen. Much of his spare time was spent at the Lowndes County sheriff's office, and he was friendly with Jim Clark, the swaggering sheriff from Selma, in nearby Dallas County, who was infamous for deputizing Klansmen for his "special posse." (Years later, and long out of office, Clark went to prison for smuggling marijuana.) Another bosom pal of Coleman's was Colonel Al Lingo, head of the tough Alabama state troopers under Governor George Wallace and a self-described "good friend" of the KKK. In 1961, Coleman's son became a state trooper and was swiftly appointed to serve as Lingo's personal driver and bodyguard. Back in Hayneville, Tom Senior carried a card identifying him as a "special" deputy sheriff, entitled to pack firearms and enforce the law. He was also an ardent member of the racist White Citizens' Council, and while he publicly denied membership in the Klan his actions spoke louder than words. Civil rights leaders and Alabama's state attorney general alike would later describe Tom Coleman as "a known Klansman." He was, in the words of one observer, "maddened by the prospect of Negroes voting in Lowndes County." Alabama was a major civil rights battlefield throughout the troubled 1960s, and while "Bloody Lowndes" held the color line longer than some counties, "invasion" by "outside agitators" was not to be avoided. In August 1965, federal voting registrars descended on Lowndes County, to make sure that blacks received equal opportunity under the new Voting Rights Act, and state attorney general Richmond Flowers visited the county on August 10th, to check on their progress. A "liberal" by Alabama standards, pledged to investigate and prosecute the terroristic KKK, Flowers had few white friends in Lowndes County. That Tuesday afternoon, Tom Coleman confronted Flowers at the Hayneville post office, launching into a near-hysterical racist tirade. "Ain't nobody down here gonna tell you anything, Richmond," he sneered. "Ain't none of these folks down here gonna tell you a damn thing." In case Flowers missed the point, Coleman warned him to "get off the Ku Klux Klan and get on these outfits down here trying to get these niggers registered. If you don't get off this Klan investigation, we'll get you off!"

Four days later, on August 14, a group of civil rights demonstrators was arrested in Fort Deposit, and transported to the larger jail in Hayneville for safekeeping. Most of the prisoners were local blacks, but their number included two white clergymen — Father Richard Morrisroe, a 27-year-old Catholic priest, and Jonathan Daniels, a 26-year-old Episcopal seminarian. The protesters were held until Friday, August 20, when they were suddenly released with orders to appear for a court date in Fort Deposit on September 11. Deputies who ushered them out of the jail refused to say who had posted their bond. Daniels, Morrisroe, and several blacks began walking toward the Cash Store, 100 yards from the jail, one of the few shops in Hayneville where black customers were welcome.

Tom Coleman was idling around the courthouse when word came that the demonstrators would soon be released. Anticipating "trouble" through some kind of psychic vibe, he drove to the Cash Store and posted himself in the doorway, sporting a pistol on his belt, semiautomatic shotgun in hand. He was ready and waiting when Daniels and Morrisroe approached the store, accompanied by two black girls, Ruby Sales and Joyce Bailey. Their intent, as afterward described by the survivors, was to purchase soft drinks and snacks, but Deputy Coleman was having none of it. Blocking the door with his body and hardware, he ordered the quartet to "get off this property or I'll blow your goddamn heads off, you sons of bitches." Jon Daniels had time to push Ruby out of the way, before a shotgun blast ripped into his chest from point-blank range, killing him instantly. Father Morrisroe grabbed Joyce's hand and turned to flee, cut down in his tracks as buckshot slammed into his back.

Apparently satisfied with his handiwork, Coleman left his shotgun at the store and drove back to the courthouse. Sheriff C. Frank Ryals was out of town, but Coleman was happy to fill in, himself answering the first telephone call that reported the shooting. That done, Coleman called Al Lingo and told Alabama's top lawman, "I just shot two preachers. You'd better get down here." Lingo, in turn, alerted Coleman's son and picked up a bail bondsman identified as a member of the KKK before he drove to Hayneville. Sheriff Clark popped over from Selma to offer moral support, and three attorneys soon arrived from the state capital in Montgomery, to safeguard Coleman's civil rights. Sheriff Ryals returned in time to tell reporters that Coleman had been acting as a special deputy, responding to reports of a disturbance at the store, when the shooting occurred. Al Lingo, for his part, preferred stonewalling the press, answering all questions with a terse "It's none of your damn business!"

By midnight that Friday, County Solicitor Carlton Perdue had decided to charge Coleman with first-degree murder, but he made the move with obvious reluctance, telling newsmen that if Daniels and Morrisroe "had been tending to their own business like I tend to mine, they'd be living and enjoying themselves today." Richmond Flowers, for his part, sent assistant Joe Gantt to supervise the investigation, accusing Al Lingo of a cover-up and describing Coleman's act as "another Ku Klux Klan murder." Pressed for details, Flowers said, "Everything points to another Klan killing, as the accused is strongly believed to be a Ku Klux Klan member."

Coleman was arraigned on Saturday morning, August 21, in a hearing that lasted all of 15 minutes. Bond was set at $10,000 on the murder charge, with another $2,300 on a second count of assault with intent to murder, and Coleman was promptly bailed out by his brother-in-law. A grand jury session was scheduled for September 13. Local whites rallied to Coleman's defense, one Lowndes County deputy sheriff speaking candidly of Father Morrisroe to visiting reporters: "I hope the son of a bitch dies. That'll give us two of them, instead of one."

The state's case against Coleman was prepared by Carlton Perdue, assisted by Circuit Solicitor Arthur Gamble. Richmond Flowers challenged Perdue's fitness to try the case, based on early statements to the press, and a group calling itself Concerned White Citizens of Alabama echoed that opinion, declaring that Perdue "could not possibly execute justice impartially," and that "there is no doubt about the immaturity and incapability of a county solicitor who implies that emotional outrage is justification for killing." The group's leader asked Flowers to remove Perdue as prosecutor, but Flowers demurred on grounds that such a move "would ruin any chance you might have for a conviction." Grasping at straws, Flowers expressed the hope that Perdue "would not let his personal beliefs interfere with his prosecution of the case."

By that time, FBI agents were on the case, working overtime despite active obstruction from Lingo's state troopers. In essence, the G-men were interested in three things: 1) Coleman's official status as a deputy sheriff acting "under color of law"; 2) the possibility of a KKK conspiracy behind the shootings; and 3) allegations that the demonstrators had been armed when Coleman gunned them down. Sheriff Ryals was regretting his certification of

Coleman as a "special deputy," worried now that his whole department might be implicated in the shooting, or perhaps even hit with federal charges of civil rights violations. Hastily rewriting history, Ryals now declared that he had issued the I.D. card to Coleman in lieu of a conventional gun permit, using Coleman and other "special" deputies as part-time clerical help, without official status or police powers. It was a blatant contradiction of the sheriff's first statement, and it would be further challenged in court, by sworn testimony from regular deputies, but it seemed to do the trick. Before bailing out of Lowndes County, FBI agents concluded that Coleman had not acted in an official capacity, nor was there any credible evidence that his victims were armed.

On September 13, a grand jury composed of 17 whites and one black heard testimony from 20-odd witnesses, before returning an indictment that reduced Coleman's original murder charge to one of first-degree manslaughter (defined in Alabama law as a killing performed "intentionally but without malice"). The charge of assault with intent to murder was likewise reduced to assault and battery. Instead of facing the electric chair, Coleman now risked a maximum of ten years in prison on the manslaughter charge, or six months and a $500 fine for assault. He pled not guilty and bond was continued, with jury selection for his trial scheduled to begin on September 27.

The watered-down indictments "shocked and amazed" Richmond Flowers, who declared, "If this is not murder, it is no case at all." Flowers pledged steps to secure a murder charge, but his statements drew flack from Carlton Perdue, himself committed to the sanctity of the local grand jury system. In Perdue's words, the grand jury had decided that Coleman acted "spasmodically" in defense of the Cash Store's female proprietor, rather than as a cold, calculating murderer. From Montgomery, Flowers fired back with allegations that Lowndes County grand jurors were "just as guilty as the man who pulled the trigger." Finally, in lieu of recalling the panel, Flowers used his power as attorney general to supersede prosecutors Gamble and Perdue, assigning Joe Gantt to handle the state's case.

The trial opened on schedule, before Judge T. Werth Thagard, in the same courthouse where other Klansmen had recently scored their first mistrial in the drive-by slaying of civil rights worker Viola Liuzzo. Another trial was pending in that case, and the three Ku Klux triggermen were on hand as spectators when Judge Thagard began to poll prospective jurors in Coleman's case. They had a laugh when Coleman's name was noted on the jury list, and yet another when Thagard asked the panel if anyone present had preconceived opinions on the case. "I do," a Hayneville mechanic told the judge. "Not guilty!"

Joe Gantt moved for a continuance, voicing his opinion that a fair trial was impossible with the present jury, but Thagard denied the motion. Next, Gantt sought a delay while Father Morrisroe recuperated from his wounds, but Thagard was stubborn, ordering the state to proceed without its key witness. When Gantt stood fast, refusing to go on with the deck so clearly stacked against him, Judge Thagard chastised him for "trifling with the court" and removed him from the prosecution, handing the case back to Carlton Perdue.

Testimony began on September 28th, with deputy sheriff Joe Jackson admitting that Coleman was a duly authorized policeman, empowered to enforce the law in Lowndes County. He also recalled Jon Daniels kissing a "nigger girl" soon after his release from jail. Was that a kiss on the cheek, or on the mouth, Jackson was asked. "Right in the mouth," he said, to snickers from the audience. No, Jackson hadn't seen the shooting victims bearing arms, but there had been a crowd of blacks around their bodies when he reached the scene, and someone could have made off with a weapon in the confusion. Dr. C.J. Rehling described the fatal wound as having been inflicted from a range of six to eight inches, but defense attorney Vaughn Robinson was more interested in Jon Daniels's clothing. His shoes, for example, "were such as no man of God in Lowndes County ever wears," and his undershorts "smelled of urine," although Dr. Rehling agreed that "there had not been any post mortem urination."

On September 29, KKK "imperial wizard" Robert Shelton drove to Hayneville with a retinue of Kluxers to observe the wrap-up of Coleman's case and the next scheduled trial in Viola Liuzzo's murder. Friends of Coleman took the witness stand to testify that Jon Daniels had carried "a knife of some kind" as he approached the Cash Store, while Father Morrisroe held something "that looked like a gun barrel." After the shooting, one witness saw "a Negro boy" who "seemed to be putting something in his pocket when I met him. It looked like a knife." Another "colored boy," likewise unidentified, had "picked up something from the ground" and "stuck it in his britches." Art Gamble himself seemed to buy the defense argument, making frequent references to "this object" and "this knife," while Carlton Perdue described Daniels "attempting to force his way" into the store. Gamble's summation for the state reminded jurors that "There is no evidence here at all that Jonathan Daniels was making any attempt to actually cut [Coleman] with that knife," but he never saw fit to challenge the existence of the knife itself. Coleman's defense attorney, meanwhile, told the jury, "You can believe that knife was there or not. I believe it was there whether it was or not." More to the point, he raved, "I think we ought to thank Almighty God that we have got such a man as Tom Coleman in our midst."

The panel agreed, one juror winking at Coleman as they filed out to deliberate, and the verdict of acquittal was a foregone conclusion. Richmond Flowers described the verdict as a "license to kill, destroy and cripple," but it was too late to turn back the clock. Coleman's second trial, for assault and battery on Father Morrisroe, was scheduled for May 1966, but Judge Thagard postponed it until such time as Morrisroe was well enough to travel. That September, Flowers asked the county grand jury to reindict Coleman for assault with intent to murder, but the panel needed only five minutes to reject that request. Next, Flowers asked Judge Thagard to nol-pros the case, thereby clearing the way for prosecution at a later time, but Thagard chose instead to dismiss the case "with prejudice," thus barring any future charge with regard to Morrisroe's shooting.

Cleared of all charges, Tom Coleman returned to his job with the highway department and stayed on until his retirement in 1977. Meanwhile, it was reported that he gave up drinking in 1971 and began to attend church more often, although there is no evidence that his racial views ever changed. Living on into the late 1980s, Coleman survived bouts of skin and bladder cancer, idling away his hours at the courthouse and enjoying his reputation as a local hero of the white race. He died of natural causes at age 86, on June 13, 1997.

# Corbitt, Michael J. and Keating, James

Born March 17, 1944 in Oak Park, Illinois, Michael Corbitt was raised and spent the rest of his life in the Chicago suburbs of Willow Springs and Summit. A high school dropout who left home at 17, he found his first employment with a vending machine company, installing gambling paraphernalia in mob-owned dives around Cook County, and moved on from there to operate a filling station. At 21, he joined the Willow Springs Police Department, an agency whose reputation for corruption defied its small size. In Willow Springs, patrolmen could be fired for failure to warn illegal gambling clubs and whorehouses before a raid by county sheriff's deputies. His first year on the job, Corbitt was one of three Willow Springs officers briefly detained by county cops to prevent them from alerting vice operators of sweeping raids in progress. No charges were filed, and he returned to duty the next day, but the incident provided Corbitt's introduction to James Dennis Keating, a sheriff's deputy who shared Corbitt's fondness for easy money.

Seven years older than Corbitt, James Keating was the son of a Chicago cop, born March 10, 1937, who joined the Chicago P.D. in 1962. He was fired a month later, reportedly after beating a prisoner, and went to work as a detective for the Santa Fe Railroad. In 1964, with some assistance from a political "rabbi," Keating found a post with the Cook County Sheriff's Police, and soon gravitated to the vice and gambling unit, where graft proliferated. Known among his fellow officers as "the most personable guy you could meet," Keating always had his hand out and his eyes wide open for another scam, another opportunity to fatten up his bank account. By 1984, he was earning $34,000 a year on the job, supplementing that income with an estimated $2,000 to $8,000 each month on the side. His specialty was selling protection to bookies, gamblers, pimps — anyone, in short, who had reason to fear the police.

While Keating was learning the ropes on vice, Mike Corbitt was well on his way to becoming a local hero. In April 1967, he shot it out with three burglars at a Willow Springs cabinet shop, wounding one and forcing them to drop a bag with some $2,000 in loot. Eighteen months later, he shot and killed an alleged Peeping Tom who resisted arrest and grabbed Corbitt's gun. The dead man's family called it murder, but investigation by the U.S. Department of Justice failed to make a case. A few months later, Corbitt shifted his allegiance to the Summit P.D., but returned to Willow Springs when Mayor John Rust offered him the job of chief. Sadly for Corbitt, Rust died before the April 1969 election, and his successor named Corbitt as a lowly sergeant, instead. In September 1971, Sgt. Corbitt killed a drunken trucker who was shooting up a Willow Springs saloon. The death was ruled justifiable, and in 1973, with the election of William Bucki as mayor, Corbitt finally attained the chief's position he had craved for so long.

Already working countless dirty deals with Keating — himself promoted to lieutenant within the sheriff's office — Corbitt broadened his horizons as chief by openly consorting with notorious mobsters, collecting a fleet of fast cars, and enjoying an open line of credit at Las Vegas casinos. A striking figure at six foot two and some 240 pounds, Corbitt preferred cowboy garb or an open shirt and gold chains to the traditional police uniform, and his lifestyle was equally unorthodox. When Chicago gangster Joe Testa lost his legs in a Florida car bombing, Corbitt flew down to say goodbye in person, remaining at Testa's bedside until the mobster died. It was clearly no joke, then, when Corbitt told a journalist that "Willow Springs is unique."

One of the men who made it all happen, both for Corbitt and Keating, was attorney Alan Masters. Born March 9, 1935, Masters was a "fixer" in the best Chicago tradition, "greasing" cops and criminals alike, serving both with fine impartiality. Police in Willow Springs illegally referred drunk drivers to his office and got kickbacks in return, while others knew him as a contact for protection in the murky realm of vice and gambling. Masters consorted with mobsters, hosting hit men at his dinner parties, but lawmen were never neglected, either. Cops have a high divorce rate, and Masters was always available to help out. By the end of 1981, he had handled divorce proceedings for Jim Keating and one of his subordinates, Lieutenant Howard Vanicki (the latter free of charge). In the mid-1970s, Masters sold his own $45,000 house to Keating at a substantial discount; when Keating turned around and sold it for $88,000 in 1981, Masters handled the closing. A year later, when Keating was promoted to head of the sheriff's Intelligence Unit, Masters and mobsters alike were delighted. As one thug later said, "Everyone was pleased, because he wasn't greedy and he would do almost anything."

And *anything*, as it turned out, included plotting murders for his friends.

Mike Corbitt's lucrative career hit a snag in April 1981, when Mayor Frank Militello was elected on a promise to clean up Willow Springs, beginning with the graft-ridden police department. His first move, that May, was to fire Corbitt and 15 other cops, but Corbitt fought the dismissal in court, defiantly hanging onto his job for another 13 months. In June 1981, a grand jury subpoenaed

Corbitt's financial records, going back six years, but he had covered his tracks well enough to avoid indictment. While the court battle dragged on, Corbitt told his underworld friends not to worry: if worse came to worse, he expected an appointment as chief of police in Summit, where he would soon resume business as usual. One of those who accepted Corbitt's assurances at face value was Alan Masters.

If Masters had a weakness, it appeared to be in the realm of his personal life. The lawyer had abandoned his wife of 17 years, in September 1975, to live with girlfriend Dianne Turner — whom he met while representing her in a 1969 divorce action — but he kept the affair so secret that his wife knew nothing of Dianne's existence for another seven years. By that time, Masters and his mistress had been married for two years, had a 5-year-old daughter, and were living in their second home — the first having been sold at bargain-basement rates to Lt. James Keating — but things were far from idyllic with Alan and Dianne. In fact, Masters could never be satisfied with one woman, soon revealing himself as a brutal philanderer who beat Dianne and sometimes threatened her with guns. Chronic depression over their relationship drove Dianne into therapy in October 1972, three years before Masters left his wife, and the psychiatric sessions continued sporadically for a decade, until the week before her death. The flip side of Alan's womanizing was obsessive jealousy, prompting frequent accusations of infidelity against Dianne. Ironically, despite his reputation as a ladies' man, Masters frequently suffered from impotence, requiring Dianne to perform elaborate dances and strip shows before they could have sex. In March 1977, when Dianne's mother was fatally injured in a fall downstairs at her home, Masters called it an accident; Dianne's brother suspected the old woman may have been pushed.

Friends and relatives were unanimous in their opinion that Alan Masters initially "bought" Dianne, but by January 1982, she was looking for something new in her life. She found it in the person of Jim Koscielniak, a professor of economics she met while running for a post as trustee of Moraine Valley Community College. Dianne won the election and Koscielniak's heart at the same time. By March 1982 she had retained an attorney and informed Alan of her plan to start a new life without him. Predictably, Masters did not take the news well. Dianne had already told friends and relatives about Alan's ties to the mob, including his purchase of a brothel called the Western Health Spa in 1978. Now, with divorce in the air, Dianne believed she was being followed. More to the point, she named the man who was tailing her: he was, she said, "an off-duty cop" named Mike Corbitt.

On March 19, 1982, Alan filed a missing person report on his wife with the Cook County sheriff's office. She had last been seen at 1:15 that morning, leaving a late dinner with fellow board members and college administrators, but she never made it home. Alan's good friend Howard Vanicki was placed in charge of the case, with Jim Keating looking over his shoulder, and Masters tried to help things along with a $10,000 reward for information leading to Dianne's safe return. Oddly, in the circumstances, he refused to speak with the press, and Cook County officials cooperated by keeping a lid on the case, suppressing information on Dianne's disappearance even while her brother demanded a more strenuous investigation. That was a problem in itself, however: Lt. Vanicki reported his opinion that Dianne "did not voluntarily disappear," announcing his suspicion that Masters was somehow involved, but Jim Keating promptly reprimanded Vanicki for "not being objective," threatening to remove him from the case.

Detectives caught a break on December 11, 1982, when a scuba diver found Dianne's yellow Cadillac in a Willow Springs canal. The diver had been hired to locate sunken cars — some 70 in all — which had been submerged as a result of a long-running insurance scam. No sooner was the yellow Caddy back on dry land than rancid odors from the trunk led police to Dianne's corpse. She was naked from the waist down, her panties and stockings missing, blouse unbuttoned, expensive jewelry intact. Dental charts confirmed the identity, and autopsy results showed that Dianne's skull had been crushed with a blunt instrument, after which she was shot twice in the head with a .22-caliber pistol. In short, the crime had all the earmarks of a syndicate execution.

If Alan Masters was shocked by the news, he recovered swiftly, moving to have Dianne cremated in defiance of her brother's protest. Prosecutors blocked that effort, in the interest of their ongoing murder investigation, but they could not prevent Masters from collecting $6,500 insurance on Dianne's Cadillac or cleaning $4,900 out of her savings and checking accounts. It was January 1983 before Masters learned about Dianne's $100,000 life insurance policy, provided for all college trustees, and in the absence of official declarations that he was a suspect in her murder, the insurance company was forced to pay off.

By that time, investigation of the crime had passed from Cook County authorities to the Willow Springs P.D., where new Chief James Ross organized a special task force, taking care to exclude the county sheriff's office. Before long, local papers reported that FBI agents were also involved in the case.

In fact, federal interest in Masters dated from before Dianne's murder, when FBI agents had launched "Operation Safebet" in Cook County, trolling for corrupt policemen in a classic sting designed to net bribe-takers. The point man was Special Agent Larry Damron, a.k.a. "Larry Wright," who struck bargains with James Keating and Michael Corbitt for protection on a string of imaginary bookie parlors and brothels. The initial payoff was $600 a month to each officer, with higher price tags attached to special projects. Jim Keating told "Wright" that Alan Masters was "the man who runs things" around Willow Springs, and he had mentioned Alan's marital problems in passing. When Dianne disappeared, Keating noted that she would be missing a scheduled court hearing on her divorce. As "Wright" recalled the moment, "He chuckled and thought it was kind of humorous, because it was so convenient."

By 1985, the federal noose was rapidly tightening around Corbitt and Keating. One of the cars dredged up at Willow Springs belonged to Chicago policeman Anthony Barone, Mike Corbitt's brother-in-law. Barone had reported the car stolen in 1981, collecting an insurance check, but under FBI grilling, he described the scam as Corbitt's brainchild. The feds had Corbitt now, but they bided their time, collecting more evidence, burrowing deeper into the morass of lies and obfuscation that surrounded the death of Dianne Masters. On August 29, 1985, James Keating was arrested on federal charges of bribery and racketeering. As the handcuffs closed on his wrists, he quipped, "Well, I guess this ruins my chances to go to the FBI Academy." Convicted at his trial in May 1986, Keating faced a maximum 133 years and a $140,000 fine, but he got off "easy" with a sentence of 15 years in federal prison. Alan Masters picked up the tab for Keating's defense, presumably acting from the goodness of his heart.

On July 13, 1986, the *Chicago Tribune* reported that FBI agents were investigating Dianne Masters's death. In fact, a federal grand jury had been secretly reviewing the case for 18 months, learning much that had been heretofore concealed. The G-men knew Dianne was being followed, for example, and that she had named Mike Corbitt as her shadow. They also located private investigator Ted Nykaza, an alcoholic ex-cop who boasted (falsely) of killing four men on the job. More recently, he had worked for Alan Masters, mounting surveillance on Dianne and tapping the phones at Alan's home in an effort to identify her lover. It had worked, and Cook County sheriff's officers helped out by running a background check on Jim Koscielniak. More to the point, Nykaza had taped a conversation between Diane and her lover, including explicit discussion of their last sexual encounter, and played the tape back for his boss. Masters "went berserk" while listening to the tape, Nykaza said, and had decided on the spot to kill Dianne. Jim Keating had participated in surveillance of Dianne and her boyfriend, reporting their movements to Masters. As for the hit itself, he told the G-men, "Corbitt is your man."

On May 20, 1987, Mike Corbitt was indicted on federal charges of bribery and extortion, related to the "Operation Safebet" sting.

He pled not guilty, but it didn't help. It looked suspicious when, a month before his trial, Corbitt purchased a $300,000 yacht and a $35,000 Corvette. At trial, he was convicted on all counts, and the yacht came back to haunt him, sending him to jail as a flight risk pending sentencing. Coming down to the wire, Corbitt presented the court with a stack of 40 letters from politicians, priests, and school-teachers, all pleading for leniency, and the judge took them under advisement, finally sentencing Corbitt to four years in prison. At that, he could have been out in 16 months, but time drags in prison. After three months in a cell, Corbitt admitted dumping Dianne's Cadillac in the Willow Springs canal, but denied any knowledge of a body in the trunk. As far as Corbitt was concerned, it had all been part of the ongoing insurance caper. Oddly, the ex-chief *did* admit agreeing to kill Dianne for Alan: he had gone so far as to accept a house key from the lawyer, initially planning to make the murder look like a random home invasion, but his nerve had failed, Corbitt said, and he had backed out of the plot. As far as who had done the deed, he couldn't say. As proof of his innocence, Corbitt produced a rental car receipt from Florida, but payroll records showed that he was on the job in Illinois that fateful night, and FBI agents had no problem exposing the receipt as a crude forgery.

On Monday, June 13, 1988, Masters, Corbitt and Keating were indicted on federal charges of plotting Dianne's murder, soliciting potential killers, and concealing the crime. Keating was specifically accused of offering $25,000 to one prospective shooter (who rejected the job), while Corbitt was charged with dumping Dianne's Cadillac in the Willow Springs canal. The three defendants were also charged with bribery in the referral-kickback scheme, while Keating stood accused of splitting various gambling "protection" bribes with Masters. The attorney was hit with an additional charge of mail fraud, related to Dianne's life insurance.

It took the best part of another year before the long-awaited trial began in Chicago federal court, on May 18, 1989. FBI agent Larry Damron was the lead prosecution witness. Others described James Keating stalking Dianne Masters and Jim Koscielniak on March 2,

1982, confirming their routine, but the first scheduled murder date was scrubbed when snow canceled a prospective rendezvous. Defense attorney Patrick Tuite began presenting his case on June 6th, and it went to the jury a week later. All concerned were expecting lengthy deliberations, but the panel surprised them, returning with verdicts after only five hours on June 13th. Alan Masters was acquitted of mail fraud, but convicted on two racketeering counts, including bribery of police and conspiring to murder his wife. James Keating was likewise convicted on two counts, for accepting bribes from Masters and soliciting the hit man who refused to kill Dianne. Mike Corbitt was convicted of accepting bribes and dumping Dianne's car in the Willow Springs canal. Back in court for sentencing on August 24, Masters drew a prison term of 40 years, together with a $250,000 fine; Keating and Corbitt were sentenced to 20 years each, those terms to run concurrently with their previous jail terms. On May 18, 1993, the U.S. Supreme Court rejected Alan Masters's appeal.

# Courtright, Timothy Isaiah

Born sometime in the mid-1840s, in either Iowa or Illinois, Timothy Courtright was one of the Old West's more colorful gunmen, best known for his handsome face, twin pistols, and the blond hair that gave him his nickname of "Longhair Jim." During the Civil War, Courtright served as a scout under General Logan. After Appomatox, he drifted into Texas and became marshal of Fort Worth in the early 1870s. Little is known of his career in Fort Worth, but rumors persist that Courtright supplemented his income by shaking down gamblers and saloonkeepers. Fired for excessive drinking in 1878, he moved on to serve briefly as marshal in Mesilla, New Mexico, before signing on as a guard for the American Mining Company. In 1883, he shot and killed two would-be robbers, the shootout bringing him to the attention of his old wartime commander, now a prosperous New Mexico rancher.

Employed as a "foreman" on the Logan ranch, Courtright's real job was the elimination of squatters. Raiding a camp at American

Valley in 1883, Longhair Jim and another shootist killed two unarmed nesters, but there were witnesses to the slayings, and Courtright fled the state. Manhunters tracked him to Fort Worth and jailed him pending extradition, but his knowledge of the lockup served him well, and Courtright escaped with the aid of two smuggled six-guns, absconding to South America. He remained outside the country until 1886, when word reached him that the prosecution witnesses had scattered, at which time it was safe to return to Socorro for trial. The charges were dismissed, and Courtright headed back to Fort Worth, stopping off in El Paso en route for an impromptu display of marksmanship.

In Fort Worth, Courtright founded the T.I.C. Commercial Detective Agency, but there was little work for private investigators in that town, and he nearly went bankrupt. Briefly employed as a railroad strikebreaker, he was left at loose ends once again when the strike was settled. Desperate for money and increasingly ill-tempered, his natural mean streak aggravated by liquor, Courtright returned to his old trade of extorting "protection" money from Fort Worth's saloons.

The racket was only effective if everyone knuckled under, however, and Courtright met stiff resistance in the person of Luke Short, himself a notorious gunman and owner of the White Elephant Saloon, who was regarded by some as the "gambling king" of Fort Worth. Unimpressed with Courtright's credentials as a killer, Short refused to ante up his share of the "insurance," and Longhair Jim brooded over the insult, boozing and biding his time.

Around 8 p.m. on February 8, 1887, Courtright appeared outside the White Elephant, calling for Short to come out. Luke took his time, slipping into his fancy vest and double-checking the gun in his pocket. When he emerged, Courtright berated him, setting the stage for a plea of self-defense when he shouted, "Don't you pull a gun on me!" The ruse was a waste of time, both men yanking their pistols and blazing away. Short's first bullet sheared off Courtright's thumb and sent his gun spinning into the street. Three more bullets, squeezed off at close range, ripped into Courtright's chest and forehead, killing him where he stood. No charges were filed against Short, leaving him free to resume business as usual.

# Crafts, Richard Bunel

A native of New York City, born December 20, 1937, Richard Crafts served in the U.S. Marine Corps and later went to work for the Central Intelligence Agency as a pilot for the agency's covert "Air America" operation in Southeast Asia. Returning to civilian life, he became a pilot for Eastern Airlines and settled in Newtown, Connecticut, where he was also employed as a part-time constable. Married in 1975, he fathered three children, but the relationship was a stormy one, and Helle Crafts had filed for divorce by 1986, accusing her husband of carrying on an affair with a stewardess from a rival airline. Richard told friends that he would never agree to the divorce; Helle, meanwhile, advised one acquaintance that if she disappeared, it should not be considered an accident.

Sure enough, Helle Crafts dropped out of sight that November, Richard spreading the tale that she had run off with an Asian lover. No one who knew the couple bought his story, and police asked Crafts to take a polygraph test, results of which were inconclusive. Meanwhile, a quiet background check disclosed that Crafts had rented a large wood chipper shortly before his wife vanished. He had also purchased a new freezer, along with replacement carpet and mattresses for the master bedroom of their home. The final pieces of the puzzle fell into place when a snow-plow driver told authorities that he had seen a man on the banks of the Housatonic River, feeding brush into a wood chipper in the predawn hours of November 19.

A search was undertaken on the river bank, recovering 2,660 hairs, shreds of flesh, chips of bone including a human thumb tip, and a gold-capped tooth. Altogether, the remains weighed less than a pound and could fit in the palm of one hand. Nearby, beneath a bridge, searchers found a chainsaw with the serial number clumsily removed, and the saw was finally traced back to Crafts. Police and prosecutors now believed that Crafts had bludgeoned Helle in the bedroom of their home, afterward freezing her body to minimize splatter of flesh and bone as she was first dismembered with the chain saw, then ground into mulch with the chipper. Arrested on January 13, 1987, Crafts was held on $750,000 bond — a new record for Connecticut, at the time. Tabloid publicity surrounding his case resulted in a change of venue to New London, where the televised trial began on April 4, 1988. Scientific evidence was the key to the prosecution's case, including identification of the single gold-capped tooth as Helle's to a "reasonable scientific certainty," but the jury deadlocked for a grueling 17 days. Finally, on July 16, a mistrial was declared when one of the jurors walked out on deliberations, angrily insisting that Helle Crafts was still alive.

A second trial began in Norwalk, Connecticut, on September 7, 1989, and lasted nine weeks, including testimony from 115 witnesses and some 380 exhibits. This time, however, the jury was more decisive, deliberating only three days before Crafts was convicted of first-degree murder on November 21. Sentenced to 50 years in prison, Crafts is required by state law to serve at least 20 years before he is considered for parole.

# Davis, Len

Len Davis was a problem cop from Day One. Before he ever applied for a job with New Orleans P.D., he had already been arrested on charges of assault and urinating in public. Admitted to the police academy against all logic, in 1987, he was kicked out for disciplinary infractions, but then was allowed to return and complete the course. On the street, he quickly amassed a file of civilian complaints, ranging from simple discourtesy to theft, physical intimidation, and outright brutality. By 1994, he had logged two reprimands and four suspensions — including a 51-day suspension in 1992 for striking a woman in the head with his flashlight. On the side, it was rumored, he also dealt drugs, and residents of the Desire public housing project dubbed him "the Desire Terrorist," because of his quick-trigger violence.

It is, perhaps, a commentary on the state of law enforcement in New Orleans that a cop like Davis could retain his badge despite such extreme behavior. As one disgusted fellow officer explained the situation, "He had an internal affairs jacket as thick as a telephone book, but supervisors have swept his dirt under the rug for so long that it's coming back to haunt them."

The haunting in question began on October 11, 1993, when Davis and patrol partner Sammie Williams assaulted and pistol-whipped 17-year-old Nathan Norwood. A friend of Norwood's, 32-year-old Kim Marie Groves, witnessed the assault and filed a brutality complaint against Davis and Williams the following day. Less than 24 hours later, on October 13, the complaint went up in smoke when Groves was murdered on the street, gunned down with a single 9mm gunshot to the head at point-blank range.

It might have been a lucky break for Davis, but this time the local brass would not have time to cover his tracks. Unknown to New Orleans officials, FBI agents were even then investigating charges of police corruption in the Crescent City, including allegations that police were selling drugs stolen from the department's evidence locker. Davis was among the targets of that probe, and G-men were monitoring his cellular phone on the night of October 13, when Kim Groves was killed.

What they heard — and recorded — was nothing less than a murder plot in progress. Specifically, the tape caught Davis directing a hit team in pursuit of Kim Groves, describing her movements and clothing on the fatal night, then waiting for word that the job had been done. When it came, Davis burst out exultantly, "Yeah! Rock-a-bye!"

Aside from Davis, participants in the murder scheme were identified as triggerman Paul ("Cool") Hardy, a 27-year-old drug dealer, and lookout Damon Causey, age 24. On December 5, all three were arrested on federal charges of violating their victim's civil rights. Two days later, Davis and eight other cops were indicted on additional narcotics charges, which alleged that they had accepted $97,000 in bribes for looting a police warehouse of cocaine, afterward distributing the dope from their patrol cars. New Orleans District Attorney Harry Connick, Sr. declined to file state murder charges, telling the press that the feds were in charge. (Connick had earlier used the same excuse for his failure to indict a Catholic priest on charges of producing child pornography. The federal charge in that case never materialized, and reporters went back to ask Connick when the priest would be indicted. His reply: "Never, as long as I'm district attorney.")

On December 13, Davis, Hardy, and Causey were formally indicted for conspiring to violate Kim Groves's civil rights. Eight days later, the trio pled not guilty before U.S. Magistrate Louis Moore, Jr. Trial was set for February 13, 1995, with Assistant U.S. Attorney Constantine Georges announcing his intent to seek the death penalty on Davis and Hardy. On January 7, 1995, 25-year-old Steve Jackson was charged as an accessory after the fact, for driving the getaway car. Jackson quickly "rolled over," maintaining that he had cooperated with the killers because he feared for his life, offering to testify as a prosecution witness in return for leniency in sentencing.

Trials are rarely held on the first date scheduled, and the Davis case was no exception. On March 24, 1995, new indictments were filed on Davis, Hardy, and Causey, accusing them of conspiracy to kill Nathan Norwood. Once again, the plot had been discussed via cellular phone, recorded by the FBI on October 17th. Hardy had been all for killing Norwood, but Davis had postponed the hit, reserving lethal action "unless [Norwood] persisted in complaining" to Internal Affairs.

On December 13, nearly a year after his trial was supposed to begin, Davis fired attorney Curklin Atkins, claiming that their relationship had "deteriorated beyond repair." More specifically, Davis charged that Atkins wanted him to lie under oath, concerning legal fees, in a scheme that would inflate the lawyer's tab. No charges were filed against Atkins, but he was allowed to retire from the case, replaced by new court-appointed counsel.

Jury selection for Davis, Hardy, and Causey finally began on April 8, 1996, and lasted a week before Judge Ginger Berrigan. Opening statements were heard on April 16, and a forensic pathologist, Dr. Susan Garcia, kicked off the prosecution's case with testimony on the cause of death. Defense attorneys grudgingly admitted that Davis had celebrated the news of Kim Groves's death, but they dismissed the cheering as "misplaced emotion," simple venting of his anger over her complaint to the New Orleans brass. Steve Jackson also testified for the government, admitting that he had lied to FBI agents the first time around, "to keep myself out of trouble."

On April 17, jurors heard the tapes of Davis in action, telling Hardy, "After it's done, go straight uptown and call me." Another surprise prosecution witness was Patrolman Sammie Williams, testifying against Davis as part of his own plea bargain with the feds. It was Williams who told the court that Davis had paid Hardy $300 for the murder contract, but "Len didn't have to pay him the money. Paul would have done it anyway."

Defense attorneys suggested an alternate suspect in the murder, recalling that a witness to the shooting resembled a former boyfriend of the victim, but the jury didn't buy it. On April 24th, after deliberating for one day, the panel convicted all three defendants, moving on to the penalty phase of the trial on April 25th. Davis and Hardy were condemned to die, while Causey drew a life sentence for his role as the triggerman's sidekick.

Len Davis had not seen the end of his troubles yet, however. On September 13, 1996, he was convicted on federal narcotics charges. By that time, five other cops in his drug ring had already pled guilty, drawing prison terms that averaged seven years per man. Formally sentenced to death for the Groves murder on November 7, Davis told Judge Berrigan, "I'm innocent of these charges. Y'all are sending an innocent man to death row." Six weeks later, his tune was the same when he received a sentence of life plus five years on the narcotics conviction. This time, the former Desire

Terrorist accused Judge Berrigan and his prosecutors of participation in a "lynching."

# Davis, Robert

Davis, a detective with the New York City police department, was arrested on February 14, 1976, as the alleged triggerman in the October 1975 murder of a Denver, Colorado, businessman, Harold Levine. At the same time, Michael Borelli, a retired NYPD detective and one-time partner with Levine in a holding company called U.S. Hamel Corporation, was jailed in Denver, charged with paying Davis $5,000 to commit the murder. As outlined by investigators, Borelli's motive had involved a $5.2 million life insurance policy on Levine, purchased by the corporation a short time before the murder. Two others arrested for allegedly participating in the plot were reputed Mafia members Anthony D'Prero and Anunzio Saccone. Davis was held without bond in New York, pending extradition, while the NYPD launched a hasty probe of possible police-mob connections.

By February 19, indictments had been issued in Denver, naming Robert Davis as Levine's actual killer, while Borelli, D'Prero and Saccone were charged as conspirators in the crime. On June 17, still in New York, D'Prero testified under a grant of immunity, describing how he assisted Davis in killing Levine. At his trial that September, Davis was acquitted of murder but convicted of conspiracy on September 23. Nine months later, on June 3, 1977, he was sentenced to life imprisonment for his role in the crime. Michael Borelli and Anunzio Saccone were tried separately and sentenced to long prison terms of their own.

# Delacruz, Guillermo

Suburban El Cajon, in San Diego County, California, had never seen a police officer murdered off-duty before Friday, June 7, 1996, when *two* were shot and killed. Even more shocking than the double homicide, however, was the identity of the triggerman: another policeman, this one from Los Angeles.

It was 12:11 p.m. when police in La Mesa, another San Diego suburb next door to El Cajon, received a 911 emergency call from a private home on Blackton Drive. A woman's voice blurted out, "I need help!" before the line went dead, but it was enough. Police dispatchers already had the phone number, and the address was quickly determined, patrol units rolling toward the scene. No one answered the door when patrolmen came knocking, and the drapes were shut, preventing them from seeing anything inside. Rather than crash the door without due cause, the officers waited outside until a search warrant arrived, around four p.m.

For those inside, the wait made no difference at all. Officers who finally entered the house found three corpses and no one alive. In one bedroom, 33-year-old Mark Amato, an El Cajon policeman, lay dead on the bed, his body punctured by multiple gunshot wounds. In the other bedroom, there were two bodies. Patricia Garcia, a 26-year-old El Cajon police officer, lay sprawled beneath the corpse of LAPD rookie Guillermo Delacruz, age 29. Because of the positioning and wounds — only Delacruz had died from a single shot to the head — investigators called the case a double murder followed by the killer's suicide.

As far as motive went, the best they could come up with was apparent jealousy. Delacruz had shared the house with Garcia, commuting 120 miles each day to his job in Los Angeles, and they had described themselves to various friends as "engaged." Still, something had gone wrong in paradise. Garcia's ex-husband told police that the relationship between Delacruz and his former wife had recently soured. On Friday morning, shortly before the massacre, a neighbor recalled seeing Delacruz loading the back of a pickup truck with personal items, as if he were preparing to move out.

Delacruz, an ex-marine who joined the LAPD in April 1995, had only completed his academy training in November of that year. With less than a year on the job, he was still a rookie, though no longer "green." Already, he had begun to discuss a transfer, hoping to join the El Cajon force, when his probationary period with the LAPD was completed. Amato and Garcia, meanwhile, had graduated from the El Cajon police academy together, and were known as friends. The problem, apparently, stemmed from the fact that Delacruz could only live in El Cajon on weekends, sharing a room with other cops in L.A. during the regular week. In short order, the relationship deteriorated to the point that Delacruz told his brother, Alfi, that Patty Garcia "was verbally abusive and slapped and hit him." Investigators surmise that Delacruz had come to retrieve his belongings on Friday, but found Garcia with Amato in the house, which made him "snap." Alfi Delacruz, for one, had no doubt in his mind that Amato and Garcia were secret lovers.

Whatever the case, three deaths left two police departments reeling. El Cajon P.D., with only 129 officers on the roll, felt the loss most acutely, but LAPD spokesmen also professed to be stunned. Deputy Chief Mark Kroeker, commanding the LAPD's South Bureau, told reporters, "This is the worst of all worlds, here. For us to lose one of our officers, and for another agency to lose two of theirs at the same time — it doesn't get much worse." Down in El Cajon, meanwhile, Capt. Bill McClurg said, "We're all very down, here, overwhelmed by a sense of loss and hopelessness. This is a tightly knit department — we all know each other, and we all feel like family. This is the worst kind of grieving."

And so much worse, for all that, because the damage had been inflicted by one of their own.

# Duncan, Joe Cecil, Jr.

Alabama state trooper Elizabeth Cobb was assigned to work from 2:00 P.M. until 11:00 p.m. on Sunday, October 11, 1987. It was supposed to be a routine shift, as always, on the quiet roads of Selma and surrounding Dallas County. Selma's last big claim to notoriety had been in 1965, when troopers and a group of sheriff's deputies had gassed and beaten civil rights protesters on the Edmund Pettus bridge, while TV cameras filmed the action for posterity. But things had changed in Selma, over twenty years — if not the attitudes, at least the action.

Trooper Cobb, at thirty-one, could count on speeders, possibly a drunk or two, to break up the routine of cruising endlessly, assisting motorists whose cars broke down, or checking out the odd abandoned car. It was a mystery, therefore, when she dropped out of touch with the dispatcher following a brief contact at 7:32 p.m. When Cobb did not report herself off-duty at 11:00 p.m., or by midnight, the dispatcher grew concerned. A phone call to Cobb's home got no response, so the dispatcher called another trooper, 32-year-old Joe Duncan, with the knowledge that he was supposed to be a friend of Cobb's. Duncan's telephone was busy, though, so the dispatcher sent a squad car to Cobb's house. There was nobody home, and the patrolman drove to Duncan's home, where Joe informed him that he had not spoken with Elizabeth since seven o'clock Sunday night.

A search began at once, climaxed at 9:38 on Monday morning, when her patrol car was found behind a rural church, not far from town. Still slumped behind the steering wheel, Cobb had been shot three times in the head. Her car keys, ticket book, and service revolver were missing from the crime scene. Autopsy results identified the murder weapon as a .22-caliber pistol, pegging the time of death between seven and nine o'clock, Sunday night.

Investigators knew that Cobb had been alive at 7:32 p.m., when she checked in by radio, and they soon heard from a trucker, who told them Cobb had stopped him for speeding around eight p.m. Instead of writing him a ticket, though, she left him sitting on the roadside, with an order to remain in place, after a Trans-Am with loud tailpipes sped past on the highway. Dutifully, the trucker waited for three-quarters of an hour, finally giving up and going on his way when Cobb did not return.

Authorities were briefly hopeful when they learned about a Trans-Am stopped in Okaloosa County, Florida, not far across the Alabama line. Its driver, Charlie Shoemaker, was jailed on firearms charges when a .22 equipped with an illegal silencer was spotted in the car. It was a tantalizing lead, but subsequent ballistics tests cleared Shoemaker of any possible involvement in the homicide, and so the search resumed, closer to home.

By that time, homicide detectives knew that Cobb and Trooper Duncan had been something more than friends. In fact, the word was out that they were lovers, possibly engaged to marry, and investigation soon identified Joe Duncan as the beneficiary on Cobb's $250,000 life insurance policy, which took effect ten days before her death — with an additional $100,000 scheduled for payment in case of accidental death (a category that included murder). Duncan's fingerprints were found on certain documents, inside Cobb's squad car, and while Duncan first said he was playing cards on Sunday night, he later changed his story. In the second version, he described himself discovering his lover's body, at the church, then told investigators he had panicked, leaving her for someone else to find.

Detectives from the Alabama Bureau of Investigation didn't buy the story, noting that Duncan was heavily in debt and could have used the fat insurance payoff to resolve his difficulties. Duncan was arrested on October 20, following his attendance at Cobb's funeral. The warrant, charging him with capital murder, alleged that Duncan had supplied investigators with information on "circumstances surrounding her death which would be unknown to anyone other than the perpetrator."

Duncan faced more embarrassment on November 10, when a panel of state troopers recommended his dismissal from the force. Attorney J.L. Chestnut protested the closed hearing, telling reporters that "The state of Alabama suspended the Constitution of the United States yesterday morning. The state became the prosecutor, judge, and jury." Captain Roy Smith had a rather different take on Duncan's situation, though, reminding newsmen that "He had knowledge of a homicide and where the victim was and failed to take proper action." A letter from Colonel Tom Wells, Alabama's director of public safety, reminded Duncan that "you by your own admission came upon the still warm and bleeding body of trooper

Elizabeth Cobb and then without so much as a single word to another living human being, you abandoned her." Such action was "unacceptable and despicable," as far as Colonel Wells was concerned, bringing "shame and embarrassment" upon the force at large.

Judge Charles Thigpen, meanwhile, issued an order on November 12, requiring Duncan to undergo psychiatric examination by a two-member lunacy commission at Taylor Hardin Secure Medical Facility, in Tuscaloosa. Judge Thigpen cited "reasonable grounds to believe that Duncan was insane, either at the time of the commission of the offense or presently," but Dallas County prosecutor Ed Greene disagreed. "There's nothing wrong with him," Greene told the press, "and we're ready to try him tomorrow."

In fact, it would be four months more before Greene got his chance. Jury selection for Duncan's trial began in Selma on March 8, 1988, after Judge J.C. Norton rejected defense motions for a change of venue. At trial, prosecutors stressed the profit motive and Duncan's record of lying to investigators, using circumstantial evidence to compensate for their lack of the still-missing murder weapon. Defense attorneys, for their part, contended that Trooper Cobb was shot by anonymous drug dealers, after she stopped them for speeding. Duncan's failure to report discovering her body, the defense maintained, was simple panic — reprehensible, perhaps, in a policeman, but still understandable in one who has discovered his fiancée slain by criminals. A videotape of Duncan's statement to police was played in court, Duncan alleging that he kept a lover's rendezvous with Cobb the night she died, but found her dead — ironically, dumped by her killers at the very spot where she and Duncan were supposed to meet.

The jury didn't buy it, deliberating for barely three hours on March 21, before convicting Duncan of first-degree murder. A day later, completing the penalty phase of the trial, jurors required only 15 minutes to recommend a sentence of life imprisonment without parole, but Judge Norton had other ideas. A jury's recommendation is not binding under Alabama law, and when Duncan next stood before him, on April 12, Norton imposed a sentence of death. Tearfully, Joe Duncan told the court, "I loved Elizabeth. I loved her dearly. I stand before you an innocent man. I will face one other judge — Saint Peter. Standing behind me will be Elizabeth, and we will walk arm in arm to meet our savior."

Perhaps, but before he went to his reward, Duncan was entitled by law to an automatic appeal of his death sentence. The Alabama Court of Criminal Appeals overturned Duncan's conviction in August 1990, based on the prosecution's failure to produce a yellow legal pad, on which state troopers had recorded several tips about a blue or black Trans-Am, initially believed to be the killer's vehicle. In theory, the omission had prevented Duncan from obtaining a "fair trial," and he was granted a new hearing on the case. The second trial was initially scheduled for 1992, but defense motions dragged the proceedings out until June 1995, when Duncan pled guilty on a reduced charge of second-degree murder, accepting a 25 year prison term.

## Earp, Wyatt Berry Stapp

Few characters of the American West have been credited with more heroic deeds than Wyatt Earp, including feature films and television series, novels and laudatory biographies. A few, like Jesse James and Billy the Kid, were known outlaws, their lives presented as an object lesson, even among those who regarded them as victims of circumstance. In Earp's case, though, the legend is a nearly total fabrication, concocted decades after the fact. Those who knew Wyatt Earp in his heyday had a very different view of the man who would become an American icon.

One of five rugged brothers, Wyatt Earp was born in Illinois, but his family moved to California in 1864. There, he worked as a stagecoach driver, bartender and gambler, before he was indicted for horse theft in 1871 and fled the state after posting a $500 bond. Thereafter, he shot buffalo for a while, then became a policeman in Wichita, Kansas. His record there was undistinguished, despite later embellishments, and he was fired in 1874, after his superiors noted that fines collected by Earp rarely reached the town treasury.

**Wyatt Earp**
*Courtesy of Mercaldo Archives.*

From 1876 to 1879, Earp served as marshal in Dodge City, where legend once more outdistanced reality. In fact, he killed only one man in Dodge, a drunk named George Hoy (or Hoyt) who may or may not have been trying to collect a bounty placed on Earp's head by a disgruntled Texas rancher. The famous Dodge City "cleanup" conducted by Earp and Bat Masterson was half-hearted at best, since both men spent off-duty hours gambling and pandering, widely known in Dodge as the "Fighting Pimps." Brother James Earp and his prostitute wife ran one saloon-brothel, which enjoyed Wyatt's special protection and kicked back a share of the profits.

By 1879, Dodge City had become more civilized, and the income from vice was declining. Wyatt struck off for the silver-rich wilds of Arizona Territory, stopping along the way in Mobeetie, Texas, where he joined part-time lawman **Dave Mather** in selling phony "gold bricks" to ignorant cowboys. The scam was short-lived, however, and they were soon run out of town by Sheriff James McIntire.

In Tombstone, Arizona, Wyatt opened a saloon with brother James tending bar, while several of the Earp women opened brothels. Another Earp brother — Virgil — became temporary town marshal when Tombstone's regular lawman was killed, and Wyatt quickly stepped in as his deputy. The stage had been set for one of the Wild West's most infamous feuds, paving the way for the most notorious shootout of all time.

Crime in the vicinity of Tombstone was clearly divided between the "townie/gambler" element, now dominated by the Earps, and a rural clique of rustlers and highwaymen, the Clanton gang. Newman ("Old Man") Clanton ran the outfit from his spread at Lewis Springs, robbing travelers and shuttling stolen cattle back and forth across the Mexican border. Besides Clanton's sons John — known as "Ike" — and Billy, the gang also included such worthies as Billy Claiborne, John Ringo, Frank Stillwell, the McLowery brothers, and William Graham — better known as Curly Bill Brocius. The Clantons had no real use for Tombstone, except when it came to drinking, whoring, and generally raising hell, but the Earps were tightening their grip in town, enforcing new, strict regulations in an effort to drive Clanton's "cowboys" out of business.

Both sides, in 1881, were anxious to control the sheriff's office for newly created Cochise County, a post worth $40,000 a year when graft and diversion of tax money was considered. Wyatt Earp coveted the job, but it went instead to John Behan, an open ally of the Clantons, thus paving the way for disaster. Frustrated in his primary goal, Earp muscled his way into part ownership of the thriving Oriental Saloon and Gambling House, his ferocity earning him a share of the profits with no cash investment.

By early 1881, the Earp-Clanton feud was heating up in Tombstone, with four Earp brothers in town, supported by the tubercular dentist and quick-trigger gunman John ("Doc") Holliday. That March, a Kinnear and Company stagecoach was robbed outside town, with two men shot and killed. Doc Holliday was named as a suspect in the holdup, and briefly jailed in June, but the charges were dismissed for lack of evidence. Wyatt Earp, meanwhile, had three different suspects in mind — all members or associates of the Clanton gang. Unable to find them himself, Wyatt approached Ike Clanton and offered to give up the $6,000 reward Wells Fargo had offered for the bandits, if only Ike would hand them over and let Wyatt take credit for the arrest. Clanton agreed, but he never had a chance to make good on the deal. That August, one of the fugitives was killed — along with Old Man Clanton himself — when Mexicans ambushed the gang at Guadalupe Canyon. The other two, Bill Leonard and Harry Head [!], were shot and killed during a bungled holdup in New Mexico.

Deprived of his headlines, Earp next spread the story that Ike Clanton had offered to sell out his friends, a report that infuriated Ike and made him swear vengeance on the Earps. A series of near-miss encounters followed, members of each side taunting and threatening the other, until the trouble came to a head on October 26, 1881. That morning, Ike Clanton and Tom McLowery were "buffaloed" — that is, pistol-whipped and arrested — by the Earp brothers in Tombstone. Ike wound up in court, fined $25, with his weapons confiscated, and the taunts continued, Morgan Earp offering to pay Clanton's fine if he would only agree to a shootout. (Most of the Clanton gang were considered inept gunmen, by comparison with Holliday and the Earps.) Later the same day, word reached Wyatt that Ike and Tom McLowery had been seen at the O.K. Corral, together with Billy Clanton, Billy Claiborne, and Tom's brother Frank. Arming themselves and swearing Doc Holliday in as a deputy, the Earps moved out to settle their feud with the Clanton gang once and for all. John Behan tried to head them off, promising to disarm Ike's group himself, but the Earps had no interest in peaceful solutions.

The rest is history — or, rather, mythology: thirty seconds of action followed by a century of propaganda, ranging from dime novels and Earp's own self-serving biography, through at least six motion pictures and an episode of *Star Trek*. Each description of the fight (or massacre) presents a slightly different twist, and little can be said with certainty today, except that three men died and three were wounded. It is, however, possible to draw at least some general conclusions.

First, the famous shootout did not occur at the O.K. Corral, but nearby, in an alley adjacent to Camillus Fly's photographic studio. Two of the Clanton group — Ike and Tom McLowery — were certainly unarmed when the Earps and Holliday arrived, Virgil Earp confusing matters at the start with a shouted order to "Give up your arms or throw up your arms!" Billy Clanton and Frank McLowery may have reached for their guns at that point, but neither had drawn yet, when Virgil said, "Hold! I don't mean that. I have come to disarm you." Tom McLowery responded by yanking open his vest, showing himself defenseless, and replying, "I have nothing."

It is still unclear who fired the first shot, but Wyatt Earp is a likely suspect, his bullet striking Frank McLowery in the stomach. Frank staggered away, his gun still holstered, as the alley exploded in a blaze of gunfire. Billy Clanton fired at Wyatt and missed, while Tom McLowery ducked behind his brother's horse for cover and Billy Claiborne ran for the cover of Fly's studio. Billy Clanton was the next to fall, shot in the wrist and chest by Morgan Earp; he slumped against a wall and switched his pistol to his left hand, desperate to stay in the fight. Unarmed, Ike Clanton dodged a shotgun blast from Holliday and followed Billy Claiborne's example, running for cover at Fly's. Meanwhile, the noise from Doc's ten-gauge spooked Frank McLowery's horse, exposing Tom to a charge of buckshot that killed him where he stood. Frank had his gun out now, as Holliday approached him, revolver in hand, and they exchanged shots at close range, Doc falling with a bullet in his hip. Billy Clanton, meanwhile, was still blazing away, striking Virgil Earp on one leg and wounding Morgan in the shoulder. Wyatt and Morgan both returned fire, and Billy was dying, still begging for more ammunition, when Camillus Fly removed the empty pistol from his hand. He was dying, the two McLowery brothers already dead.

Tombstone's citizens and newspapers quickly chose up sides, the pro-Earp *Tombstone Telegraph* burying a small report of the gunfight on page three, while the dead men were laid out at a local undertaker's parlor, beneath a sign that read MURDERED ON THE STREETS OF TOMBSTONE. Wyatt and Doc Holliday were ultimately charged with murder, but the charges were dismissed by a friendly justice of the peace.

The Earp-Clanton feud was not finished, however. Curly Bill Brocius had assumed control of the gang when Old Man Clanton died in Mexico, and he was hungry for revenge against the Earps. On November 28, 1881, Virgil Earp was ambushed on a city street, cut down by five shotgun blasts that permanently disabled his left arm. Four months later, Morgan Earp was playing pool when unseen gunmen shot him in the back. Wyatt blamed the murder on Brocius, Frank Stillwell (himself a deputy sheriff under John Behan), and a halfbreed named Florentino Cruz, who allegedly received $25 to hold the killers' horses.

Revenge for Morgan's death was not long in coming. Wyatt and brother Warren were putting Virgil and his family on a train to California when they spotted four gunmen lurking in the shadows. Wyatt's first shot killed Pete Spence, a member of the Clanton team, and moments later he cornered Frank Stillwell, blasting the renegade deputy with both barrels of a shotgun at point-blank range. From there, the hunt was on, and there would be no mercy. Wyatt led the posse that riddled Florentino Cruz with bullets, and he is generally given credit for the death of Bill Brocius as well, though reports of that shooting vary. Johnny Ringo, the best — or worst — gunman of the Clanton gang, was found shot in the head by persons unknown at Turkey Creek Canyon, in July 1882. A short time later, the weight of public opinion encouraged Wyatt to depart from Tombstone, leaving the field to his rival John Behan, but his rival's triumph was brief. Before the year's end, Behan resigned his post in lieu of facing trial for financial irregularities, but he still couldn't keep his nose clean. Indicted for collecting taxes after he left office, Behan fled one jump ahead of his arrest and never returned to Tombstone.

As for Wyatt, he was back in Dodge City by 1883, joining the misnamed Dodge City Peace Commission under corrupt mayor "Dog" Kelly. Despite its label, the Peace Commission was, in truth, a team of mercenary gunmen hired to support Kelly's saloon, gambling and brothel interests against would-be "reformers" — most of whom, it must be conceded, were more interested in seizing control of the lucrative vice trade than shutting it down. With notorious gunmen such as Earp, Doc Holliday, Luke Short, Bat Masterson, Shotgun Collins, and "Dark Alley Jim" on the team, it took minimal persuasion for Mayor Kelly's side to carry the day. It is worth noting, perhaps, that Dodge City's newspaper did not remember Wyatt as the man who "cleaned up" Dodge in the 1870s, preferring to describe him as a gunman "famous in the cheerful business of depopulating the county."

By 1884, Earp had surfaced in Idaho Territory, where he ran a couple of saloons with brother James, further involving himself in a consortium that specialized in claim jumping. Before long, he was "encouraged" to sojourn elsewhere, making his way back to California, where he spent the rest of his life (aside from four years of fruitless gold prospecting in Alaska). In the 1920s, Earp haunted the Hollywood movie lots, befriending stars such as Tom Mix and William S. Hart in an effort to promote his own fading legend. In 1927, he began collaborating with a writer on a glorified autobiography, but Earp died on January 13, 1929, before the book was published.

# Erler, Robert John, Jr.

At 6:18 A.M. on August 12, 1968, an anonymous caller told the sheriff's office in Fort Lauderdale, Florida, "I just killed three people! Please catch me before I kill more!" Despite pleas to "come and get me," the male caller refused to give his name or location, signing off with the advice that "I'm going to kill more tonight, too!"

A short time later, security guards at Fort Lauderdale's airport found a woman slumped in her car, in an airport parking lot. She had been shot five times in the head, apparently from close range, but she was still alive. Rushed to the nearest hospital, she was identified as 42-year-old Dorothy Clark, from Clarkston, Georgia. While surgeons were fighting to save her life, Patrolman Robert Erler, of the Hollywood Police Department, was dispatched to a local industrial park, allegedly responding to a motorist's report of a body lying in a field. It proved to be Clark's daughter, 12-year-old Merilyn, shot five times in the head and certified dead at the scene. Police felt certain they had found two of their anonymous caller's victims, but no third body was ever located to round out the score.

Bob Erler was a rookie with the Hollywood P.D., born July 1, 1944, in Adam, Massachusetts, whose family had relocated in Phoenix when he was a child. A black-belt karate expert who enlisted in the U.S. Army after high school, he signed up for training as a Green Beret, but received a premature hardship discharge when his father fell terminally ill. Soon married in Phoenix, he found wedded bliss elusive, and moved his bride to Florida in search of a fresh start. Starting off as a patrolman in the tiny town of Dania, Erler clashed repeatedly with black officers on the force, disgusted by their on-duty flirtations with white barmaids. Coming home one night to find a black cop sitting in his living room with Erler's wife, Bob ordered him out of the house and resigned the next day, transferring to Hollywood P.D. He made good grades at the police academy — his first real training, since the Dania department offered none — and seemed to enjoy his new job. Now, in August 1968, he was in the thick of a double murder investigation, assigned to supervise a voice recognition campaign using tapes of the anonymous "Catch-Me Killer's" telephone call.

By August 19, Dorothy Clark had recovered sufficiently to describe her attacker as a young man in a police uniform. He had approached the car while Clark and her daughter were sleeping on

Dania Beach, shined a flashlight in their eyes, and demanded money. Her assailant had been husky, with a blond crew cut, but the rest of it was vague, due to Clark's head injury. Still, it was enough for Erler, whose marriage was now on the rocks, and he surprised his supervisor with the news that he was quitting, moving back to Arizona, where his mother needed help around the house. He had been gone a week, when one of Erler's former coworkers from Dania identified his voice on the "Catch-Me Killer" tape and fingered Bob as the anonymous caller. Hollywood detectives checked Erler's log for August 12 and discovered that he had no name, address or license number for the "motorist" who had spotted Merilyn Clark's body. Furthermore, the field was too dark at night for any passing driver to notice a corpse on the ground. But if Erler had not been tipped-off to the girl's whereabouts, how had he known where to find her?

Unless....

The case was broken when Dorothy Clark picked Erler's photo as a likeness of her attacker, and a warrant for his arrest was issued on September 13. Arrested in Phoenix two days later, Erler kicked a press photographer in the groin at his arraignment, then smashed his manacled hands through a window, severing an artery in his left wrist. It was all in vain, and he was held in lieu of $85,000 bond pending extradition to Florida. An indictment for second-degree murder awaited him there, Erler basing his defense on contradictory statements from Dorothy Clark, before she identified his photograph. Physical evidence was sparse, but Clark stood ready to testify for the prosecution, still carrying the would-be killer's bullets in her head. Erler was briefly encouraged on September 24, when the victim failed to pick him out of a lineup, and defense attorneys were still seeking an alternate suspect when his trial opened on January 27, 1969.

In court, Dorothy Clark's story was very different from the initial report, made within days of her shooting. Now, she described Patrolman Erler approaching her car on Dania Beach, informing her that it was illegal to sleep out in public. Instead of forcing them to move along, however, he had invited Dorothy and Merilyn back to his trailer, explaining that he was married, with an infant son. Clark had been surprised, therefore, to find no wife or child waiting for them in the mobile home, but Merilyn had lain down to sleep on one of Erler's two sofas. Drawing Dorothy aside, Erler had propositioned her, then drew a pistol and began to masturbate in front of her when she refused to have sex with him. After he finished, he escorted mother and daughter back out to their car, still brandishing the gun, and *then* demanded money. Clark had turned to Merilyn with a rueful smile, saying, "Boy, I can sure pick them," and that was the last she remembered before she awoke in the hospital, more than three weeks later.

Defense attorneys tried to shake her story, but in vain. Erler took the stand on his own behalf, denying any part in the crime, while his counsel summed up by stressing the lack of forensic evidence. The jury convicted Erler on January 31st and recommended a prison term of 99 years, to which the presiding judge added another six months for good measure.

Confined at Raiford prison, Erler refused protective custody, his dual status as an ex-policeman and a convicted child killer prompting repeated inmate attacks, costing him several teeth, a broken jaw, and a head wound requiring more than 100 stitches. His blankets and clothing were also burned more than once, before he was finally transferred to the medium-security Bell Glade Correctional Institute, on Lake Okeechobee. There, in August 1973, Erler escaped through the swamp and made his way to Miami, where he organized a loose-knit gang of mercenary hoodlums. On March 31, 1974, authorities were alerted to a package containing marijuana and a pistol, addressed to one "Bruce Strickland" at the Mathison, Mississippi post office. When Erler showed up to collect it, sporting black-dyed hair and fake I.D., he was pursued by sheriff's officers in a high-speed chase, until he crashed his car. Trying to escape on foot, the "Catch-Me Killer" finally surrendered after a rifle slug drilled him through the buttocks.

Returned to prison under surveillance as an escape risk, Erler reportedly experienced a jailhouse religious conversion, confessing his attack on the Clarks and withdrawing the appeal of his conviction. Before long, he was recognized as leader of the Christian Men's Fellowship at Florida State Prison, and he also organized an inmate chapter of the Jaycees. In 1977, he was transferred to Arizona's state pen, where he continued his career as an evangelist, baptizing more than 100 convicts in an irrigation ditch on prison grounds. A year later, Arizona's parole board recommended his release, but Florida officials demanded that he serve a minimum of 25 years on his sentence. All the same, he was released from custody on July 19, 1983, to resume preaching as a free man. "Religion," he likes to say, "is the best armor that a man can have, but it is the worst cloak."

## Fioretti, Robert

Born August 9, 1949, Robert Fioretti took a civilian job with the New York City Police Department in 1968, as part of the same program that enlisted wife-killer **Mark Stahl** (and which was later canceled, largely based upon the poor quality of recruits obtained). Two years later, shortly after turning 21, Fioretti became a full-fledged patrolman with the NYPD and hit the mean streets with a gun on his hip. In the fall of 1971, he met Rita Hauser on a blind date, and she was pregnant when they wed, in March 1972. Oddly, Rita only met Fioretti's family after the wedding, and they seemed to despise her on sight, a feeling that soon became mutual.

Within a month of the wedding, Rita and Robert were having trouble at home. For one thing, she disliked guns, while Robert collected them, displaying a fondness for weapons which Rita viewed as "bordering on the erotic." Robert also began to display a dangerous "Jekyll and Hyde" personality, soft-spoken and gentle one moment, violently angry the next. Infuriated by the most trivial incidents, he soon progressed from verbal abuse of Rita to vicious beatings, the latter invariably followed by tearful promises to mend his ways. Before they were married a year, Rita had already fled their Bronx home once, in fear for her life, but Robert wooed her back and truly seemed to change... until the next time. Through it all, Rita was grimly determined to make her marriage "work."

Robert, meanwhile, was busy enacting a peculiar charade in 1974, huddling with an attorney to plan his divorce. Another officer provided Fioretti with a false affidavit, swearing that he and Robert had served Rita with divorce papers on May 20 of that year. A month later, citing her "failure to respond," Fioretti petitioned the court for immediate dissolution of his marriage. The decree was granted on July 22, but it had no legal effect, being returned by the post office as "undeliverable." In February 1975, Fioretti moved his "ex"-wife and son into a new $75,000 home, paying $15,000 down in cash, with a $30,000 mortgage. His new neighbors quickly learned to avoid him, regarding him as "weird" and dangerous. Out walking his police dog one night, Fioretti allowed the animal to attack a neighbor's dog, then pulled a sawed-off shotgun from beneath his coat and warned the other man, "Get that mutt out of here, or I'll blow your fucking dog away."

Fioretti's behavior at home was a mirror-image of his conduct on the job, marking him early on as an erratic, rogue cop. Devoid of ambition and virtually friendless on the job, except for a handful of misfits such as Mark Stahl, Fioretti logged a series of disciplinary citations for sleeping on duty, forging stolen property vouchers, and lying about his location to avoid work details. Punished with loss of vacation time and extra duty assignments, Fioretti might have been fired except for the blizzard of traffic tickets he wrote on each shift — an average of 50 or 60 per day, producing more revenue for the city. Even so, his brother officers noted that Fioretti avoided "high-risk" traffic stops, confining his attention to women, young teens, and the elderly, writing them up for the most part on trivial violations such as burned-out taillights or improper display of license plates. Many of his targets, like the black nurse he addressed as a "nigger cunt," complained of verbal abuse from Officer Fioretti, and other cops branded him "that asshole" when he began harassing tow-truck drivers answering police calls. Once, he was beaten up on the street after stopping and insulting an off-duty policeman. Other cops responded to the "assist officer" radio call, then stood by and watched Fioretti taking his licks; not one of them saw fit to record the incident in their patrol logs.

Finally, even the friendly brass had their fill of Bob Fioretti, and he was transferred from traffic patrol to an undercover assignment, investigating allegations of money laundering through a Bronx armored-car company. While so engaged, he managed to miss an $11 million robbery arranged by the company's owners, an oversight so flagrant that the Bronx D.A. suspected Fioretti of conspiracy. The disastrous episode climaxed with Robert breaking his own arm and claiming a job-related injury, later recanting the lie under pressure from his superiors. The next transfer sent Fioretti to Queens, where he was teamed with policewoman Maureen Brooks in a new experimental program, placing male and female officers together in the same patrol car.

Relations had stabilized between Robert and Rita, following their move to the new house, and nearly two years passed before Fioretti resumed beating his wife. Now, his son was also a target, Fioretti raging at Robert Jr., "Who the fuck knows *who* your father is? Your mother is a fucking whore!" Against Fioretti's wishes, Rita enrolled at Fordham University in 1980, often showing up for class with bruises on her face, arms and legs. By 1983 she was pregnant again, giving Fioretti a second son, but Robert couldn't be bothered to attend the baby's baptism, telling her he was involved in " a very dangerous undercover assignment." In fact, the only undercover work he did was crawling into bed with Maureen Brooks, a divorcée with two daughters. The NYPD's Internal Affairs Division learned of the affair when an outraged citizen reported Brooks performing oral sex on Fioretti in their cruiser, parked on a public street, but both cops denied it, and the case was dropped for lack of evidence.

By the fall of 1985, Rita knew Robert was cheating on her, but she likewise had no proof, until she found an unfamiliar telephone number in his pocket. The number led her to Maureen Brooks' apartment, where she surprised them together one afternoon. Brooks was presumably surprised, since she had seen Fioretti's "divorce papers" and believed him to be a free man. Fioretti responded by telling Brooks that Rita was "nuts," yet he stalled until October 1985 before finally moving out of their home. It was enough for Rita, and despite her staunch Catholicism, she vowed to file for divorce.

To that end, she retained an attorney and had him prepare the necessary paperwork. On February 14, 1986, Rita withdrew $17,000 from a joint bank account she shared with Robert, placing it in a new account of her own. By early April, the money had found its way back to the original account, and Fioretti was visiting Rita again, all the while assuring Maureen Brooks that he was "only using" Rita for some vague police assignment. Maureen swallowed the lie and prepared for their wedding, seemingly undismayed when Robert failed to show up for the ceremony in June 1986. Around the same time, Rita Fioretti was telling her friends, "Don't be surprised if Robert puts a bullet in my head." Another friend was cautioned, "Look, if I should suddenly die, make sure they do an autopsy on me."

In fact, the autopsy would have to wait. Rita's friends last heard from her in a telephone conversation, on Saturday, August 9, 1986. She missed work on Monday, September 11, and never returned, but Robert was back that Thursday, moving Maureen Brooks and her girls into the house he had formerly shared with Rita. It was September 22 before the NYPD showed an interest in the missing woman, and only then after her friends and co-workers mentioned Fioretti's name to Internal Affairs. Questioned about his wife's disappearance, Fioretti branded Rita as a "drunken whore" who "runs away every so often." He believed she was romantically involved with "some old guy," but didn't know the phantom lover's name. In Fioretti's version of events, he last saw Rita on August 10, leaving the house with two suitcases, various papers including her birth certificate, and "thousands of dollars" in cash. His lack of concern was occasioned, he said, by the fact that she had left him "many times" before.

Police were still waiting for Rita's body to surface, when they received a peculiar report from her bank. According to the institution's paperwork, Rita Fioretti had withdrawn $17,000 from her account on October 7, suggesting she was still alive and well. The *really* odd part, though, was that her husband had come in nine days later and opened a new account of his own, with an initial deposit of $20,000. Checking further, detectives learned that Rita had not, in fact, withdrawn the cash herself on October 7th; rather, Bob Fioretti had shown up with pre-signed withdrawal slips in Rita's name, removing the cash himself. Examination of the slips in question showed the signatures were forgeries.

Fioretti had begun to feel the heat, by now, and he was in the process of filling out his retirement papers when a pair of IAD detectives arrested him at police headquarters, on January 14, 1987. It took another three months for the NYPD to dismiss him, but they still had no case in the disappearance and presumed murder of his wife. Maureen Brooks was questioned about the hasty change of domicile, a mere four days after Rita supposedly "ran away," but the policewoman seemed unconcerned about the possibility of Rita's return. After all, Robert had promised her that "we would deal with it when it happened."

The prospect grew more remote in April 1988, when a headless woman's torso, weighted and wrapped in plastic, washed ashore on the bank of the Hudson River, at the northern tip of Manhattan. The partial remains displayed no fatal wounds, and cause of death remains undetermined to this day, but X-ray examination of the available bones positively identified the victim as Rita Fioretti. That summer, one of Fioretti's neighbors reported the ex-cop grappling with a manhole cover in the street, late at night, and detectives went underground in search of further evidence, retrieving shredded lingerie and three cut-up credit cards, which Fioretti swore his wife had taken with her when she "ran away." Bronx D.A. Paul Gentile held a press conference, publicly describing

Fioretti as the "chief suspect" in his wife's murder, but there was still no evidence strong enough to support an indictment.

Investigators caught an unexpected break on March 13, 1989, when Maureen Brooks' daughters approached a teacher at school, accusing stepfather Bob Fioretti of beating and sexually molesting them. A medical examination turned up rectal and vaginal scars, while the girls — age nine and 12 — tested positive for venereal disease. Arrested for child molestation, Fioretti denounced his accusers as "fucking little whores," and Maureen stood by her man, fronting the $25,000 bond required to get him out of jail. She also supported Fioretti's legal bid to regain custody of the girls, but a court hearing put an end to that pipe dream, also costing Bob the custody of his younger son. Trial was still pending on the sex charges in 1990, when federal authorities indicted Fioretti for bank fraud, relative to his forgery of the withdrawal slips in 1986. Once again, Maureen Brooks posted bond.

By 1992, the star-crossed lovers had seemingly run out of luck. Brooks was dismissed from her job with the NYPD, and Fioretti was convicted of bank fraud in federal court on January 21, sentenced on August 27 to a ten-year prison term, plus five years probation. In the meantime, on March 17, Fioretti pled guilty in state court on child molestation charges; on September 15, he drew another prison term of five to 15 years, that sentence to run concurrently with his federal time. To date, no murder charge has been filed in the death of Rita Fioretti, although police and prosecutors alike remain unanimous in their affirmations of Fioretti's guilt.

# Fisher, John King

Texas-born in 1854, John Fisher grew up hating the stepmother who hung him by his suspenders in the doorway of their Collin County home, leaving him to squall and wriggle while she went about her daily chores. The family moved to Goliad when Fisher was sixteen, and there he experienced his first brush with the law, sentenced to two years in prison for horse theft and burglary. At that, he served only four months of his term before he was pardoned by the governor, moving on to Pendencia in 1871. Briefly employed as a mercenary "regulator," hounding rustlers from the range, he soon founded a ranch of his own. The spread quickly became known as a hangout for rustlers and gunmen, with Fisher rated the worst of the lot, described by one acquaintance as "the most perfect specimen of a frontier dandy and desperado that I ever met." A sign at the crossroads near his ranch proclaimed THIS IS KING FISHER'S ROAD — TAKE THE OTHER ONE, and those who knew him found it wise to follow that advice.

**John King Fisher**
*Courtesy of*
*Western History Collections,*
*University of Oklahoma Libraries.*

Fisher profited from an alliance with Mexican revolutionary (later president) Porfirio Diaz, running stolen cattle back and forth across the border, but his temper made him dangerous even to his own employees. Once, when one of his *vaqueros* accidentally jostled Fisher near a fire at branding time, King brained him with a branding iron, then drew his pistol and killed three more Mexicans sitting on a nearby fence. Considering the race of his victims, and their unsavory reputation, no charges were filed, but such was not always the case. In 1876, Fisher and nine of his men were arrested for rustling, but charges were dropped before trial. A year later, King was jailed on three counts of rustling and four counts of murder, spending five months in a cell before he was released on $25,000 bond. Altogether, over the next three years, he was indicted 21 times, but six juries released him, one after another. In 1881, King Fisher seemed to mend his ways, signing on as a deputy sheriff in Uvalde County, Texas. His boss was soon indicted for embezzlement, and Fisher took over as acting sheriff, planning to run on his own in the 1884 election, but he never got the chance. That March, visiting Austin on official business, he ran into a friend and fellow trigger-happy lawman, tough **Ben Thompson.** On a whim, they rode to San Antonio to visit the Vaudeville Variety Theatre, a gambling hall whose owner Thompson had murdered two years earlier. The dead man's surviving partners had long memories, and an ambush was waiting for Thompson inside. Provoked by a drunken tirade and flourish of pistols from Thompson, six-shooters cut loose on the lawmen, riddling Thompson with nine shots and Fisher with 13. Both died instantly, Fisher without ever firing a shot.

Back in Uvalde County, reports of Deputy Fisher's sudden death were not entirely unwelcome. Long afterward, it is said that the mother of a man murdered by Fisher visited the lawman's grave each year, on the anniversary of her son's death, lighting a brush fire atop the plot, then dancing around it "with devilish glee."

# Ford, Richard and Von Villas, Robert A.

Richard Ford was a natural actor, starring in several high school stage plays, but upon his graduation in 1957, he passed up a chance to study at the Pasadena Playhouse in favor of joining the U.S. Army. He served ten years in olive drab and once considered making the army his career, with postings in Japan and Germany before he volunteered for two tours of duty in Vietnam. There, as a helicopter gunner, he was wounded twice and decorated for bravery, discharged in 1968 with the rank of master sergeant. Accustomed to uniforms and adventure, Ford quickly joined the Los Angeles Police Department. In June 1969 he was wounded again, this time by a suspected car thief who disarmed him, shooting Ford and his partner with Ford's own service revolver, before the gunman himself was killed.

By the early 1970s, Ford was working vice, auto theft, and narcotics, utilizing his dramatic skills for undercover stings, earning numerous evaluations like the one which noted that "His pleasant and witty personality has kept the unit laughing." In 1972, Ford married LAPD records clerk Lillian Roeder, the second marriage for both, and Richard made detective in 1977. A year later, Ford surprised his supervisor with the announcement that he was having emotional problems and trouble with booze. If he was not removed from his present inner-city narcotics assignment, Ford said, he was afraid he might "end up shooting a coon." Referred to a police psychologist, Ford told the shrink that "something is going on inside of me that isn't right." He expressed an increasing desire "to kill drug dealers," prompting a diagnosis of "stress overload" with recommendation for transfer to "a less dynamic area."

In retrospect, some would say that Ford had merely used his acting skills to work the system, bailing out of the ghetto in favor of a posting to the LAPD's relatively peaceful Devonshire Division, in the San Fernando Valley — dubbed "Club Dev" within the department. Oddly, the move didn't seem to help: Ford's first evaluation in his new division was strictly mediocre, prompting him to snap at his commander, "This is bullshit! I'm the best detective in the world!"

The one positive aspect of his transfer was Ford's meeting with Officer Bob Von Villas, another decorated Vietnam veteran who had earned the Bronze Star by rescuing members of his platoon from a burning helicopter. Von Villas worked juvey at Devonshire, where he was rated outstanding, and moonlighted as a security guard at private homes, shopping malls, concerts and movie sets. When not so employed, brother cops recall that Von Villas was pushing real estate or selling things out of his car trunk, the stock ranging from kitchen appliances to sunglasses and sporting goods. Von Villas had joined the LAPD within six days of his army discharge, and spent nine months as the personal bodyguard of Mayor Sam Yorty. Like another of L.A.'s finest, **William Leasure**, Von Villas had a way with women, often bedding vulnerable females he met on the job. He was known to scan police reports at Club Dev for incidents of assault against women, later calling up to offer himself as a personal bodyguard. Some of the clients wound up in his bed, unknown to Bob's wife, and one such infraction earned him a two-week suspension in November 1982. By that Christmas, financially wounded in the commodities market, Von Villas told a female friend, "I'm tired of being an honest cop. If you hear of any job I can do for money, let me know. There isn't any job I wouldn't do for money, including murder. I'll do anything for money."

Unknown to his wife and fellow officers, Richard Ford was coming to the same conclusion. Whatever was cooking with Ford, things went from bad to worse, when his wife — now a city bus driver — was beaten, raped, and left for dead in an L.A. alley. In the wake of that assault, the formerly vivacious woman was described as being "totally dependent, like an infant." She cringed at Ford's touch, finally advising him to "get yourself a girlfriend." At the same time, Ford was caring for his mother-in-law, terminally ill with cancer, and a five-month leave of absence, in mid-1981, failed to bring relief. A year later, in November 1982, he took fellow Vietnam veteran Bruce Adams on a "hunting trip" to Colorado, where Ford purchased a crate of illegal submachine guns and silencers. He needed the weapons for a jewel heist, Ford explained, and cautioned Adams to keep his mouth shut. "I've knocked people off before," Ford said. "It wouldn't bother me at all." A few days later, he introduced Adams to Bob Von Villas, described by Ford as his "partner" in the upcoming robbery.

On November 18, 1982, Ford and Von Villas picked up two wigs and fake beards from a Hollywood wigmaker, explaining that they needed the disguises for undercover police work. Four days later, two armed robbers wearing salt-and-pepper wigs and beards raided a Northridge jewelry store, leaving three female employees bound and gagged in a storeroom before they escaped with $200,000 worth of gems, mostly loose diamonds. Instructions issued to employees by the robbers struck L.A. police as sounding like "cop talk," but they were naturally reluctant to believe fellow officers could have committed the crime.

The winter of 1982-83 was a busy time for Ford and Von Villas. That December, Von Villas gave Bruce Adams $500 in cash, with instructions to scout locations for an auto shop, which they would jointly own, with Adams doing most of the work. Once a location was chosen, Von Villas covered rent and startup costs with three loose diamonds valued at $1,200. The shop was barely up and running when Von Villas and Ford announced their intention to open an escort service, dubbed "Classy Ladies," which wound up operating from a back room of the garage, with part-time stripper Joan Loguerico manning the telephone. Adams wound up repairing cars by day and chauffeuring hookers around town at night, the girls charging a $45 hourly "modeling" fee in addition to an average $150 extra for sex. The prostitution racket was shut down after six weeks, deemed too risky by Ford and Von Villas, but they had already cleared some $25,000 from the business.

Another source of illegal income, that winter, was Dr. Jan Ogilvie, a successful laboratory clinician and businesswoman whose 11-month marriage to husband Thomas Weed was heading for divorce court by October 1982. They fought habitually and took turns filing charges of assault against one another, a circumstance that was exacerbated by their partnership in Ogilvie's lab, and the fact that Weed worked on the premises. That December, a friend of Ogilvie's named Julie Rabold "jokingly" suggested that Jan should have her husband killed. If she decided to go through with it, Rabold suggested, she knew a police detective in Devonshire Division who could "take care of" Weed. Two months later, on February 23, 1983, Weed disappeared without a trace. Around the same time, Bruce Adams witnessed Von Villas handing Richard Ford

$10,000 in cash at the shop. Ford explained to Adams that the money came from a murder contract on Tom Weed, remarking that "Weed's bones are bleaching out in the desert."

On May 25, 1983, Adams and Von Villas had a falling out, Adams refusing to pick up a shipment of stolen grenade launchers from the U.S. Marine Corps base at El Toro. Von Villas threatened his life, and Adams retaliated by contacting the U.S. Treasury Department's Bureau of Alcohol, Tobacco and Firearms (ATF). He met with feds the first time on June 21st, and while they were initially skeptical of his bizarre story — including allegations of conspirators within the LAPD — the agents finally took him seriously and persuaded Adams to meet with trusted L.A. police brass. Reluctantly, Adams agreed to remain in contact with Ford and Von Villas, wearing a concealed microphone to their subsequent meetings.

In the meantime, L.A.'s rogue cops had a new job in the works. Von Villas had recently helped Joan Loguerico out with a messy divorce, using his real estate know-how to save her some money by purchasing her house himself. As a precaution, supposedly to safeguard his investment, Von Villas insisted on taking out a joint $100,000 mortgage insurance policy, with Von Villas named as Joan's beneficiary and vice versa. That was in April 1983, and a $600 premium payment was due on the policy in late July, but Von Villas never planned on spending the money. Instead, he planned to collect at the earliest possible date.

Soon after they signed for the policy, Joan met a free-spending, bearded stranger at the strip club where she danced. He introduced himself "Dr. Anderson," tipping her a hundred dollars per dance while he pestered her for dates. Intrigued but suspicious, Joan discussed the prospect with Von Villas, who encouraged her to take the "doctor" for as much as she could, while his infatuation lasted. Joan agreed to a motel "date" on June 17, enjoying a strenuous bout of sex before she caught "Dr. Anderson" pulling on latex surgical gloves, reaching toward her face with "something black" in his hand. It was enough to send Joan running for her car, and she met with Bruce Adams on July 6th, reporting that she thought someone — perhaps Bob Von Villas — was trying to kill her. Adam's was convinced of it when she described "Dr. Anderson's" skull-and-crossbones tattoo, identical in all respects to one worn by Richard Ford.

Adams reported the apparent murder plot to ATF and LAPD, prompting acceleration of the sting on Ford and Von Villas. One day after his meeting with Joan Loguerico, Adams was wired for sound when Von Villas approached him about helping to kill the dancer. The price-tag was $12,500, confirmed in a tape-recorded phone call from Ford. On the telephone, Ford described his plan to drug Joan and kill her in a van, afterward disposing of the bloody carpet in a garbage dumpster. In Ford's words, the murder "ain't gonna be no big fuckin' thing. It's gonna be like taking candy from a baby."

At 9 o'clock that night, Adams and his microphone joined Ford in the would-be murder van, Bruce driving while Ford waxed eloquent on his plans. Ford meant to force pills down Joan's throat, then rape and mutilate her body in simulation of an attack by a psychotic who had "fucked her body up, beat the shit out of her, ended up fuckin' killing her and dumped her in a fuckin' alley in Hollywood. So the whole thing is supposed to look like a sex crime." They drove on toward their target, Ford rambling on, "As for killing assholes, I just do it for kicks. Instead of being depressed, going out and shooting at fuckin' rocks and squirrels, I go down south and shoot niggers. I think it's fun, but I'd rather get paid for it." Ford was in the back, hidden under a blanket and ready to spring on his prey, when Adams drove him into a police trap and the scheme fell apart. An hour later, Bob Von Villas was arrested at his home in Simi Valley, 20 loose diamonds retrieved from his attaché case.

L.A. Police Chief Daryl Gates was stunned the next morning, as he listened to the tapes of Dick Ford plotting murder, discussing his many alleged kills. On July 12, Ford and Von Villas were arraigned on one count each of attempted murder, conspiracy to commit murder, attempting to administer a stupefying drug, and carrying concealed weapons (two commando daggers found with Ford in the van, a part of his self-described "murder kit"). Both pled not guilty and were held without bond. A month later, on August 12, the two officers were arraigned on ten charges related to the November jewel heist. Again, they pled not guilty and remained in L.A. County's jail. Their preliminary hearing opened on September 26; four days later, Judge Michael Sauer ordered the defendants to stand trial for robbery, conspiracy, and attempted murder.

Meanwhile, another noose was tightening around the necks of L.A.'s not-so-finest. Homicide detectives interviewed Jan Ogilvie about her husband's disappearance on August 2, 1983, but she denied all knowledge of his whereabouts. According to her statement, Tom Weed was either in Canada or Mexico — she wasn't sure which. Bruce Adams quickly identified her recorded voice as that of a woman who had called the combination auto shop and escort service several times, thus confirming his earlier report of the Weed "contract." On February 15, 1984 — six days after Von Villas resigned from the LAPD — he and Ford were indicted for Tom Weed's murder. Additional charges of murder and conspiracy were also filed against Jan Ogilvie and Joyce Reynolds. All four pled not guilty, and on March 15, the D.A.'s office announced its intent to pursue the death penalty. Three months later, Jan Ogilvie cracked from the strain, agreeing to testify against Ford and Von Villas in return for leniency.

On March 7, 1985, Judge Larry Fidler ordered Ford and Von Villas to stand trial for the murder of Thomas Weed. It would not be that simple, however, as California justice ground along its sluggish, laborious course. Most of 1986 was consumed with a nine-month preliminary hearing, ending on October 14, and the rogue cops had to face trial on their first indictment before they went to court on Weed's slaying. The first trial opened on April Fool's Day, before Judge Alexander Williams III. Joan Loguerico had died of cancer, waiting for her day in court, but there were still 140 witnesses to be heard, some 400 exhibits to be examined. It was October 22 before the defense began presenting its case, and Richard Ford alone spent two weeks on the witness stand. Von Villas also testified, denying any criminal activity, claiming that the diamonds found at his home were obtained by trading with a man no one could find. Jurors began deliberating on January 4, 1988 and returned with a verdict three days later: Ford and Von Villas were each convicted on 13 identical counts, including conspiracy to kill Joan Loguerico, dual counts of attempted murder (for June 17 and July 7, 1983), robbery, conspiracy to commit robbery, false imprisonment (of the jewelry store employees), and assault with a firearm on each of the three. Ford was also convicted of attempting to administer a stupefying drug, while Bob Von Villas was acquitted on that charge. At his sentencing, on March 11, Ford made a rambling, tearful speech, including the remark that "I don't know why I feel guilty about having been found guilty when I'm not guilty." He received a sentence of 36 years to life, and Von Villas got 35 years to life.

On April 12, 1988, a peculiar trial opened before Judge Darlene Schempp, on the murder of Thomas Weed. Judge Schempp had rejected defense motions to sever the trials, instead picking a separate jury for each defendant, both of which would occupy the same courtroom. Selection of those jurors consumed three months, with opening arguments heard on July 5. Ford's jury began deliberations on October 4, 1988 and returned a week later, convicting Ford of first-degree murder and conspiracy to murder, each with the "special circumstance" of murder for financial gain which left him open to the death penalty. Von Villas received an identical verdict from his jury on November 3. At the penalty phase of his trial, five psychologists described Ford as a long-term victim of post-traumatic stress syndrome dating back to Vietnam, adding that his wife and children "would never recover" if Ford was sentenced to die. On November 29, after 13 hours of deliberation, the jury deadlocked 11-to-1 in favor of life, and that sentence was formally imposed on February 22, 1989, with Ford still claiming innocence. Bob Von Villas heard his jury recommend life without parole on

December 15, 1988, with formal sentencing completed on March 8, 1989.

# Fox, J.M.

A captain of the Texas Rangers who despised Hispanics, J.M. Fox found a ready excuse to exercise his bigotry along the Tex-Mex border, in the paranoid years of the First World War. Texans were inflamed by Pancho Villa's border raids, ongoing revolutions in Mexico, and the infamous Zimmerman Note that hinted at an alliance between Mexico and Kaiser Wilhelm's Germany. Rangers and racist vigilantes alike terrorized Mexicans on both sides of the border, with estimates of the Latino body count ranging from 500 to 5,000, but the worst single incident was the Ponvenir Massacre of December 1917.

On Christmas Day, a band of 40 or 50 bandits raided Brite's store, outside the small village of Ponvenir, in the Big Bend country. While they were looting the store, a stagecoach unexpectedly arrived, and the raiders opened fire, killing the driver and two Mexican passengers. From Brite's, they rode on to besiege a nearby farmhouse, but armed settlers repelled the gang, inflicting heavy losses.

It was a victory of sorts, but not enough to satisfy the likes of Captain J.M. Fox. Assigned to investigate the raid, he heard reports that Chicanos in Ponvenir were sporting shoes of the same kind looted from Brite's. A Mexican in new shoes was cause for dire suspicion in those days, and Captain Fox swiftly organized a posse consisting of eight fellow Rangers and four white civilians. Boozing all the way to Ponvenir, they were in a killing mood by the time they arrived, torturing some two dozen villagers "for information," finally choosing 15 at random and gunning them down in cold blood. When reports of the massacre spread, Fox described the killings as self-defense, claiming that his men had come under fire from *banditos* while making arrests.

The truth came out in 1919, before a Texas state legislative committee investigating allegations of wholesale civil rights violations by the Texas Rangers. No charges were filed in the Ponvenir case, but Fox and his eight fellow gunmen were sacked from the Rangers. At that, widespread corruption and brutality continued for years afterward, until Governor Miriam ("Ma") Ferguson fired the whole force en masse and started over from scratch, putting state law enforcement on a professional basis for the first time in living memory.

# Frank, Antoinette

At 1:00 A.M. on March 4, 1995, New Orleans policewoman Antoinette Frank ate supper at the Kim Anh Vietnamese restaurant, on Bullard Avenue, where she worked part-time as a security guard to earn extra cash. The meal was prepared and served by two children of the family that owned the restaurant, 24-year-old Ha Vu, and her 17-year-old brother Cuong Vu. Frank left when she had finished eating, then returned about an hour later, and knocked on the door, which was locked at the time. Another moonlighting policeman, 25-year-old Ronald Williams II, let her in. Frank was accompanied by 18-year-old Roger Lacaze, and they wasted no time in getting down to business.

Ronald Williams was the first to die, shot once in the head at close range, then twice more, for insurance, as he lay on the restaurant floor. The children knelt and pleaded for their lives, with guns in their faces, finally lapsing into tearful prayer. (Cuong Vu, a high-school junior, also served as an altar boy at St. Brigid's Church; his sister, meanwhile, planned to be a nun.) The prayers were answered with violence, Cuong Vu pistol-whipped and shot six times, his sister killed by three shots at point-blank range. That done, Frank and Lacaze proceeded to rob the restaurant, then fled. Frank proceeded to the Seventh District station house, where she picked up a squad car and returned to the Kim Anh restaurant, answering an emergency distress call to 911.

By the time she arrived, the place was crawling with police, including new Chief Richard Pennington, called out from home with the news that a patrolman had been slain. Unknown to Frank, two more siblings of the Vu family had also been present when the massacre went down, listening and watching the murders from hiding, in the kitchen. Chau Vu, another daughter, recognized Frank in a flash and instantly pointed her out as she entered the restaurant. Arrested at the scene, Frank was driven back to jail, this time in handcuffs, and soon named her accomplice in the crime.

It was the nadir for a police department already racked by scandal and disgrace. The New Orleans P.D. had long suffered from image problems, well known for its corruption since the 1930s, when New York mobsters under Frank Costello moved their slot machines south, as part of a bargain with "Kingfish" Huey Long. Racism and police brutality against black citizens were rampant in New Orleans, and women of all colors were unsafe in jail, where officers were said to line up and rape attractive prisoners in order of rank, with lowly patrolmen waiting their turn after captains, lieutenants, and sergeants. By the 1990s, though, police scandals had gone from an open secret to a public running sore. Citizen complaints, ranging from simple rudeness to savage beatings, hit an all-time peak at the end of 1993, and the following year, New Orleans was rated as America's "murder capital," with 421 reported homicides. In two years time, four local police officers had been charged with first-degree murder, and 30 others were awaiting trial on various felony counts.

Antoinette Frank, for her part, had come to the end of the line. On September 11, 1995, she was convicted on three counts of murder; two days later, she was formally sentenced to die. In mid-November of that same year, already on death row, she fell under suspicion of yet another killing. Skeletal human remains had been found beneath the floorboards of her former home, and while Frank denied any knowledge of how they got there, investigators speculated that the bones might belong to her father, Adam Frank, reported missing back in 1994. At this writing, no further charges have been filed in that case, and ex-Officer Frank awaits execution by lethal injection.

# Fratta, Robert

Robert Fratta was working as a ticket agent for American Airlines in 1983 when he met his future wife on the job. At first, it seemed like an idyllic union, which produced three children in 1987, 1989, and 1991. Things had turned sour by the time the youngest was born, however, with Fratta — now a public safety officer in Missouri City, Texas — displaying proclivities that grew increasingly bizarre over time. First, he set about rebuilding wife Farah with plastic surgery, insisting on a nose job and breast enhancement which she grudgingly accepted. Still dissatisfied, he next suggested "open" marriage or the possibility of threesomes in the house, scouting Houston bars for a willing young female to fill out the cast.

Farah finally drew the line and filed for divorce in March 1992. Bob Fratta, in typical fashion, told anyone who would listen, "She'll never divorce me. She's mine, and I'm not going to let anyone else have what I paid for." On June 28, 1994, a masked stranger burst into Farah's home and shocked her with an electronic stun gun, leaving her sprawled on the floor. The intruder escaped, and while Bob Fratta had a rock-solid alibi, his wife believed the attack was a deliberate ploy to make her give up the divorce and child-custody fight. The kids were visiting their father on November 9, when Farah came home from work and found a gunman waiting outside her garage. The first bullet grazed her skull, eliciting a scream, before the second dropped her in her tracks. Neighbors were quick enough to see a small car racing from the scene, its two passengers dressed all in black, but they were too late to save Farah Fratta, and she died an hour later, at Herman Hospital. Two days after the murder, Bob Fratta tried to cash in his wife's $235,000 life insurance policy, appearing stunned when he was told that she had named their three children as the sole beneficiaries.

Farah's parents, Lex and Betty Baquer, wasted no time in filing for custody of the three Fratta children. Both believed that Fratta was behind their daughter's murder, and they spared no effort to protect their grandchildren from the man they regarded as a cold-blooded killer. A special custody hearing was held before Judge Robert Hinojosa, in December 1994, and the testimony recorded was less than flattering to Robert Fratta. Friends of the family described Fratta's obsession with kinky sex and three-way affairs, along with his negligence where the children's safety was concerned. According to witnesses, Fratta often left guns and live ammunition lying about the house; he also collected exotic reptiles, including a large snake which had recently bitten one of his sons. The capper, though, was delivered by acquaintances of Fratta from a gym where he worked out on a regular basis. The body builders told Judge Hinojosa that Fratta had asked them for referrals to a hit man, later offering to pay them $3,000 for the murder, if they could not suggest a professional. It was enough for the court, and the Baquers were granted temporary custody pending an outcome of the murder investigation.

Harris County homicide detectives had been hoping for a break, and now they had one. Fratta predictably denied any role in the murder, but testimony at the custody hearing got him fired from his policeman's job in Missouri City, and detectives placed him under round-the-clock surveillance. Still, they needed something more to make the case, and they got lucky again in March 1995, when anonymous tips led them to two men named Howard Paul Guidry and Joseph Andrew Prystash. Both, they were told, had been bragging about the murder of Farah Fratta, 18-year-old Guidry describing himself as the triggerman, while Prystash, 20 years his senior, drove the getaway car. Prystash was also fingered as the home invader who had attacked Fratta's wife with a stun gun, back in June of 1994.

As luck would have it, Howard Guidry was already in jail, one of four men arrested following a chaotic bank robbery on March 1. Joe Prystash, a paroled Alabama burglar, was also a known friend of Robert Fratta, who had worked out at the gym where Fratta was soliciting hit men in 1994. Arrested for murder on March 13th, Prystash tried to tough it out, but a .38-caliber pistol found at his home was quickly identified as the murder weapon, its serial number traced back to Robert Fratta. Guidry, for his part, was already talking, anxious to cut a deal, describing how he and Prystash had been hired to commit the murder and make it look like a random burglary gone wrong.

Another six weeks elapsed before Robert Fratta was finally arrested on charges of soliciting a murder, the charges relating to his original offers, rejected by friends at the gym. Held without bond, the 37-year-old ex-cop told reporters, "I didn't do it. I'm praying for justice." Lex Baquer had a different view of his one-time son-in-law. "He is truly psychotic," Baquer declared. "I just want him off the streets, so I can sleep and walk and breathe freely again." On June 28, the charge against Fratta was upgraded to capital murder. As prosecutor Casey O'Brien explained, "He is indicted specifically for hiring those that did the killing. The difference is that he is now appropriately charged. He was charged [in April] with soliciting someone other than the killer, and was indicted again for succeeding." Guidry and Prystash where formally indicted, at the same time, as the actual killers. Defense attorney Richard Frankoff, meanwhile, blamed Fratta's indictment on "a jailhouse snitch, the trash of the trash. These guys are unbelievable. They make up stories as they go."

Fratta's trial opened on April 9, 1996, before Judge Bob Burdette in Houston, with prosecutor Kelly Siegler seeking the death penalty. In her opening statement, the D.A. described Fratta as a man who had everything a husband could wish for, and still wasn't satisfied. "He wanted an open marriage," Siegler told the jury, "meaning he could date other women. He made disgusting, revolting sexual demands she could not meet." Attorney James Beeler, who had represented Farah Fratta in divorce proceedings, described Bob Fratta's outspoken boredom with traditional marriage and his relentless pressure on Farah, seeking her collaboration in deviant sex. Telephone records showed frequent calls from the defendant to Joe Prystash, and nine-year-old Bradley Fratta appeared as a key prosecution witness, describing how his father was repeatedly paged and returned numerous phone calls on the night of the murder. Mary Gipp, a girlfriend of Joe Prystash, was allowed to testify in her lover's absence, describing Fratta's offer of $1,000 and a new Jeep as payment for the murder. Dueling psychologists testified for both sides, Edward Friedman telling the jury that he found no evidence of deviant sexuality in his interview with Fratta, while Laurence Abrams described the ex-cop as a man who regarded all women as "little girls" in need of strict domination.

Jurors deliberated for 50 minutes on April 17, before convicting Fratta of murder, and the penalty phase of his trial began the next day. Fratta's attorney called the trial unfair, since neither Guidry nor Prystash had appeared in court, but Prosecutor Siegler had a simple explanation for the jury. "You wouldn't have been able to stomach the deal we'd have had to cut," she said, pointing at the empty witness stand, "to put them in that chair." Betty Baquer testified on April 19, telling the court, "We don't have a life any more, thanks to that monster right there." Defense attorney John Ackerman, for his part, blamed the murder on a bitter divorce fight, ironically asking that Fratta's life be spared for the sake of his children. The jury disagreed, and sentenced Fratta to death on April 22.

An ironic sidebar to the Fratta case was recorded on May 8, 1996, when Bill Planter — himself a former sheriff's deputy and constable, one-time police chief of Splendora, Texas — was convicted of approaching the Baquers and offering to kill Bob Fratta in return for a payment of $10,000. The offer had been made before Fratta was arrested, and Lex Baquer promptly reported it to police. At the time of Planter's arrest, detectives found guns, a knife, and high explosives in his car. Upon conviction of soliciting a murder, the three-time ex-cop was sentenced to 17 years in state prison.

Justice scored a clean sweep two months later, on July 10, when Joe Prystash was sentenced to death for his part in Farah Fratta's murder. Jurors were unimpressed by the antics of defense attorney Gerald Bourque, who waved a bible overhead and quoted passages about forgiveness in his final summation. They were having none of it, and the panel deliberated barely two hours before condemning the hit man to death by lethal injection.

# Glen, Herschell

Herschell Glen, age 24, had three years on the job as a patrolman with the Elgin, Illinois, Police Department in February 1982, when he was briefly hospitalized with a case of accidental carbon monoxide poisoning. Three months later, he had more serious trouble to worry about, but the accident would prove convenient, giving him at least a marginal excuse for his participation in a strange and brutal crime.

James Wright and Lillian Final were out on a date Friday night, May 7, when they stopped at a park in Elgin. They never made it home, but Wright's bullet-punctured body was found at 4 a.m. on Saturday, behind a vacant building north of town. Another five and a half hours would pass before Lillian's body was found by a farmer, plowing his field in neighboring Cook County, but by that time, authorities in Elgin already had their suspect in custody. A wallet, found ten feet from Wright's corpse, had been traced to Herschell Glen, and the officer was arrested when he showed up for work at seven o'clock Saturday morning.

Detectives initially pondered a racial motive in the double slaying, since Glen was black and his victims were white, but autopsy results confirmed that Lillian Final had been raped by her killer. A search of Glen's home produced the murder weapon and a set of bloody clothes. With the discovery of Wright's abandoned pickup truck, detectives theorized that Glen had abducted the victims at gunpoint, driving them to their deaths in his car.

Held without bond in Kane County, Patrolman Glen was indicted on two counts of first-degree murder, with additional charges of kidnapping, rape, and deviate sexual assault. His defense attorney claimed that Glen had suffered brain damage from his February accident, promoting an insanity defense, but a medical exam in August failed to support the claim. A year after the murders, in May 1983, Glen went to trial for Wright's murder. Ballistics evidence and matching blood types sealed his fate, along with two witnesses who had seen the policeman standing over Wright's body, and jotted down his license number as he drove away. It was enough to convict him on May 11th, jurors deliberating less than two hours before they returned the guilty verdict. Despite the brutality of his crime, Glen was spared the death penalty, drawing a sentence of life imprisonment.

## Griffith, Michael

The Always and Forever Flower Shop and Wedding Chapel had been serving residents of Houston, Texas, for 20 years at the same location, on Mangum Road, but times had changed in the Lone Star State over two decades. Five robberies in recent years had prompted owners of the family business to keep their doors locked, even during normal business hours, admitting only persons whom they recognized or who appeared trustworthy. At that, the locked doors were no great inconvenience, since most of Always and Forever's business was conducted via telephone. And besides, it was a small price to pay for personal safety.

On the morning of October 9, 1994, 44-year-old Deborah Jean McCormick and her daughter, Elizabeth Barnett, opened the flower shop as usual, then locked the doors securely behind them. Deborah went out to run an errand, shortly after they arrived, and the shop was silent when she returned at 8:45 a.m. Moments later, she was horrified to find her daughter sprawled on the floor of the shop's reception hall, nude from the waist up, her body smeared with blood that formed a spreading puddle on the floor. A call to 911 brought police and ambulance attendants racing to the scene, but it was already too late. Elizabeth had been killed by nine stab wounds to her chest, side and back. Her sweater lay nearby, and her brassiere, still fastened in the back, had been yanked down around her thighs. There was no evidence of "normal" rape, but autopsy results showed that Elizabeth had been forced to perform oral sex before she died. In parting, the killer had stolen an estimated $400 in cash and several credit cards from Deborah's purse.

On October 14, a telephone tip to Houston's "Crime Stoppers" program pointed detectives in the direction of Michael Griffith, a former deputy with the Harris County sheriff's office, fired from his job in 1993, after ten years in uniform, when he was sentenced to one year's probation on criminal charges for beating his wife. (An additional weapons charge had cost him three days in jail and a $300 fine in March 1993.) Before moving to Texas, Griffith had also been a deputy in Florida, where he was once named "Lawman of the Year." That didn't stop him from abusing the women in his life, however, including the girlfriend who had recently charged him with assault, following a punch-out at their apartment down the street from Always and Forever. Soon after that charge was filed, Griffith had dropped out of sight, along with $1,000 from the office-cleaning business he had run since his dismissal from the force. His partner missed the money more than Griffith, and had placed the call to "Crime Stoppers."

Homicide detectives had been hunting Griffith for two weeks, when a burly dark-haired man entered another Houston bridal shop, on October 28. He forced the 18-year-old female clerk to remove her blouse and bra, then kneel and perform oral sex until she vomited. When the man asked her age, the terrified girl shaved four years off the total and asked if he planned to kill her, whereupon the man replied, "You're too young to die." Instead of finishing his victim off, he masturbated over her supine body, then looted the cash register and fled. Without hesitation, the victim identified Michael Griffith's mug shot from the 1993 arrest as a likeness of her assailant.

For reasons unknown, the ex-cop turned killer refused to leave town while he had the chance. Between October 31 and November 1, he used Deborah McCormick's credit cards repeatedly, at various Houston shopping malls, with police always lagging a few steps behind their quarry. Again, Griffith's ex-partner came to the rescue, reporting that a woman had been calling Griffith's pager, left behind in their office when he robbed the till and fled. Detectives traced the woman through her call-back number and learned that Griffith had lived with her for three weeks, beginning on October 7. She had not seen him since the October 28, but another battered girlfriend tipped police that he was hiding out at a local motel.

When raiders came knocking on November 4, Griffith answered the door himself and was jailed on charges of aggravated rape and robbery, stemming from the October 28 attack. Held without bond while prosecutors put their case together, Griffith had another turn of bad luck on November 9, when an alert detective recognized his face on the security videotape which had captured a bank robbery in progress, back on October 12. The stickup artist had shot and wounded a female teller as he was leaving the bank, and new charges were added to the growing list, but Griffith's fate would hinge upon the capital murder count involving Elizabeth Barnett.

At his trial, in December 1995, Griffith was described by witnesses who knew him as a "vicious control freak" who hated his hard-drinking mother from childhood, once telling a relative that he couldn't wait to become a policeman, so that he could arrest his mother and clap her in jail. Jurors convicted Griffith of murder, rape and robbery in the Barnett case, deliberating barely three hours before they imposed the death sentence. On January 2, 1996, Griffith pled guilty on two counts of aggravated robbery, related to the bank and second flower shop, receiving two concurrent 60-year prison terms before he went back to death row.

## Hayes, Frank

Frank Hayes was the police chief of Castroville, Texas, when he shot and killed a defenseless Chicano prisoner, Richard Morales, on September 14, 1975. Fearing prosecution for the crime, Hayes enlisted his wife to drive the body some 350 miles from Castroville, planting it in a shallow grave in east Texas. The corpse was found, even so, and while Hayes was charged with capital murder, he described the shooting as an "accident." A local jury swallowed the line and refused to convict him, opting for a reduced charge of aggravated assault. The ex-police chief was sentenced to a prison term of two to ten years. Dorothy Hayes pled no contest on a misdemeanor charge of tampering with evidence and was sentenced to one year's probation.

At that, it was more justice than Hispanic Texans had come to expect from cases involving abusive lawmen, but the Morales case produced angry demonstrations in the Latino community. By August 1976, agents from the U.S. Department of Justice were on the case, pursuing federal charges of civil rights violations. On February 23, 1977, Frank Hayes was indicted for a violation of civil rights resulting in death; Dorothy Hayes and her sister, Alice Baldwin, were charged as accessories after the fact, for helping to conceal the body. All three were convicted in Waco, on September 30. Chief Hayes received the maximum sentence of life imprisonment, while his wife was sentenced to three years and his sister-in-law to a term of 18 months.

# Helm, Jack

The facts of Jack Helm's early life are vague. We know that he was born in 1838 and fought for Dixie in the War Between the States. On one occasion, while the conflict was in progress, Helm reportedly shot and killed a black man for the "crime" of whistling a Yankee tune. By the early 1870s, Helm was serving simultaneously as sheriff of DeWitt County, Texas, and as a captain in the Texas state police, well on his way to nailing down a reputation as "the most cold-blooded murderer ever to wear a badge."

Helm's chief claim to fame — and his ultimate downfall — sprang from his involvement in the deadly Sutton-Taylor feud. Sheriff Helm threw in his lot with the Suttons, fielding a private army of 200 deputies and mercenary gunmen against the rival Taylor clan. The war came to a head in 1873, when Helm's posse arrested two Taylor supporters on a misdemeanor charge of disturbing the peace, then left their bullet-riddled bodies sprawled beside a country road. Several deputies swore the prisoners were shot "while trying to escape"; Helm, for his part, denied any knowledge of the double killing. Under fire from the press, Governor E.J. Davis cut Helm from the state police payroll, but Jack retained his sheriff's badge and full authority to enforce his own brand of law in DeWitt County.

Matters went from bad to worse in 1873, with the arrival of prolific killer John Wesley Hardin on the scene. A distant relative of the Taylors, Hardin was credited with 35 or 40 homicides, "not counting Mexicans," and he soon added Helm's chief deputy to the list, twice narrowly missing the sheriff himself. Helm sought to negotiate a truce, but the first meeting erupted in gunfire, leaving two of the Sutton men dead. At a second meeting, held in a saloon, Hardin grew suspicious and pulled a gun on Helm, backing out of the bar. Their final confrontation occurred at the local blacksmith's shop, including Helm, Hardin, and Jim Taylor. All were heavily armed, and Helm sealed his fate by drawing a knife and stabbing Taylor. Hardin responded with a sawed-off shotgun, flattening Helm with two blasts, after which Taylor drew a pistol and pumped six shots into the fallen sheriff's head. Thus, as Hardin's memoirs related with unintentional irony, died the man "whose name was a horror to all law-abiding citizens."

# Hickok, James Butler "Wild Bill"

**James Butler "Wild Bill" Hickok**
*Courtesy of Mercaldo Archives.*

Described by one enthusiastic biographer as "the most dangerous gunman who ever lived," James Hickok was born May 27, 1837 in Troy Grove, Illinois, to a family transplanted from Vermont. His long nose and protruding upper lip earned him the nickname "Duck Bill," and while there is no evidence that he was gay, Hickok's high-pitched voice and effeminate mannerisms led some wags to call him "Maudie." It would take a thick mustache and much publicity about his prowess with a gun before "Duck Bill" Hickok won the more respectful sobriquet "Wild Bill."

At age 18, still living in Troy Grove, Hickok got into a fistfight with a teamster who insulted him, both men tumbling into a murky canal. Hickok dragged himself from the water, wrongly believing that his assailant had drowned, and fled westward to escape a nonexistent murder charge. He wound up in Leavenworth, Kansas, at a time when factional disputes over slavery had transformed the territory into a war zone. Hickok worked as a teamster and buffalo hunter, becoming friendly with Buffalo Bill Cody, before he signed on with the Pony Express in 1861, operating from a small station at Rock Creek, Nebraska.

The station property had once belonged to 40-year-old David McCanles, a North Carolina native who disliked Hickok on sight, frequently teasing him about his appearance and manners. The trouble only worsened when Hickok began courting his enemy's girlfriend, and McCanles vowed to get even. One afternoon, McCanles turned up at the station with his 12-year-old son, demanding money which he claimed was owed to him by the freight company. Insults were exchanged, but Hickok stayed inside the station, lurking behind a curtain. When he refused to come out, McCanles entered the station, and Hickok shot him from hiding. Two friends of McCanles, James Woods and James Gordon, came running at the sound of gunfire, Gordon entering the station to find his pal dead on the floor. Hickok chased him outside, brandishing a pistol, and wounded the unarmed man as he ran for his life. Another shot nailed Woods, the injured man collapsing in a patch of weeds, where the wife of station master Horace Wellman finished him off with a hoe. James Gordon ran until his strength failed, slumping down against a tree, and was dispatched with close-range shotgun blasts from two other station employees.

At Hickok's murder trial, the young McCanles boy was not allowed to testify, and the presiding judge acquitted all concerned. The triple killing was forgotten for a time — no big deal in Nebraska, in the early 1860s — but it was later revived to Hickok's advantage, as the first myth in a body of legend that made him one of the West's most notorious gunmen. As retold by Hickok, long after the fact, his battle with "the McCanles gang" had been a heroic struggle, pitting Wild Bill against nine desperadoes, all of whom he killed single-handed, while stopping 11 bullets in the process. It was blatant nonsense, but it stuck, and so the myth was born.

By October 1861, Hickok was long gone from Rock Creek, serving as a scout and wagon master for the Union army. There is no good evidence that he saw any action in the Civil War, but stories circulated — probably from Hickok himself — that he had killed 50 Confederate soldiers with 50 shots in a single engagement.

His next verified killing dates from three months after the end of the war. Hickok was gambling in Springfield, Missouri, when he lost a poker hand to 26-year-old Dave Tutt and found himself unable to cover his bet. Tutt relieved Hickok of his watch, to cover the debt, and Wild Bill muttered darkly that he would kill Tutt, if Dave so much as used the timepiece. On July 21, they met in Springfield's public square, Tutt proudly showing off the watch, while Hickok fumed and cursed. Both men drew pistols, Tutt blazing away from an improbable 75 yards and missing his mark, while Hickok took the time to aim and killed his adversary with a single shot.

Back in military service, Hickok became a principal scout and personal friend of George Armstrong Custer, in the Seventh U.S. Cavalry. Little is known of his exploits in this period, except for the lies he told to correspondent Henry Stanley from the *New York Herald*, claiming to have killed 100 men in standup fights. Stanley, still years away from his discovery of Dr. Livingstone in darkest Africa, swallowed the nonsense whole and spread it nationwide, while Hickok thrived on the publicity. Between stints with the army, Wild Bill ran for sheriff in Ellsworth, Kansas, and lost; in 1869's election, he had better luck in the small cattle town of Hays City. There, he killed a man named Bill Mulrey on August 24, followed by a teamster the next month. By November, his luck had changed, and he was voted out of office for pocketing more than his fair share of graft.

Embarrassed by the defeat, Hickok spent some more time in the army, but he was back in Hays City by July 1870. On July 17, five rowdy troopers from the Seventh Cavalry jumped him in Drum's Saloon, mopping the floor with Wild Bill before he managed to kill one of them and critically wound another. After recuperating in Ellsworth, he moved on to Abilene, and was appointed marshal there in April 1871. The job paid $150 per month, plus one-fourth of any fines paid by prisoners he arrested, but Hickok spent most of his time gambling or consorting with prostitutes, prompting a local newspaper to complain that he was letting criminals overrun the town.

One source of repeated complaints was the Bull's Head Saloon, owned by Phil Coe and **Ben Thompson**. More specifically, some locals were outraged by the saloon's garish sign, depicting a bull with huge genitals, which one wag nicknamed "the shame of Abilene." Hickok was pressured to remove or censor the sign, and while he finally achieved his objective, stories differ on whether he wielded the paintbrush himself or stood by, supervising, with a shotgun in hand, while one of Coe's employees did the work.

In either case, the antagonism between Hickok and the Bull's Head owners grew worse over time. Hickok feared Thompson's quick hand and steady eye, but Phil Coe was another story. In fact, they were dating the same woman, and Hickok flew into a rage one night, on finding her with Coe in another saloon. He slapped the woman down in front of Coe, while the saloonkeeper, unarmed, refused to take the bait.

On October 5, 1871, Coe was bar-hopping with friends when a stray dog tried to bite him in the street, and he pegged a wild shot at the cur. Marshal Hickok came running, demanding to know who had fired, and Coe was trying to explain when Hickok drew his pistols, pumping two slugs into Coe's belly. The gambler tried to return fire, one bullet snagging Hickok's coat, before he collapsed in the dust. Suddenly, Wild Bill heard footsteps closing from behind him, and he spun on his heel, blazing away, instantly killing Deputy Mike Williams. Critics blamed Hickok's eyesight, allegedly weakened by gonorrhea contracted from one of his whores, but it hardly mattered in any case. No charges were filed, and Hickok picked up the tab for his deputy's funeral, but the damage was done. Abilene's city fathers demanded his resignation, and Wild Bill was unemployed once more.

The rest of his life was a short, downhill slide, barely relieved by the publicity he garnered from dime novels and participation in Buffalo Bill Cody's Wild West Show. Hickok drank heavily, and finally abandoned show business in March 1874. Two years later, he married an older woman in Cheyenne, but soon left his bride for a fling at gold prospecting. By the summer of 1876, he had landed in Deadwood, South Dakota, making his way as a gambler. On August 2, Hickok was playing poker with three companions in Mann's Saloon Number Ten, when 25-year-old Jack McCall stepped up behind him, said "Take that!" and fired a shot into the back of Wild Bill's head. Hickok died holding his best hand of the night — aces and eights, henceforth known as the "dead man's hand."

In custody, McCall offered contradictory versions of why he had killed Hickok. His first explanation — revenge for a brother's death at Wild Bill's hands — was unsupported, and he soon changed his story, claiming that Hickok had insulted him in public. As a matter of fact, it appeared that Hickok had grubstaked McCall, displaying unusual generosity in forgiving a gambling debt, whereupon the shooter next tried to blame local citizens for hiring him to shoot Hickok. Once again, evidence was lacking, and the situation was confused enough by then that a miner's court acquitted him of murder. Hickok's friends in the army raised an immediate outcry, pointing out that miner's courts had no legitimate authority, and so McCall faced trial again, this time in U.S. district court, where he was convicted and sentenced to hang. He went to the gallows on March 1, 1877.

## Hodge, Jeffrey

A native of Northwood, Ohio, Jeffrey Hodge dreamed of becoming a policeman for as long as anyone could remember. As one friend recalled from those early days, "For Jeff, that was it, everything. He wanted to wear the badge." In high school, Hodge was a popular student, active in a campus Christian group, and if size kept him off the football team, he made up for it with his enthusiasm at pep rallies. In his senior year, Hodge met the Norwegian exchange student who would shortly become his wife. Graduating from high school in 1987, he went on to college in Toledo, and by September 1989 was serving as a student dispatcher for the Toledo University campus police. The following summer, Hodge took a full-time job with the Lucas County emergency system, manning the telephones by night and attending the police academy by day. When he graduated as a full-fledged cop in May 1990, a job was waiting for him with the TU campus force.

His first semester on the job, Patrolman Hodge chalked up some impressive arrests, prompting a supervisor to recall, "He was quite good. He was thorough and aggressive. He looked like a good one." At the same time, however, something had gone drastically wrong, although campus officials would not recognized the problem for some time. The same Jeff Hodge described by his neighbors as quiet and reserved, earned barbs from TU students calling him "cocky, gung ho and eager." Some co-eds complained of his brusqueness and arrogance, while others caught him rating them as they walked by. In October 1991, Hodge arrested a co-ed for driving while intoxicated, then suggested that they meet later, to "talk it over." She indignantly refused and filed a complaint. The mother of another busted girl remembers that, "He called my house several hours after arresting my daughter on a drunken driving charge. I told him she was still in jail. He said he wanted to discuss other possible charges with her, but it sounded as if Officer Hodge wanted to ask my girl for a date." And then, there were the "pranks." Over Labor Day weekend, in 1991, a series of nine arson fires caused some $45,000 on the TU campus. All were set during the graveyard shift, when Hodge was on patrol, and each inside a building that required a master key for access to the inner rooms. Two months later, on November 22, campus police were forced to relocate a luncheon after they received anonymous bomb threats. In retrospect, Hodge would also be linked to phony burglar reports on campus, and the false alarm of an armed man on campus. Looking back, one Toledo detective opined, "He was a loose cannon. The incidents started out as petty ones but began to escalate." Looking back with 20/20 hindsight, a campus spokesman said, "I think he was playing two roles — that of a bad guy and that of a good guy. He creates the crisis and then gets in a phone booth and puts on a Superman outfit."

The crisis on January 20, 1992, was a shooting. Late that Monday night, an unknown gunman had fired six shots from a 9mm pistol into McKinnon Hall, a resident dormitory for women. One slug narrowly missed a sleeping co-ed, and while campus police duly collected the bullets and spent cartridge cases, there was little they could do with them unless they found a suspect weapon for comparison.

A week later, at 12:20 a.m. on January 27, a night dispatcher at the Checker Cab company received an anonymous phone call, reporting the robbery of a taxi driver on the TU campus, near the Engineering Technology Laboratory. Shots had been fired, the female caller said, before she broke the connection. The dispatcher was worried, checking with her drivers on the street by radio, but none of them had suffered any problem, much less robbery at gunpoint. The call was seemingly a prank, but the dispatcher took no chances. At half-past midnight, she relayed the message to campus police, and a two-man car was on the scene by 12:40. There was no sign of any disturbance, but Jeff Hodge and his partner split up to search the area on foot. Moments later, Hodge was back, shouting for his partner in a strained, excited voice.

He had found a woman's body, lying face down in the snow behind the engineering lab. Her jeans and panties were pulled down around her knees, the Pi Beta Phi sorority sweatshirt pushed up to her armpits. Her body had been lying in the snowbank long enough that it was frozen to the ground. Autopsy results showed that the victim had been shot 14 times in the head, back and legs with a 9mm weapon, all from a range of three feet or less. As one investigator suggested, "It was somebody who definitely wanted to make sure she was dead." No drugs or alcohol were found in the young woman's system, and despite the disarrangement of her clothing, there was no sign of a sexual assault.

The killing was TU's first murder in more than 50 years, the last one involving a randy football player and a love affair gone sour in the 1930s. Thankfully, there was no problem identifying the latest victim, since she had been reported missing a day before her body was found. Melissa Anne Herstrum, age 19, was a nursing student at the university, apparently well liked by everyone who knew her. She shared an apartment with another co-ed, in the section of Toledo known as College Station, and her roommate had last seen Melissa alive on Sunday morning, January 26, around 4 a.m. As she recalled it, Melissa had returned late from a Saturday night party, and she wasn't home long — only long enough, in fact, to receive three phone calls and place one of her own. Melissa had been visibly upset when she left, with no mention of where she was going. When she failed to return by noon the next day, her roomie had filed a missing persons report with the campus police.

The I.D. on their victim gave investigators something to work with, as they began the search for her killer. Melissa's 1989 Ford Taurus had not been in the parking lot where her body was found, and police put out an all-points bulletin on the missing car. Ironically, it was Patrolman Hodge who found the vehicle a few hours later, in another parking lot, some two miles from the murder scene. Melissa's purse was in the car, the contents of her wallet seemingly intact, which ruled out robbery as a motive for the killing. A final inventory showed that Melissa's car keys and driver's license were still missing, along with the coat she had worn when she left her apartment. The keys were later found in a campus trash can, close by the scene of the crime, and a student found Melissa's driver's license on Thursday night, January 30, lying atop a bank of plowed snow on Westwood Drive, a mile from the engineering lab. Finally, a police sketch artist prepared a drawing of the lost coat, which was shown on TV. Within the hour, police had the garment, returned by a man who had found it on Westwood, close to where the driver's license was discarded.

Police, meanwhile, were working overtime on the evidence in hand. Melissa's last phone call had been made to an ex-boyfriend, who told police, "She was crying and very upset on the telephone. She said she was coming over, that she had to see me. I waited for her, but she never arrived." Ballistics tests revealed that Herstrum had been killed with the same gun that riddled McKinnon Hall a week before her slaying. On February 1, detectives traced the "prank" call to the Checker Cab company, discovering that it had been made from a pay phone on campus, *inside* a building locked up for the night. The removal of Melissa's driver's license from her wallet suggested a possible traffic stop by police, and the suspicion deepened after Lucas County Coroner James Patrick reported finding abrasions on the victim's wrists, consistent with handcuffs. One of the bullets retrieved from her body was also deformed, as if from striking metal before it had entered her flesh.

All things considered, homicide detectives thought it would be wise to take a closer look at Jeffrey Hodge. They learned that Hodge had worked an automobile accident on Sunday, January 26, and that Melissa had been on the scene when he arrived, giving first aid to one of the injured drivers. Soon after her killing, Hodge had joined a number of his colleagues at a Super Bowl party, haranguing them with questions about techniques of ballistic testing until they finally told him to shut up and watch the game. Before the sun went down on February 1, Jeff Hodge was in custody for questioning. A search of his police locker turned up handcuffs scarred with "a smear of lead and copper consistent with a bullet found underneath the body at the crime scene," while examination of his uniform disclosed microscopic drops of blood and bits of flesh that matched Melissa Herstrum's blood type. At a press conference that evening, TU Security Director Frank Pizzulo and Toledo Police Chief Martin Felker announced the arrest. A question was raised concerning the female caller who had telephoned the Checker Cab company, but Captain Thomas Gulch assured reporters, "It was no woman. It was Mr. Hodge impersonating a woman."

A grand jury agreed, indicting Hodge for aggravated murder and kidnapping on February 10. Use of a firearm in the crime, under Ohio law, permitted prosecutors to seek the death penalty at trial. Hodge had been suspended with pay following his arrest, but now, in the wake of his indictment, Director Pizzulo secured his dismissal by order of the university's president. Attorney Alan Konop, meanwhile, seemed disdainful of the accusations linking his client to offenses ranging from simple malfeasance to arson. "If they're so damn sure he has committed these crimes," Konop told newsmen, "why don't they just charge him with these crimes? It's so easy to come up with all these other charges after he's gone. There have been links made as though he's committed every crime on campus for the past two years."

Held under suicide watch in the Lucas County jail, with his trial scheduled for October 13, Hodge and his lawyer were confronted with an ever-mounting pile of evidence. Hair similar to Melissa Herstrum's was recovered from Hodge's patrol car, and while the murder weapon was still missing, friends recalled that Hodge had spoken of owning a 9mm pistol. In September, a DNA report on the blood and bits of flesh from Hodge's uniform made a positive match with the victim, prompting lawyer Konop to seek a continuance for independent testing. The trial date was pushed back to March 1993, but it didn't help. On November 25, another lab report identified microscopic traces of Melissa's skin on Hodge's handcuffs. Konop sought and secured another delay, this time until June 1993, but his client was quickly running out of nerve.

In May 1993, Hodge instructed his lawyer to seek a plea bargain, and prosecutors — still lacking a murder weapon — agreed to waive the death penalty in return for a full confession. Hodge pled guilty before Judge Judith Lanzinger, on May 16, explaining that he had stopped Melissa on suspicion of drunk driving, but found she had no driver's license with her in the car. Hodge drove her back to her apartment, waiting outside while she fetched her I.D. "When she came back down," he told the court, "I drove back to the lot where her car was parked. I came to turn towards her car, but I went back and turned the other way. We proceeded to the Scott Park Campus, at which time I handcuffed the victim and shot her." When the body had not been recovered the next day, Hodge had faked the emergency call to Checker Cab, thus giving himself an excuse to "discover" Melissa's remains. When asked the reason for the brutal slaying, Hodge replied, "At the time of the actual incident, I don't know."

Melissa's father was allowed to speak out at the hearing, telling Hodge, "You don't deserve to live. We agreed to this negotiated plea because it is important for us to know that it is you who really are the killer and to hear you publicly confess that you are the kidnapper and murderer." The confession was enough to earn Hodge a life sentence for aggravated murder, with no parole for the first 20 years, plus ten to 25 years for kidnapping and a mandatory three years for using a gun in commission of a crime. It added up to a minimum of 33 years behind bars, making Hodge eligible for parole in 2026 A.D., at age 57.

Even that may be too soon, if UT sociology professor James King is correct in his assessment of the ex-cop's character. An expert in deviant behavior, Dr. King is convinced that Hodge would have kept on killing indefinitely, if circumstantial evidence had not prompted his arrest. In King's words, "He fits every single profile of a serial killer. The Herstrum murder was just the beginning."

# Horton, Billy Ray: See Ladner, Thomas

# Hudson, Jack Ray, Jr.

The oldest of four children, born in 1958, Jack Hudson grew up in Waxhaw, North Carolina, some 20 miles from Charlotte. His father died while Jack was still a child, whereupon his mother married one of the late man's brothers, but Jack appeared to survive the upset with no ill effects. He was an Eagle Scout and science buff, whose high school career included stints with the band, football team, and Future Business Leaders of America. Upon graduation, in 1976, he joined the U.S. Marine Corps, serving both at home and in Japan. His first marriage didn't last long, but Hudson soon re-married — this time to Becky Hoover, the sister of his best friend in high school. In January 1991, with the rank of sergeant, Hudson transferred to the marine air station at Yuma, Arizona, where he supervised air traffic controllers. Major Steve Harris, at Yuma, called Hudson "pre-eminent as a Marine leader," and wrote in one performance evaluation that Hudson's "problem-solving skills are the best I've ever seen." It came as a surprise to everyone, then, when Sgt. Hudson was arrested on June 5, 1992, for drunk driving on base. It was the end of any meaningful advancement for him, in the Corps, and he took early retirement less than a year later.

Fortunately, Hudson already had a new career lined up and waiting for him. While still a marine, he had begun working part-time as a communications operator for the Yuma Rural/Metro Fire Department and a reserve sheriff's deputy. The Yuma County Sheriff's office hired him full-time in August 1993, and October 1994 saw Hudson honored as "rookie of the year." In short order, he found himself attached to the Southwest Border Alliance, a narcotics task force which included local officers, along with agents of the Customs Service, Border Patrol, and the Drug Enforcement Administration (DEA). Hudson was placed in charge of inventory records, logging in confiscated drugs and guns at headquarters, along with certain cash earmarked as "marijuana eradication funds." The job also included undercover work, with biker gangs, and Hudson soon underwent a radical change, transformed from a crewcut, spit-and-polish cop, to something more along the lines of a long-haired, grungy-looking doper. When fellow officers remarked on his precipitous weight loss, Hudson replied that he was "working out" to keep himself in shape. Still, his first six-month performance review showed Jack doing an "excellent job" on the task force, and supervision of the new guy was relaxed almost to the point of nonexistence.

By June 1995, something was obviously wrong at SBA headquarters. Money, guns and drugs were disappearing from the lockup Hudson supervised. Barring a break-in, which had not occurred, no one but cops had access to the stash. Unknown to Hudson, task force technician Jim Erhardt was ordered to rig a covert surveillance camera inside the evidence vault. On the night of July 4, 1995, the hidden eye caught Jack Hudson prowling the stash, well after hours, and a quiet alarm was sounded.

Those responding at 10:50 p.m. were 42-year-old Dan Elkins, a lieutenant with the Yuma P.D. and the task force commander, plus 41-year-old Mike Crowe, a 15-year veteran of the Arizona Department of Public Safety. On arrival at the SBA's rural headquarters, they were joined by Erhardt, emerging from a nearby building that served as his makeshift surveillance post. Entering the office, they were met by Hudson, who was carrying a heavy pair of bolt cutters. When Lt. Elkins asked what he was doing, Jack replied that he was working on his monthly inventory statement. That said, he quickly ducked into the evidence room once more, and returned seconds later, with a 9mm MAC-10 machine pistol in his hand.

The rest was chaos. Crowe apparently ordered Hudson to drop the gun, then turned to flee, three bullets slamming into his back. Elkins, curiously unarmed, ducked into another room, while Hudson turned his gun on Erhardt. The weapon jammed, and Erhardt watched, frozen in horror, as Jack tried to clear the action. No sooner was he done, though, than a sound outside the open door distracted Hudson, and he turned away from his trembling victim to follow Mike Crowe. The wounded officer was crawling toward his car, when Hudson walked up behind him and fired another shot into his head.

Jim Erhardt saw his chance and took it, sprinting from the office to his separate building, where he kept a shotgun. Hudson, meanwhile, went back for Elkins, who was still inside the command post. He found Elkins in one of the offices and killed him on the spot. Unknown to Hudson, though, his second victim had already used the telephone, dialing 911 to report "an agent who's gone 918" (mentally unstable). "He's shooting guns!" Crowe told the operator. "He's firing rounds! Hurry up!"

The call was logged at 10:53 p.m. and lasted 40 seconds. Emergency units were rolling toward the scene within another minute and a half, sirens wailing. At SBA headquarters, near Yuma National Airport, the officers found Mike Crowe stretched out in the parking lot. He was alive, but just barely; less than three hours later, he was pronounced dead at Yuma Regional Medical Center. Inside the headquarters, Dan Elkins was already dead, shot several times at close range. The evidence locker, as later described to the press, "looked like a bomb had gone off" inside.

Jack Hudson, blood-spattered and seemingly dazed, surrendered without a fight. In his car, nearby, arresting officers found a submachine gun and two other weapons, a smoke grenade, cellular telephones and radios, unauthorized keys to the evidence locker, and $2,034 in cash; the trunk gave up another $49,800 in hundred-dollar bills. A subsequent search of his home revealed 43 guns (more than half of them stolen from the evidence locker), telescopic sights for rifles, and a variety of stolen drugs, including marijuana, cocaine, and methamphetamines. A breathalyzer found Hudson sober, but his blood tested positive for both amphetamines and methamphetamines.

Charged with first-degree murder, aggravated assault, burglary, and theft, Jack pled not guilty on all counts and was held in lieu of

$15.5 million bond. Local lawmen were in shock, Chief Robby Robinson of Yuma P.D. describing the incident as "a major tragedy for all police departments and law-enforcement officers in Arizona." Sheriff Ralph Ogden could only reiterate that Hudson seemed to be "doing a fine job," before he suddenly went berserk. When the lab test came back on Hudson's blood, Sheriff Ogden declared himself "very surprised that a person of his caliber would use drugs." Investigators noted that "meth" often produces severe paranoia as its effects begin wearing off.

Hudson's trial began in mid-November 1996, Judge Tom Cole overruling prosecution objections to permit a defense of "involuntary intoxication." As outlined by the defense, Hudson had been "forced" to take illegal drugs on the job, in order to infiltrate various bike gangs, and the drugs had rendered him legally insane. Deputy District Attorney Conrad Mallek countered that argument with evidence that Hudson was deeply in debt, owing some $5,000 in back taxes, while writing a series of 25 bad checks between November 1994 and January 1995. The debts only worsened when his wife gave birth to a second child, Mallek said, and Hudson had begun looting the task force storeroom for profit, finally turning to murder when he was caught. The first theft, Mallek showed, had taken place in February 1995, when $1,630 vanished from SBA's evidence locker, followed quickly by a deposit of $1,500 to Hudson's bank account. The raids escalated from there, with Hudson allegedly planning to torch the headquarters, thereby covering his tracks, on the night he was cornered.

Jurors were unmoved by the defense pleas for sympathy. On January 13, 1997, they deliberated barely three hours, before convicting Hudson on two counts of first-degree murder and seven additional felony counts. In Arizona, murder of a lawman on duty carries the death penalty.

# Hyden, James: See Ladner, Thomas

# Keating, James: See Corbitt, Michael

# Ladner, Thomas

A native of Sabine County, in "Deep East" Texas, Thomas Ladner caught his first glimpse of the outside world in 1967, when the U.S. Army drafted him five months after his graduation from high school. Vietnam was a shock to this intensely racist "good ol' boy," and he arrived in time for the brutal Tet Offensive of 1968. Upon returning to civilian life, in 1971, Ladner made a beeline back to familiar territory and soon found employment as the town constable in tiny Yellowpine.

At a glance, the six-foot-one, 270-pound Ladner appeared to be the sort of lawman who could quiet trouble by his very presence. Unfortunately for the residents of his jurisdiction, he also possessed the personality of what one prosecutor would call a "psychopathic bully," quick with his fists and favorite blackjack on the flimsiest excuse. Nor was his violence necessarily limited to lawbreakers: in 1974, he pulled a gun on Hemphill City Marshal Andy Helms, to liberate a drunken driver who was one of Ladner's friends. (Helms resigned over the incident, when Ladner's bizarre action was supported by Mayor Charlie Rice and Sheriff Blan Greer.) Four years later, after his appointment as Hemphill's chief of police, Ladner acquired a reputation for harassing teenage girls, often stopping them on lonely roads outside his jurisdiction, arresting them on trumped-up charges and subjecting them to crude interrogations. Between Ladner and Sheriff Greer — first elected in 1965 — blacks were particularly at risk in Sabine County. "Outsiders" of color were sometimes escorted from Hemphill by police, and white residents who befriended blacks were likewise targets of harassment. Ladner and Sabine County's chief deputy, Billy Ray Horton, were both reported to the FBI for civil rights violations, Ladner logging at least three complaints, but witnesses generally declined to testify, and none of the cases were prosecuted.

On the night of December 25, 1987, Loyal Garner Jr. and two friends, brothers John and Alton Maxie, made the critical error of driving the half-dozen miles from their Louisiana home town into Sabine County, Texas. The three men were black, and at least two of them had been drinking; reports differ as to whether Garner, driving the pickup truck, had consumed any alcohol. Chief Ladner and 34-year-old sheriff's deputy James ("Bo") Hyden were on their way back to Hemphill, after helping a clumsy neighbor retrieve his keys from a locked car, when they spotted the pickup with three blacks inside. Ladner would later testify that the truck was weaving erratically; Loyal Garner, for his part, saw the flashing red lights in his rearview mirror and thought he was being stopped for a defective taillight. All three were taken into custody, without explanation, and soon found themselves in the detox tank of the Sabine County jail. Next door, in a separate cell, five other prisoners were wide awake and listening when the three new arrivals began shouting, demanding their right to a telephone call.

Billy Ray Horton was first to respond, threatening to "kick some ass" if the racket continued. Alton Maxie, drunk enough to be courageous, challenged his keeper: "What you gonna do, bring four or five with you?" The prisoners kept shouting until Chief Ladner appeared, with James Hyden in tow. Brandishing his trusty black-jack, the chief demanded, "Which one of you's beating on the motherfucking door?" At that, Loyal Garner made the mistake of a lifetime. "I was," he told Ladner. "I just want to call my wife."

Next door, the other inmates heard distinctive sounds of a beating in progress, Ladner clubbing Garner with the sap, while Hyden watched the Maxie brothers, one hand on his gun. When Garner was properly subdued, the officers dragged him out of the cell, Hyden sneering at Garner's companions as the cell door slammed shut. "See, boy," he gloated, "it didn't take no four or five of us." The cops dragged Garner to the nearby jailer's office, where Billy Ray Horton was manning the desk. When they brought him back to the drunk tank ten minutes later, Garner was barely conscious, eyes unfocused, his shirt drenched in blood. Next, it was

Alton Maxie's turn, marched to the office where blood stained the floor, threatened with a nightstick and ordered to keep his mouth shut. A sudden attack of humility allowed Maxie to escape a beating... or, perhaps the officers were simply tired. Trusty Trent Taylor was summoned to mop up the blood in the office; he noticed a blackjack on the floor, its stitches torn, one of the lead weights missing, and one of the cops joked, "They just don't make 'em like they used to." Near midnight, Alton Maxie was finally allowed to phone home, Deputy Horton permitting the call on condition that Maxie simply tell his mother where he was "and that she can't do anything about it until morning."

At breakfast time, day-shift jailer Clyde King found Garner still unconscious, sprawled on the floor of his cell, and summoned an ambulance. Transported to the emergency room at Sabine County Hospital, Garner was examined by Dr. Grover Winslow. Controversy continues over exactly what that examination involved, but Dr. Winslow quickly determined that Garner needed more help than Sabine County could provide. Another ambulance transported him to Tyler, 100 miles northwest of Hemphill, where he was diagnosed with a massive brain hemorrhage. For all intents and purposes, he was dead on arrival, officially pronounced at 12:15 p.m. on December 27.

Within an hour of Garner's death, an ambulance from Hemphill had arrived in Tyler, to retrieve his corpse, but Justice of the Peace Bill Beaird was properly suspicious, refusing to give up the body without a full autopsy. A Sabine County judge called up, insisting that Garner had been in a jailhouse "accident," but Beaird stood his ground. Back in Hemphill, meanwhile, the Maxie brothers were released after paying $22.50 each on charges of public intoxication, their freedom conditional on signing affidavits which described Chief Ladner and company as "acting like gentlemen and kindly." Both would later recant the statements, claiming they had signed them unread, and there is reason to accept the denials as genuine: both statements were, in fact, typed up by State Trooper Bill Bradberry, disciplined in 1979 for falsifying official reports to conceal the misbehavior of his patrol partner. By the time Bill Beaird began fielding angry phone calls in Tyler, the Maxie brothers were already back in Louisiana, counting themselves lucky to be alive.

Chief Ladner, for his part, expected a storm. He hired attorney John Seale, who had represented Ladner's first wife during their divorce, and staunchly refused to speak with FBI agents investigating the case. A short public statement described Loyal Garner as an abusive, belligerent drunk who was "driving very erratic" when stopped on the highway, later assaulting Ladner and Bo Hyden in jail, when they kindly escorted him to the jailer's office for a phone call. Ladner admitted striking Garner once with his blackjack, but insisted that "I didn't even get a good lick at him." While they were scuffling, Ladner and Hyden getting the worst of it — despite a total lack of injuries — Garner had slipped and fallen, "hitting his head against the wall." He had seemed fit enough when they walked Garner back to his cell, Ladner said. "The next thing I know, they say he's in a coma, and the next thing I know, they say he's dead. I just can't believe it."

On December 31, the Maxie brothers appeared before a Sabine County grand jury investigating Garner's death. They came reluctantly, honoring subpoenas only on the condition that they be escorted by a friendly Louisiana sheriff, for protection. Under oath, they recanted their prior affidavits, staunchly denying that Garner had crossed the Texas line "to pick up and deliver some drugs." Five other inmates, clearly fearing for their safety in the Sabine County lockup, described Ladner's noisy beating of Garner, and even Sheriff Greer admitted his was "disappointed" in Deputy Horton for failing to prevent the incident. In Greer's view, Horton "should have checked this patient a little closer." Dr. Winslow, from the county hospital, described Garner as "probably brain dead practically" when he reached the ER, then digressed to speculate on "some very freakish accidents" that could have caused the fatal injuries. Pathologist Virgil Gonzalez dismissed the "accident" scenario, confirming the cause of Garner's death as violent blows to the head. None of the three accused officers testified, submitting written statements instead. On January 5, 1988, all three were indicted on two counts each, accused first of beating Loyal Garner, and then denying him medical treatment.

Soon after the indictments, civil rights attorney Morris Dees and his Southern Poverty Law Center joined forces with Corinne Garner, assisting her in preparation of a civil suit for wrongful death in her husband's beating. By mid-January, Ladner, Horton and Hyden had been served in that case, with the city of Hemphill named as an additional defendant. Some locals dismissed the SPLC staff as "those meddling bastards from Alabama," but Chief Ladner had no shortage of enemies in Sabine County, some of them inclined to believe that Garner's death was, as described in the lawsuit, a "brutal, racially motivated killing." On January 31, deputies Horton and Hyden were suspended without pay, pending resolution of their case; a short time later, the Hemphill City Council reluctantly followed suit with Chief Ladner.

Eight days after the first two suspensions, Justice of the Peace Bill Beaird convened his inquest into Garner's death, in Tyler, Texas. Dr. Gonzalez and the Maxie brothers repeated their previous testimony. Complaints from John Seale notwithstanding, the jury of four men and two women deliberated only 20 minutes before finding that Loyal Garner "died of injuries to his head as a result of homicide." Smith County D.A. Jack Skeen took the case to a grand jury, resulting in murder indictments against all three defendants on March 3. Already under bond at home, the officers were booked again and released on $25,000 bail pending trial.

The news was encouraging, but Corinne Garner and Morris Dees still had their doubts about justice in Sabine County, where one observer had remarked, "Nobody's got rights if they ain't from here." The district attorney was clearly reluctant to pursue civil rights charges against the three accused lawmen, but a quirk of Texas law permits crime victims or their survivors to employ a special prosecutor at their own expense, providing that the duly appointed D.A. is unable or unwilling to proceed. Dees and company took full advantage of the law, securing the services of U.S. Attorney John Hannah to ramrod the prosecution in Hemphill. Jury selection for the first trial, before Judge O'Neal Bacon in Sabine County, began on July 5, 1988, with testimony starting two days later. It was an uphill battle for John Hannah from the start, Judge Bacon barely able to conceal his fondness for the cops on trial. The judge excluded autopsy photos and other medical evidence, in what Hannah called "an obvious attempt to aid the defense," and his behavior quickly became so egregious that Hannah drafted a motion to disqualify Bacon as "so biased and prejudiced against the State of Texas that a fair trial cannot be had by the prosecution." He stopped short of filing that complaint, though, preferring to soldier in the face of brutal odds. Dr. Winslow returned to describe Loyal Garner as hopelessly drunk at the time of his arrest, but his credibility took a nose-dive when it was revealed that he had signed bond for at least one of the defendants; somehow, Dr. Winslow "couldn't be positive" if he had helped to bail out more than one. A string of prosecution witnesses described Garner's beating, and similar acts of brutality committed by Garner, but an all-white jury was unmoved. On July 15, the three defendants were acquitted on all counts.

John Seale was back in court the next day, this time in Tyler, trying to convince Judge Joe Tunnell that murder charges should be dismissed on the theory of "collateral estoppel" — i.e., that a second trial would rehash the same issues already litigated in Sabine County. Tunnell rejected the theory, ordering Ladner to stand trial on August 8, but the case was postponed while Seale carried his argument to the Texas 12th Court of Appeals. On September 13, that court threw out the indictments, but now it was Jack Skeen's turn to appeal. On October 25, the Texas Court of Criminal Appeals, in Austin, reinstated the murder indictments on all three defendants, ruling that the issues — murder vs. civil rights violations — were "far from identical." Seale tried again, with a claim that the second trial would constitute double jeopardy, but that argument was struck down by the same court a year later, on October 25, 1989.

In the meantime, Deputies Horton and Hyden were filing some writs of their own, suing Morris Dees and the SPLC on charges of malicious prosecution and conspiracy. Tom Ladner abstained from the lawsuit, on advice of his attorney, and the case was soon dismissed as a transparent sham. On November 23, 1988, the city of Hemphill settled out of court with Corinne Garner, terms of the settlement sealed by order of Judge Robert Parker.

Things were heating up in Deep East Texas by the spring of 1990, with Ku Klux Klansmen rallying in support of the accused lawmen, while the NAACP organized angry counter-demonstrations. Chief Ladner's mobile home went up in flames one night, the fire blamed on arson, and more violence seemed imminent by the time trial convened on April 16. This time, when Dr. Winslow trotted out his tale of a drunk-and-disorderly victim, Jack Skeen countered with autopsy results that showed no alcohol in Garner's blood. Skeen described Tom Ladner to the jury as a man "on a mission," who had beaten his helpless prisoner to death "for hollering." On May 3, all three defendants were convicted of murder. The following day, Tom Ladner was sentenced to 28 years in prison, while Hyden drew a term of 14 years and Horton was sentenced to ten years. Ladner's appeal of the conviction was denied on September 21, 1991.

# Larn, John

A native of Mobile, Alabama, born in 1850, John Larn followed Horace Greely's advice as a young man, drifting westward until he found himself in Colorado. His first recorded act there was the murder of a cattleman who objected to Larn "borrowing" his horse without permission, and he also killed the sheriff who tried to arrest him. Fleeing into Texas, he stopped at Fort Griffin and signed on with a trail drive headed for New Mexico. Along the way, it was reported that he killed three men and dumped their bodies in the Pecos River "to feed the catfish." Back at Fort Griffin, Larn quarreled with his trail boss and led several renegade drovers on a rampage through the camp, leaving two men dead and seven wounded when the smoke cleared. Since the victims were suspected rustlers themselves, authorities ignored the incident.

In February 1876, Larn ran for sheriff in Shackleford County, Texas, and won on the basis of his vow to "clean up" the district. The campaign began on April 2, when Larn's posse rounded up a gang of rustlers led by one Joe Watson, summarily lynching four of the thieves. Two others fled to Dodge City, but Larn brought them back under warrants and lodged them in the Fort Griffin jail, where they in turn were soon lynched by "persons unknown." By year's end, 11 more rustlers were hanged without trial, and Shackleford County had calmed down enough for Sheriff Larn to try his hand at ranching, in partnership with Deputy **John Selman.**

No one who knew the lawmen would have been surprised to learn that they were stealing cattle from their neighbors, but Larn was never satisfied with simple theft. Two stone masons who built a wall on Larn's property were found dead in a river before they were paid for the job, and several other disappearances were also traced back to the ranch. Larn finally resigned after two of his cowboys shot up Fort Griffin, leaving three men dead, with a deputy and the county attorney wounded. Retirement left him free to steal cattle full-time, fielding nightriders to terrorize his growing legion of critics. In June 1878, Larn was finally arrested at his ranch, while Selman managed to escape the dragnet. At 10 o'clock that night, in a scene that must have conjured memories from his own glory days, the former sheriff was removed from jail and executed by a firing squad of nine masked men.

# Leasure, William Ernest

Bill Leasure did not fit the standard mold of the Los Angeles Police Department, as portrayed on *Dragnet* or the headlines that have branded the LAPD as a violent, racist institution in the wake of cases such as the O.J. Simpson murder trial and Rodney King affair. Nicknamed "Mild Bill" by his associates, he boasted a spotless personnel record, including numerous letters of praise from citizens who met him on the street and one sergeant's assessment that Leasure's "easy-going personality" often had "a calming effect in stressful situations." In custody for triple murder, Leasure described himself to one interviewer as "the nicest, quietest, mildest guy you'll ever want to meet. I'd never hurt a fly."

Humans were something else, as it turned out.

A native of Wayne, Michigan, born in 1946, Bill Leasure was the third of five children, painfully shy, an indifferent student who tested well in school but stubbornly refused to do homework. After high school, Leasure went to work at General Motors for a year, but Vietnam was heating up and the draft board was hot on his trail. In 1966, he joined the U.S. Marine Corps and was sent to Camp Pendleton, in southern California, for training. While there, in 1967, he met a local girl and married her on a whim. They were virtual strangers when he shipped out for Asia a short time later. Mild Bill managed to avoid combat duty in Nam, and was discharged from the service in 1969. Jobless and devoid of prospects, he learned that the LAPD was actively recruiting military veterans, and he joined the force a few months after his discharge from the Marines. In 1970, he was assigned to Central Traffic, where he spent the bulk of his police career.

Most cops view traffic duty as a launching pad to something bigger, better, more adventurous and lucrative, but Leasure seemed completely satisfied with his assignment. He preferred the night shift, sometimes aggravating supervisors with his slow, painstaking style of writing accident reports. Leasure told one associate that he had failed the sergeant's test deliberately, in order to avoid promotion and protect his precious leisure time. He wasn't on the street for long before he started dating women whom he stopped for speeding, sometimes those he met at crime scenes. Leasure liked the weak and vulnerable ones, some of them in their teens, and he enjoyed his reputation as a "pussy hound" among his fellow officers. The game went sour on him, briefly, during 1972, when a self-appointed moralist in the department started phoning wives of various adulterous patrolmen, exposing their affairs. By year's end, Leasure was separated from his wife, their divorce finalized in April 1975. By that time, however, Mild Bill had already found himself a new "main squeeze." Betsy Mogul was an L.A. city attorney who met Leasure in 1974, while she was prosecuting one of his cases. They hit it off and started dating while Leasure was still married, tying the knot soon after his divorce became final in 1975. It was a step up for Leasure, financially, their combined income topping $100,000 per year in the early 1980s, but the newlyweds still seemed to live beyond their means. They had a $250,000 waterfront condo and boat slip in Long Beach, a three-bedroom rental home in Sun Valley, and the primary residence in Northridge, while modest in itself, occupied a huge lot that was soon crammed with Leasure's collection of classic Corvettes. At any given time, he owned between 12 and 17 of the expensive sports cars, housing eight in a special garage at his home, farming others out to friends or stashing them in rented garages. Unknown to most of his fellow officers, Mild Bill converted one room of his house into a private armory, his stockpile of 40-odd weapons including illegal machine guns and silencers. Friends on the job assumed that he was joking when he talked about the island he had purchased, in Belize, and his off-shore bank accounts in the Cayman Islands. Just bullshit, they told themselves, playing along with the jest.

Bill Leasure's second marriage did not slow him down, in terms of cultivating girlfriends on the side. One, Cathy Chang (a pseudonym), met Bill in 1979, when he helped recover her father's stolen car. She was 18, to Leasure's 33, and while they were lovers for the next seven years, she never knew that he was married. In 1985, when she got pregnant, Leasure talked her into an abortion at her own expense. Leasure was always a tightwad, though he often spoke to Chang about his private business dealings — conversations that would finally come back to haunt him from the witness stand.

It is unclear exactly when Mild Bill went bad. The final list of charges filed against him ranged from grand theft auto to premeditated murder, and some of the Corvettes in Leasure's collection were certainly stolen. He also had a habit of collecting shady friends — among them part-time contract killer Dennis Winebaugh, paroled bank robber Robert Kuns, and all-around shady character Dennis France. Another self-described "good friend" of Leasure's was Arthur Smith, a witness in one of the cases Betsy Mogul prosecuted for Leasure in 1974. A big-time wheeler-dealer with a taste for larceny, Smith befriended Leasure, selling him a Cadillac and a Mercedes Benz at discount rates, taking Mild Bill along on outings to the Cayman Islands and Belize. Leasure made no secret of the fact that he was loyal to his friends and would do anything on their behalf, if they were in a bind... and if the price was right.

First, though, he had another friend in need. Paulette de los Reyes met Leasure in 1975, introduced by his patrol partner, and they became the very best of friends. Though married, her relationship with husband Tony was a stormy one, to say the least, exacerbated by his violent temper and flagrant adultery. To make things worse, their domestic strife was intertwined with business, Tony and Paulette's parents standing as joint owners of El Sol Tortillas, a factory serving Mexican restaurants around L.A. In June 1976 the couple separated, Tony Reyes filing for divorce, and the family business began to suffer accordingly. Paulette and Bill Leasure were watching TV at her place one evening, enjoying Charles Bronson in *The Mechanic* — a story of professional hit men — when she remarked how lovely it would be if someone killed her husband. "Piece of cake," Mild Bill replied.

On October 7, 1976, a dynamite bomb destroyed Tony's car, in the underground garage at his apartment house. No one was injured, but the blast was a clear warning. Tony fired off a letter to the police, accusing his wife of plotting to have him killed, but in the absence of hard evidence, no charges were filed. Tony Reyes began watching his back, but in the meantime, his would-be assassins had other fish to fry.

Paulette's stepfather, Gilberto Cervantes, was the other major partner in El Sol Tortillas. It is still unclear exactly who decided he should die, to clear the way for bigger, better things: Tony and Paulette later blamed each other, but both had firm alibis, and their spiteful accusations would not stand as evidence. On Sunday, March 20, 1977, Cervantes returned from early-morning Mass to his home in suburban San Gabriel. As he nosed his Cadillac into the garage, a pickup truck with two male passengers pulled up to the curb, one stepping out and moving rapidly to intercept Cervantes. The old man had barely risen from his car when a .357 Magnum bullet knocked him sprawling, dead before he hit the ground. Years would pass before Dennis Winebaugh was identified as the killer, with Mild Bill Leasure named as the mastermind and wheelman on the hit.

A few months after Gilberto's murder, Tony de los Reyes offered Winebaugh $5,000 to get rid of his wife, unaware that Paulette was then sharing the triggerman's bed on a regular basis. Winebaugh readily took the five grand, then tipped Paulette off to the plot. Betrayed and frightened, Tony wrote a second accusatory letter, this one entrusted to a friend for publication in the event of his death. Dated July 7, 1977, the latest note accused Winebaugh and Paulette of the Cervantes slaying, going on to say that Paulette had hired "someone else" to murder Tony. Almost as an afterthought, Reyes expressed his fear that the LAPD "might not properly investigate" his death. As luck would have it, though, new business had distracted those who hunted him, giving Tony another reprieve.

By early 1980, after seven years of marriage, Art Smith was in the midst of a bitter divorce from his wife Anne Marie. A full year earlier, Smith had told one of his friends, "I know two cops who will kill anybody you want for $50,000. I'm going to have them kidnap Anne and make it look like a sex-fiend killing." The friend took it as a joke, at least until he saw two plainclothes officers leaving Smith's office a few weeks later, but even then, he made no report of Smith's threat to the authorities. After all, if killer cops were involved, whom could he trust?

On May 28, 1980, Anne Marie Smith petitioned for a court order that would have evicted Arthur from the home they shared, despite their increasingly vicious divorce battle. The same day, she confided to her sister-in-law that Art had threatened to "break" her before the case was resolved. Next morning, Anne kept her appointment at a beauty salon in Highland Park. Ten minutes after she arrived, a gunman entered the shop and demanded cash, taking time to blast Anne Marie with a .45-caliber pistol before he fled. Three survivors in the shop, including two elderly women, could barely describe the killer, but a mechanic working across the street remembered the getaway car. It was a green Chevy Nova, he told police, with a white rally stripe down each side. It was coincidence, perhaps, that Bill Leasure called in sick on the day of the murder, while Dennis France paid $70 a few days later, to have his green Nova painted bright red.

Tony and Paulette Reyes, meanwhile, were still embroiled in their own domestic war. In the spring of 1981, while driving with a girlfriend, Tony was nearly killed in a drive-by shooting. The would-be killers drove a red Nova and escaped in the confusion. Tony suspected Paulette, of course, but the shooting did not prevent them from reconciling briefly. Still, they could never seem to get along for any length of time, and Tony kicked her out again on September 1. Eight days later, leaving a bar in Sherman Oaks with girlfriend Sandra Zysman, Tony was confronted by a mugger who demanded, "Your money or your life." Reyes didn't move fast enough to satisfy the robber, and a close-range shotgun blast shattered his skull, leaving him dead on the ground. Once again, police had no evidence, no leads, no suspects.

Bill Leasure had known paroled thief Robert Kuns since 1978, and while he knew all about the 35 months Kuns had served in a federal prison for bank robbery, they somehow avoided discussing any joint illegal enterprise until the latter months of 1982. Kuns had it in his mind to make a fortune selling stolen yachts, with some insurance fraud on the side, and Leasure thought it sounded good. In April 1983, with some assistance from Art Smith, the hopeful pirates formed a dummy corporation in the Cayman Islands to conceal the windfall they expected from their plan. That October, Leasure and Kuns made their first big score, flying to British Columbia with Dennis France to steal the *Peggy Rose II*, valued at some $60,000. It was weeks before the rightful owners missed their boat, by which time it had been renamed *Tortuga* and unloaded on gullible buyers.

From there, the thefts proliferated. Bill Leasure would later admit "helping" Kuns transport five yachts, denying any knowledge of the fact that they were stolen. In October 1984, the $85,000 *Tribunal* was taken from Newport Beach, sailed to the Marina Bay Yacht Harbor in Richmond, California, where Kuns had rented a slip. The sale was easy, followed by another yacht, the *Sans Souci*, in April 1985. A month later, Leasure and Kuns stole the *Billy G*, with at least four more yachts ripped off between July of that year and March 1986. At the same time, Leasure was also stealing cars — Corvettes preferred — and trading in illegal weapons on the side. Bob Kuns wanted to retire from the hot yacht racket in March 1986, but Leasure convinced him to stick it out for another year. In fact, while Mild Bill couldn't know it yet, their winning streak had barely two months left to run.

Up north, someone had blown the whistle, and police were waiting when the yacht *Holiday* — formerly *La Vita*, newly stolen out of San Diego — pulled into port on May 29. Leasure and Kuns were charged with grand theft, and while Bill's many friends at the LAPD refused to believe he was "dirty," the oh-so-nice patrolman's world was starting to unravel on all sides.

As luck would have it, on the same day Leasure was arrested, Long Beach detectives were grilling a petty crook named Jerry France. His specialty was "paper hanging" — that is, writing rubber checks — and he survived by ratting out competing thieves to save himself from doing time. The month before, in fact, Long Beach police had cleared six cases thanks to Jerry France, but now he was in jail again, with nothing left to trade. He sweated for a while, before it hit him. There was "something really heavy" he could tell detectives, after all, involving yacht thefts, contract killings, and a string of other crimes. The men responsible were Jerry's brother Dennis and "a traffic cop named Bill," from neighboring Los Angeles.

The LAPD was frankly skeptical of Jerry France's story, even with Bill Leasure sitting in the Alameda County jail. For one thing, France's physical description of the L.A. traffic cop was off by some two inches, ten years, and 170 pounds; he gave Leasure a full head of gray hair, when Mild Bill was a blond and nearly bald. Still, in the circumstances, every accusation had to be checked out. Detectives picked up Dennis France, who proved no more resilient under grilling than his brother. In short order, Dennis was spilling a marathon confession to multiple murders and sundry other felonies, tossing in a few new suspects for good measure. (One affidavit prompted security guard Lee Sandridge to cop an involuntary manslaughter plea in the August 1981 beating death of Roberto Chavez, a crime for which he was sentenced to 30 days in jail and three years probation.) France described the murder of Gilberto Cervantes first, naming Dennis Winebaugh as the shooter, Bill Leasure as the brains and getaway driver. France himself had killed Anne Smith in the beauty salon, on orders from Leasure, while Mild Bill waited outside in his green Chevy Nova. Dennis was also the shooter in both attempts on Tony de los Reyes, another hit lined up by Leasure, although he supposedly "tried to miss" with the shotgun blast that nearly decapitated Reyes on September 9, 1981.

Reluctantly, holding their noses all the way, investigators cut a deal. They had no case against Bill Leasure without France's testimony, and the price of that assistance was immunity from prosecution. In return for his freedom, France agreed to wear a wire and visit Leasure in jail, eliciting guilty comments that would drive the final nails into Mild Bill's coffin. On the first visit, however, Leasure frustrated his captors by scribbling notes to France in lieu of spoken conversation, plainly fearing a bug in the visiting room.

Once, when France turned the conversation to Anne Smith, blurting out, "I was the shooter, you wasn't," Leasure hissed at him: "Shhh!"

It was a bust, but detectives arranged a second jailhouse meeting, this time in Los Angeles, where Leasure was transferred on October 14 to face charges of auto theft. This time, they had a video camera standing by, strategically positioned to view Leasure's notes. What had become of the Anne Smith murder weapon? France inquired. Leasure's written answer: "Melted." Yet another note urged France to "Dump everything illegal."

Two days later, Leasure was back in northern California, facing arraignment for theft of various yachts. The preliminary hearing dragged on until December 4, including a parade of yacht owners, detectives, and a pregnant Cathy Chang, who described the large-scale exchange of cash between Bill Leasure, Bob Kuns, and others. On December 9, Kuns and his attorney cut a deal with the D.A., Kuns accepting a maximum prison term of five years in exchange for testimony against Bill Leasure.

While the preliminary hearing was in progress, authorities traced Dennis Winebaugh to Oklahoma City and arrested him there. A search of his home turned up firearms and notes in Bill Leasure's handwriting, but Winebaugh was made of sterner stuff than France and Kuns, refusing to squeal in return for offers of leniency. The indictments rolled on into 1987, with new charges of yacht theft and insurance fraud filed against Leasure and his patrol partner, Ralph Gerard, on February 27; at the same time, Betsy Mogul was indicted for perjury, based on false information contained in the registration papers of a car she purchased from Art Smith. Three months later, on May 22, Smith and Paulette de los Reyes were charged with conspiracy to murder their respective spouses, and the LAPD was busy trying to fire Bill Leasure, his mandatory Board of Rights hearing winding through a series of fits and starts between April 1987 and June 1988, when he was finally dismissed for conduct "totally inconsistent with his role as a police officer."

In January 1988, Dennis Winebaugh went to trial for the murder of Gilberto Cervantes, with Dennis France appearing as the key prosecution witness against him. Convicted of that crime, Winebaugh was sentenced to life imprisonment by Judge Michael Berg. That autumn, Art Smith was convicted of plotting to kill his wife, once again on the strength of Dennis France's testimony. Before the penalty phase of his trial could begin, Smith cut a deal to testify against Bill Leasure in return for a waiver of the death penalty. Paulette de los Reyes was the last to roll over, in December 1989, the D.A.'s officer accepting her offer of testimony against Leasure in return for a guilty plea on second-degree murder and solicitation of murder. Prosecutors further agreed that Paulette would be sentenced only on the solicitation charge, with a maximum sentence of six years in jail.

At long last, Mild Bill went to trial on three counts of first-degree murder on April 15, 1991. He appeared confident in court, still maintaining his innocence, but the parade of ex-accomplices and co-conspirators hammered away at his "nice, quiet" image. Deputy D.A. James Koller made his final summation on May 30, five years and one day since Leasure's arrest, and the jury deliberated over four weeks before reporting themselves hopelessly deadlocked on June 28. The final vote had been 10 to 2 for conviction on all counts.

Jury selection for Leasure's second trial began on October 31, 1991, and Mild Bill surprised the prosecution a day later, changing his plea from "not guilty" to "no contest" on two negotiated counts of second-degree murder, accepting a prison term of 15 years to life. At that, it was no admission of guilt from Leasure's perspective; rather, he informed the press, he had struck the bargain "because my wife wants me to come home someday." He will be eligible for parole, along with killer cop **Craig Peyer**, in the year 2004.

# Long, Steve

Little is known about the early life of Big Steve Long, the six-foot six-inch gunman who was one of the bloodiest lawmen in Wyoming history. He drifted into Laramie in 1867, carrying the reputation of a hair-trigger gunman, and was soon appointed to the post of deputy marshal. Within the next two months, he killed eight men, including five gunned down with no real provocation in a single incident.

The massacre occurred on October 22, resulting from the harassment of three Eastern "dudes" by four local cowboys. The seven men were brawling in the street when Long arrived on the scene, calling for them to desist. The combatants ignored him, prompting Long to draw a pair of .44-caliber revolvers and blaze away like a madman, mortally wounding two of the cowboys and all three visitors.

His ferocity notwithstanding, Long still had no luck in controlling Laramie's criminal element. A vigilance committee organized to clear the town of riffraff, and its leaders soon had reason to suspect that Marshal Long's failure owed more to deliberate neglect than simple ineptitude. In fact, Big Steve was moonlighting as a highwayman, robbing travelers in the countryside around Laramie, but his double life came to a screeching halt in October 1868. Wounded by a prospector he tried to rob, Long made it back to town, where his fiancée patched him up. He made the critical mistake of telling her the truth about his injury, however, whereupon she promptly blew the whistle on him to the vigilance committee. The response was immediate and final: Long was seized by the vigilantes next day and hanged from a telegraph pole.

# Mather, David

"Mysterious Dave" Mather hailed from Massachusetts, where he was born in 1845, a descendant of the witch-hunting tyrant Cotton Mather. Little more is known about his early years, but Mather's nickname was not a reference to his murky past; rather, it was an expression of amazement at the seeming ease with which he skated through a series of notorious escapades. From rustling cattle in 1873, he moved on to Dodge City, Kansas, the following year, dividing his time between work as a gambler and lawman. Such contradictory behavior was not unusual in the Wild West, but Mather carried the game to extremes, reputed to have killed seven men in one standup fight. By 1878, he had drifted south to Texas, teaming up with **Wyatt Earp** in a swindle that involved sales of phony "gold bricks" to gullible rubes around Mobeetie. A year later, Mather was accused of train robbery, but the charges were dropped for lack of evidence.

**David Mather**
*Courtesy of Denver Public Library,*
*Western History Division.*

When not engaged in robbery or law enforcement, Mather was known as a practical joker, the propensity illustrated by an incident from his Dodge City days. An itinerant preacher somehow elicited Mather's promise to attend a local revival meeting, and as colleague Bob Wright pointed out, "Dave would not break his word. If he promised a man he would kill him, Dave was sure to do it." Attending the revival was one thing, however; offering his soul to Jesus was something else. On the appointed evening, Mather turned up as promised, his appearance prompting the evangelist and several members of the crowd to shout that they could die in peace, now that "the wickedest man in the county" had joined their fold. On hearing that, Mather announced that dying might not be a bad idea, since it would save the preacher and his flock from any risk of backsliding. Mather offered to kill himself, after shooting all the rest, and fired a shot over the preacher's head. As all and sundry ducked for cover, Mather strolled toward the exit, scornfully declaring, "You are all a set of liars and frauds. You don't want to go to heaven with me at all."

In 1880, Mather turned up in Las Vegas, New Mexico, backing Marshal Joe Carson's drive against the Henry gang. Carson died in one skirmish, while Mather killed one of his assailants and wounded another, lodging the survivor in jail. Three days later, Mather killed another Henry stalwart. When the last two members of the gang were jailed, Mather doffed his lawman's hat long enough to lead the lynch mob that removed all three from jail and strung them up without the benefit of trial. A few months later, Mather left Las Vegas under a cloud, accused of "promiscuous shooting."

He surfaced next in El Paso, Texas, as assistant marshal, but the pay was low, and Mather soon turned to pimping on the side. Shot and stabbed by a whorehouse madam when he tried to rob her brothel, Mather made his way back to Dodge City — and another posting as assistant marshal. Mather ran saloons on the side, competing with kingpin Tom Nixon, and February 1884 saw him stripped of his badge, replaced by Nixon in a local election. Mather promptly launched a price war against Nixon's saloons, and he seemed to be winning, until Marshal Nixon cut off his beer supply. Mather retaliated by romancing Nixon's young wife, a situation that virtually guaranteed violence to come.

On July 18, 1884, Nixon waited for Mather outside a Dodge City saloon, risking one shot before he fled, believing Mather to be dead. In fact, Mysterious Dave was unscathed, and he refused to press charges for attempted murder, preferring to settle the problem himself. Three days later, Nixon was loitering on Front Street when Mather crept up behind him and shot him four times in the back, killing him instantly. Indicted for murder, Mather was acquitted at trial on a plea of self-defense, the July 18th shooting presented as evidence of Nixon's murderous intent.

In 1885, Mather killed another man and wounded two more in separate Dodge City shootings. Marshal Ben Tilghman finally ran him out of town, Mather drifting on to serve as lawman in various small towns in Kansas and Nebraska. From there, different stories place him in Canada, perhaps serving as an officer with the Royal Canadian Mounted Police. He may have been alive as late as 1915, in Alberta, but the record is unclear.

## McKenna, Mark Douglas

In the early 1990s, Atlanta, Georgia, was plagued by a ring of daring thieves who specialized in burglarizing nightclubs, warehouses, department stores and supermarkets after hours, disabling the most sophisticated alarm systems, sometimes making off with heavy safes, leaving police with nothing in the way of useful clues. At one point, the prowlers were blamed for some 500 heists around metropolitan Atlanta; their evident skill earned grudging expressions of respect from local detectives. "These guys are damn slick," one detective told reporters. "I don't think they've made a security system yet these guys can't figure out. I tip my hat. They're pros." In 1992, the holdup men began to concentrate on local topless bars, hitting five for big scores in a period of 16 months, and it was this activity that ultimately led to their undoing, exposing an unprecedented law-enforcement scandal in the process.

Somehow, the burglars always seemed to know which strip clubs had a large amount of cash on hand, and when it would be easiest to loot bars. On December 13, 1992, they hit the Gold Club on Piedmont Road, Atlanta, evading a state-of-the-art security system by entering through a rooftop ventilation grill, removing a 460-pound safe with some $40,000 inside. A month later, the target was

Diamond Legs International, with phone lines cut and the burglar alarm disabled. This time, the safe was too heavy to move, so a special saw was used to cur through the tempered steel door. A short time later, thieves raided the Tops & Tails Show Club and wheeled out a safe packed with $85,000 in cash, leaving the alarm system disabled, and no clues to assist the police.

While the other nightclub robberies were in progress, the thieves found a favorite target in 50-year-old Henry Jeffcoat, proprietor of the Goldrush Showbar, which boasted "the prettiest naked women in the South." Jeffcoat employed off-duty policemen and former U.S. Army Rangers as bouncers in his club, and while they kept a lid on trouble during business hours, they were useless to him when the bar was closed. In September 1991, burglars knocked out the Goldrush Showbar's alarm system and stole $82,000 from the safe. A year later, two masked gunmen waylaid Jeffcoat at home, as he returned from work late at night, and marched him into his house, looting a wall safe of $62,000. On January 10, 1993, the Goldrush was burglarized again, and Jeffcoat decided enough was enough. "If they try something again," he told an employee, "I'll have a surprise waiting for them."

One month later to the day, on February 10, the Clayton County Sheriff's Department received a 911 emergency call at 12:06 a.m., reporting gunfire at Jeffcoat's home in suburban Morrow, Georgia. Deputies responding to the call found Jeffcoat dead on the floor of his garage. He had been shot nine times in the back; six other slugs had missed and drilled the wall of the garage. Footprints discovered in some nearby shrubbery revealed where the assassins had been waiting for their prey when he came home.

Police assumed that Jeffcoat's murder was connected with the string of thefts he had endured, remarking that the burglaries appeared to be the work of thieves with inside knowledge of the Goldrush operation. They ran checks on various employees, grilling several, but they were still short of suspects on March 1, when they received a call from Tami Hurst, proprietor of Gold's Athletic Club in Fayetteville. Hurst fingered the killer thieves as a group of her regular customers, off-duty cops whom she had regarded as "pillars of the community" until she learned they were responsible for Jeffcoat's murder. "They had a real good thing going until this shooting," she told authorities. "Way I heard it, they only wanted to rob him, but things got out of hand." Two officers specifically involved in Jeffcoat's death, Hurst said, were Riverdale patrolmen Mark McKenna and James C. Batsel IV.

Lieutenant Doug Jewett didn't want to believe the report, but he was obliged to check it out. Goldrush employee records confirmed several cops on the payroll, and one ex-employee, 34-year-old Christopher Grantham, was on probation from a 1990 charge of possessing explosives. Detectives learned that Grantham often worked out at Gold's, where he was friendly with 27-year-old Mark McKenna and 30-year-old James Batsel. According to the Riverdale P.D., McKenna was off on emergency leave, tending a sick parent in Ohio, but neighbors reported him at home, wearing a large bandage taped to his face.

On March 2, detectives surprised McKenna at home, arresting him and searching the house, coming up with a police report that had a diagram of Henry Jeffcoat's house drawn on the back. Questioned about the bandage on his face, McKenna first claimed he had hurt himself while doing chores at home, but he soon recanted, admitting that he had been shot in the face by Henry Jeffcoat, moments before the nightclub owner was killed by James Batsel. Both killer cops agreed to spill their guts and name accomplices, if they were guaranteed exemption from the death penalty. With visible reluctance, detectives and prosecutors accepted the deal, determined to identify and jail the other members of the holdup gang. By March 5, a task force was up and running, including detectives from Atlanta and Riverdale, along with other law enforcement agencies in Fulton and Clayton Counties. Chris Grantham was nabbed in Alabama, his Pontiac seized as the getaway car in Jeffcoat's murder, and ten more arrests were logged by week's end, including eight more policemen. Chief Eldrin Bell, of the Atlanta

P.D., told the press, "I'm going to be just as venomous as a snake in handling this. If they are dirty, they can expect no mercy."

Mark McKenna was the first suspect to cut a deal with prosecutors, describing his introduction to the burglary ring. A Riverdale lawman since November 1989, McKenna had possessed a spotless record prior to his arrest, described in one evaluation as "a capable, quiet officer, often showing wisdom beyond his years." In 1990, he had been recalled to active duty as a military policeman with the U.S. Army, during Operation Desert Storm, and while he returned home with decorations for exemplary service, he also found his bank account depleted by the severe reduction in pay. Moonlighting at strip clubs failed to take up the financial slack, but McKenna noticed some of his colleagues dressing well, driving flashy new cars. James Batsel finally clued him in on their secret. "We rob drug dealers," he told McKenna. "We rip off the bad guys." It was a foolproof team effort, Batsel explained, involving officers from several departments. They planned their heists in restaurants and spent their free time pumping iron at Gold's, rock climbing, and loitering at strip clubs where a number of their gang moonlighted as bouncers, where they were casing the bars as potential targets.

Soon after joining the gang, McKenna learned that he had been recruited with a lie. The targets were not criminals at all, but rather local businesses. By that time, said McKenna, he was in too deep to change his mind — and besides, the money was great. "It wasn't unusual to make $50,000 to $80,000" in one night, he told investigators, a decent wage even when the take was split four or five ways. Of course, the midnight missions sometimes went awry. Once, McKenna said, they had wound up with a bag of hypodermic syringes instead of cash; another time, one of the cops had slipped and fallen as he scaled a store's wall, using grappling hooks. On yet another run, the raiders had accidentally broadcast their movements on a radio frequency used by traffic police, but no one had caught on. Around December 1992, McKenna felt the urge to quit stealing, but he never got around to it. "It was always one more job," he explained. "Another easy payday."

One such — though not so easy in the end — had been the bungled holdup of Henry Jeffcoat on February 10. According to McKenna, Fulton County sheriff's deputy William Roget Moclaire had trailed Jeffcoat home from the Goldrush, while McKenna, Jim Batsel and Chris Grantham waited at the nightclub owner's house. Moclaire had beeped them on the radio, to warn them of their quarry's approach, and Grantham waited in the getaway car while McKenna and Batsel closed in with drawn guns. Both were in uniform at the time, and Batsel was actually on duty when the hit went down. They only meant to rob Jeffcoat, as they had done before, but he surprised them with his gun, shooting McKenna in the face. Batsel had emptied his pistol in retaliation, then carried his wounded partner back to the getaway car. McKenna had been nursing his wound and trying to think of a logical explanation when detectives came knocking and his world fell apart.

McKenna's statement, followed by admissions from Batsel, secured charges against several of their fellow officers. Batsel, McKenna and Moclaire were indicted for Jeffcoat's murder, along with Chris Grantham, but other charges took precedence. On June 3, 1993, Moclaire, Atlanta patrolman Brett Morrill and strip club bouncer Troy Endres were tried on multiple charges, including burglaries of two nightclubs and the $30,000 armed robbery of a Home Depot store in Atlanta. Mark McKenna and James Batsel testified for the state, and while defense attorneys branded them as killers lying on the witness stand to save themselves, the jury disagreed. Morrill and Moclaire were convicted of burglary and armed robbery, sentenced to 25 years each, while Endres drew a ten-year sentence for burglary. Additional charges were waiting in Clayton County, for crimes which included the additional robberies and the Jeffcoat murder, with Moclaire and Grantham still facing a possible date with the electric chair.

McKenna, spared the threat of execution, still seemed a bit confused about how everything had gone awry. "We were just a bunch of cops working out in a gym," he said. "Then it all got out of control." Lieutenant Hugh Brown, of the Riverdale P.D., was equally dismayed. "I've seen a lot of things go wrong with police," he told reporters, "but nothing quite this bad."

Even with the main event out of the way, Atlanta's "bad cop ring" remained in the headlines through much of the following year. On June 16, 1994, ex-cops Eric Hagan and Brett Morrill, were acquitted, along with former strip club manager James Kirkland, of trying to burglarize a suburban Wal-Mart store. Mark McKenna formally pled guilty to the Jeffcoat murder on May 4, 1995, and was sentenced to life imprisonment on July 13. One week before that sentence was pronounced, on July 6, James Batsel pled guilty in the same case and was sentenced to life, with an understanding that the prosecution would not oppose any parole bid after seven years. The final wrap-up came on July 27, 1995, when multiple cases were settled: 36-year-old Donald Curtis White, once a trainer of drug-sniffing police dogs, was sentenced to five years in prison on a guilty plea to one count of armed robbery; Fulton County's D.A. dismissed burglary charges against Christopher Grantham, since he was already serving life for murder; and Mark McKenna accepted a ten-year sentence on a guilty plea to armed robbery, that term to run concurrently with his life sentence for murder.

# Miller, James B.

James Miller was a study in contradictions. Courteous to a fault, a regular churchgoer and sometime leader of prayer meetings, he was known as "Deacon Jim" to those who saw his pious, smiling side. Unfortunately, there was also "Killin' Jim," a trigger-happy backshooter who boasted of 40 or 50 homicides, at least some of them carried out while Miller was a Texas peace officer.

A native of Van Burne, Arkansas, born in October 1861, Miller lived with his brother-in-law as a youth, then killed him with a shotgun when Miller was 22 years old. Convicted of murder and sentenced to life imprisonment, Jim saw the verdict reversed on appeal and was never retried. By 1891, he was settled in Pecos, Texas, serving as a deputy to Sheriff Bud Frazer. He married a local girl and went into the cattle business on the side, rustling cattle to build up a herd. Sheriff Frazer investigated his deputy, and while he found no evidence of any crime, suspicions lingered, souring their relationship. When Frazer next left town on business, Miller left the town wide-open to criminal elements, spreading the word that he meant to kill Frazer when the sheriff returned.

**James B. Miller**
(Seated at the table
with the white hat on.)
*Courtesy of
Western History Collections,
University of Oklahoma.*

The story found its way to Frazer, and he returned to Pecos with Texas Ranger John Hughes, clapping Miller in jail on a charge of conspiracy to commit murder. Tried and acquitted in El Paso, Miller returned to Pecos and bought a hotel in 1894, spreading the word that he meant to mend his ways. One who doubted him was Sheriff Frazer, who confronted Miller with a drawn gun on April 12. Iron plates sewed into the lining of his frock coat saved Miller's life, though he was wounded twice, in the arm and abdomen.

The shooting cost Frazer his job, and the ex-sheriff moved to New Mexico, leaving Miller to boast of his "victory," once again threatening to kill Frazer if he ever came back. Six months later, when Frazer returned to Pecos on business, they met on the street and guns blazed once again. Wounded twice more, Miller pressed charges of attempted murder, but Frazer was acquitted at his second trial, on a plea of self-defense.

The feud came to a head on September 13, 1896, when Miller tracked Frazer to a Toyah, Texas, saloon and killed him from ambush with a sawed-off shotgun. Tried twice for murder at Eastland, "Deacon Jim" was acquitted the second time after ingratiating himself with the townsfolk, leading prayer meetings and spending much time in the local church.

Soon after the turn of the century, Miller took a fling at real estate speculation, with partner Frank Fore. Unfortunately for "Killin' Jim," Fore was an honest man who saw through Miller's fraudulent schemes and threatened to inform the grand jury. To silence Fore, Miller shot and killed him in a hotel men's room, afterward securing acquittal on another plea of self-defense.

Several more killings followed, and Miller is frequently named as a suspect in the ambush murder of lawman Pat Garrett near Las Cruces, New Mexico, in February 1908. (Garrett was shot twice in the back, while urinating on the roadside, shortly after quarreling with Miller over the price of some grazing land.) A year later, in early 1909, Miller accepted a $2,000 contract to murder Angus Bobbitt, of Ada, Oklahoma, performing the deed with his trusty shotgun as Bobbitt rode past in a buggy. The killing capped off a long feud, and Miller's employers were soon in custody, sharing the triggerman's name with police. Arrested in Fort Worth and returned to Oklahoma for trial, Miller showed no surprise when a mob of 40 vigilantes came for him and his confederates on April 19. They were dragged to a barn, next door to the jail, and hanged one by one, with Miller the last to go. It is reported that he smiled, standing with the noose around his neck, and told his executioners to "Let 'er rip!"

# Moclaire, William:
# See McKenna, Mark

# Morris, Carl W., Jr.

A five-year veteran of the Baltimore Police Department, 32-year-old Carl Morris was supervising seven children — four of his own, and three of his sister's — when disaster struck on Sunday, January 20, 1991. An ambulance was summoned to his home in Columbia, Maryland, where emergency medical technicians found Morris's 19-month-old son Christopher sprawled on the living room floor, barely breathing. Morris explained that the boy had fallen downstairs, a carpet-cleaning machine tumbling after him in what could only be described as a freak accident.

Christopher was rushed to St. Agnes Hospital, then transferred to Johns Hopkins, where he died in surgery on Sunday night. Physicians at Johns Hopkins were openly dubious of the father's story, and the Howard County medical examiner agreed, describing Christopher's death as a homicide caused by blunt object trauma to the child's head and abdomen. Christopher's head, back, hips, buttocks, and genitals had suffered major bruises. Already suspended from work without pay since December 1990, for causes never specified, Morris was arrested five days after his son's death, and charged with first-degree murder and child abuse.

According to Patrolman Morris, it was all a horrible misunderstanding. Seven rowdy children had been "ripping and roaring through the house" all weekend, he alleged, when Christopher suffered his fatal mishap. Public defender Louis Willemin promised to call at least two of the surviving children at Morris's trial, to verify that "nobody was hurt, nobody was harmed, everything was okay," but *something* had clearly gone tragically wrong. Prosecutor Kate O'Donnell countered with the news that she would call Christopher's mother and Morris's brother — "two people who were once very close" to Carl Morris — as witnesses for the state. Christopher's death was "more than tragic," O'Donnell told the press. "It was criminal. It was not an accident."

Morris's trial opened on Thursday, April 2, 1992, Willemin telling the jury that his client was innocent, a scapegoat jailed "because everybody jumped to conclusions." Prosecutor

O'Donnell, for her part, promised witnesses who "will describe to you how Carl Morris acted after his baby was dead. And they will tell you it was not the way someone acts when their baby has just died in a horrible accident." Ambulance attendant Joanne Rund was one of those called to testify, describing how she urged Morris to hold his son's hand and talk to the boy, despite his visible reluctance. "He just seemed so distant," she said. Howard County's medical examiner testified that Christopher had died from blunt force "equal to a 50-mile-an-hour head-on collision." As for the weapon used, it could have been "a fist, a foot, a baseball bat."

Summing up, attorney Willemin urged jurors not to "decide this case based solely on medical evidence." Alternate theories were proposed, including a bizarre suggestion that Christopher may have died at the hands of another child. "There were six other children in the house that day," Willemin reminded the panel. "Could one of those children have stepped onto the child's stomach? Could one of them have poked the child with a board? We don't know."

Kate O'Donnell, for her part, had no doubt about the killer's identity. Time and time again, she told jurors that Christopher's death was "no accident," denouncing Morris's version of events as "an elaborate, almost ingenious coverup." In her view, "none of the scenarios suggested by the defendant or counsel in any way caused the injuries in this case. Don't let the defendant manipulate you. Don't let him get away with murder."

Jurors deliberated for ten hours on Friday, April 10, before convicting Morris of manslaughter, assault and battery, and child abuse. Although acquitted on the more serious murder charge, he still faced 23 years in prison when he stood for sentencing a month later. Prosecutor O'Donnell described the verdict as "good enough," although "obviously we were hoping for a murder conviction." Christopher's mother, Angellette Friend, was inclined to agree. "Just to know he's going to be in jail is good enough for me," she said. "God had his way today."

# Mortensen, Ronald

By all accounts, 21-year-old Daniel Mendoza was enjoying himself in the early hours of Saturday, December 28, 1996. Lounging on the front steps of his apartment complex, not far from the stylish Fashion Show Mall in Las Vegas, Nevada, Mendoza was sipping beer and killing time with friends, his 17-year-old fiancée at his side. They planned to be married in August, as soon as the girl turned 18, and Mendoza seemed to enjoy the prospect of settling down.

Unfortunately, he would never get the chance.

At 1:00 a.m. that Saturday, a dark-blue pickup truck pulled up to the curb, its passenger rolling down the window and shouting, "Come here!" He seemed to be addressing Mendoza, who twice replied, "What?" A third command to "come here" was ignored, whereupon the stranger stuck a pistol out the window, squeezing off six shots in rapid fire. One bullet struck Mendoza in the chest and pierced his heart, causing near-instant death.

Police initially described the murder as a gang-related drive-by shooting, but Mendoza's friends denied the charge. Daniel had had some trouble in the past, they agreed, but he was well on the road to turning his life around. And besides, they told authorities, the shooter was a "white boy." There had been no provocation for the shooting, they insisted, and they did not recognize the triggerman.

Thirty six hours elapsed before detectives caught their break in the case, with a confession from 24-year-old Christopher Brady. A three-year veteran of Metro P.D. and the son of a retired homicide detective, Brady told investigators that the fatal shot had been fired from his pickup. He was driving at the time, said Brady, and he was taken by surprise when his passenger — rookie patrolman Ron Mortensen — had started firing through the window. Even so, Brady claimed, he thought the shots had gone harmlessly skyward. He and Mortensen had been out on the town, celebrating Ron's 31st birthday on Friday, and Brady assumed that his friend was just letting off steam. Saturday's news broadcast had told him otherwise, and Brady had consulted with his family before coming forward.

Sheriff Jerry Keller, in charge of Metro P.D., was stunned by the news. He ordered Mortensen's arrest, and the six-month rookie was arrested at 10:00 p.m. on Sunday, when he reported for the graveyard shift. Eyewitnesses reportedly had trouble picking Mortensen out of a photo lineup, but Chris Brady's story was evidence enough for the moment, and Mortensen was held without bond on a preliminary murder charge, kept in isolation for his own protection, at the Clark County jail.

Looking back, the Metro brass regretted ever hiring Ron Mortensen in the first place. One of 147 new officers recruited without the usual background checks, to compensate for rapid population growth in Las Vegas, Mortensen had graduated from the police academy in September 1995. A note in Ron's file had discouraged hiring him, based upon combative behavior displayed while he was working as a department store security guard, but the force had taken him anyway, more interested in quantity than quality.

Mortensen was arraigned on Thursday, January 9th, while NAACP spokesmen called for prosecution of the murder as a hate crime, urging charges against Brady as an accomplice. Two days later, ballistics tests confirmed Mortensen's service pistol as the murder weapon. Bond was set at $500,000 on January 15, after prosecutors announced they would not seek the death penalty, and Mortensen was formally indicted two days later, on a single charge of first-degree murder with use of a deadly weapon.

Chris Brady had been on administrative leave, with pay, since he identified Mortensen as the shooter, but publicity got the better of him, and he resigned from the force on January 24. Mortensen did likewise on February 13, the announcement coupled with complaints from defense attorney Frank Cremen, noting that Brady's pickup had been repainted and fitted with new seats before Cremen was allowed to examine it. No problem, Metro detectives replied; fingerprints and other evidence had been collected from the truck in accordance with "standard procedure," before it was returned to Brady.

By that time, Cremen had already focused on Brady as an alternate suspect in the case, his argument bolstered by other blots on the ex-patrolman's record. In July 1995, for instance, Brady had been riding a bicycle downtown, when he noticed civilian motorist Louis Nogali looking at him and challenged, "Do you have a problem?" Nogali said nothing, but Brady threw his bike in front of Nogali's car at the next traffic light, then ordered him out of the car at gunpoint and slapped the cuffs on. Nogali spent 12 hours in jail before he was released without charges, immediately filing suit against Brady and Metro. The department settled that case out of court, for one dollar less than ten grand, but it was not the only problem marring Brady's record. Shortly after his resignation, in fact, a 26-year-old woman had come forward, alleging that Brady had sexually assaulted her en route to the jail, following her arrest on an outstanding warrant. Ron Mortensen, she claimed, was also in the car and witnessed the attack. When Brady finished with her, the woman said, she asked him why he had assaulted her. Brady's alleged reply: "I am evil."

It wasn't much, perhaps, but it was enough for Frank Cremen to build an alternate theory of Mendoza's slaying, with Brady as the triggerman. On February 6, his client pled not guilty to the murder, Cremen telling reporters that the D.A.'s case was "hanging on by the thread of a hair of Mr. Brady."

Mortensen's murder trial opened on April 28, 1997, beginning with two days of jury selection. In addition to ballistics evidence and Brady's testimony, the state now had five witnesses from the shooting scene, all agreed that Mortensen was the gunman. Come May 9, Mortensen took the stand in his own defense, insisting that Chris Brady fired the burst of gunshots, using Mortensen's pistol. Afterward, Brady had allegedly explained the random outburst with familiar words: "I am evil."

The jury didn't buy it, convicting Mortensen of first-degree murder with use of a deadly weapon on May 14, 1997. The following day, after another three hours of deliberation on prospective penalties, the panel recommended life imprisonment without parole. Attorney Cremen sought a new trial, based on Chris Brady's alleged remarks to the woman who accused him of sexual assault, but the claim hit a snag on June 13, 1997, when Clark County D.A. Stewart Bell announced that Brady would not be prosecuted on that charge. According to Bell, the woman's several stories revealed certain inconsistencies, while a polygraph examination showed "a tendency toward deception," and she had admitted fabricating part of one statement to police. Whatever Brady may have done, Metro was satisfied just knowing he would never be a cop again. Ron Mortensen, meanwhile, would have to serve his time alone.

## Nevers, Larry: See Budzyn, Walter

## O.K. Corral: See Earp, Wyatt

## Outlaw, Bass

A Georgia native, Bass Outlaw fled his home state sometime prior to 1885, after killing a man in suspicious circumstances. He wound up in Alpine, Texas, where he joined the Texas Rangers, rising to the rank of corporal in 1890 and sergeant in 1892. He was, by all accounts, a conscientious lawman when sober, but whiskey stripped him of all restraint, transforming him, as one biographer has said, into "a homicidal maniac." The problem was exacerbated by his runty stature and a deep-seated inferiority complex that continually drove Outlaw to demonstrate his manhood in a series of vicious fights.

Outlaw's superiors recognized the problem, but they kept him on for years in spite of everything, since Ranger positions were difficult to fill. Ranger Alonzo Oden once described Outlaw as a friend who could "laugh louder, ride longer, and cuss harder than the rest of us; but he could be more sympathetic, more tender, more patient than all of us when necessary." On the down side, though, "Bass had one weakness which proved stronger than all his virtues. He couldn't leave liquor alone. None of us could handle him, none of us could reason with him. We just stayed nearby until he sobered up." Unfortunately, by the time that happened, there was often someone dead.

In 1893, the drinking finally became too much, and Outlaw was dismissed by Captain Frank Jones. He tried hunting buried treasure for a while, but had no luck, and soon went to work as a deputy for U.S. Marshal Richard Ware. On April 5, 1894, Outlaw traveled with Ware to El Paso on official business, but a bottle got the better of him, and he wandered into Tillie Howard's brothel. There, he met lawman **John Selman**, and they talked briefly, Outlaw still drinking, before he lurched into the alley out back. Moments later, a gunshot rang out from the rear of the house.

Anticipating trouble, Madam Tillie grabbed her trusty police whistle and sounded the alarm for help while Selman stepped out back to see what was happening. Texas Ranger Joe McKidrict came running in response to the noise, jumping a fence to confront Outlaw in the alley.

"Bass, why did you shoot?" he demanded.

Outlaw turned on him, snarling, "Do you want some, too?" and shot McKidrict twice in the head.

John Selman drew his gun at that, and more shots were exchanged. Selman suffered two leg wounds, while Outlaw took a bullet in the chest and staggered out to the main street, there surrendering to Ranger Frank McMahon. He was carried to a nearby saloon, where he died four hours later, crying out, "Oh God, help! Where are my friends?"

They were nowhere to be found, and while Selman may have been surprised by his own indictment on murder charges, he had nothing to fear at the trial. Judge C.N. Butler directed a verdict of acquittal, in October 1894, and the jury was pleased to comply.

# Pardo, Manuel Jr.

Manny Pardo was 21 years old when he joined the Florida Highway Patrol in 1978, but his first stint in law enforcement was short-lived. Accused of falsifying more than 100 traffic warnings and correction notices, he was allowed to resign a year after he joined the force, in lieu of being fired. It seemed a small concession at the time, but it was all he needed: two months later, Pardo was hired by the Sweetwater Police Department to patrol a Miami suburb. Still, his problems continued, and in 1981 Pardo was one of four officers charged in a series of brutality cases filed by the state attorney general's office. Those charges were later dismissed, but Pardo was fired on January 21, 1985, after he flew to the Bahamas to testify in defense of another ex-cop, held for trial on drug-running charges.

Still, the worst was yet to come. On May 7, 1986, Pardo and a 25-year-old punk named Roland Garcia were arrested on murder charges, accused in the execution-style slayings of drug dealer Ramon Alvero Cruz and his girlfriend, Daisy Ricard, who were shot and killed on April 23. Weeks later, on June 11, Metro Dade officials announced that Pardo and Garcia were linked to a total of nine murders — of six men and three women — dating back to January 1986. Detective Ted MacArthur told the press, "They were drug ripoffs, and quantities of cocaine were taken from the scene." The killing spree had ended with Ramon Alvero Cruz, alleged to be Pardo's underworld employer since he was fired by Sweetwater P.D. As evidence against the killer cop, prosecutors cited Pardo's diary, which included written entries about the murders, along with news clippings and photographs of several bloody corpses. Nazi memorabilia recovered from Pardo's home, together with the prisoner's own statements, revealed that he was also an ardent admirer of Adolf Hitler, who believed that blacks and Jews were inferior species deserving of extermination.

Legal maneuvering delayed Pardo's trial for two years, but prosecutor David Waksman stood by the state's original theory of an ex-cop gone bad, addicted to cocaine and easy money, killing coke dealers to rip off their stashes, eliminating any pesky witnesses who crossed his path. Pardo denied it, painting himself as a one-man vigilante squad, committed to eliminating "parasites" and "leeches" such as drug dealers from law-abiding society. His court-appointed counsel, lawyer Ronald Guralnick, was committed to a different tack, presenting an insanity defense. "The man is crazy," he told reporters. "All you have to do is listen to him to know he's totally out of his mind."

And, indeed, Pardo seemed intent on proving that point when he took the witness stand in his own defense, on April 13, 1988. Testifying against Guralnick's advice, Manny didn't bother to deny the killings; rather, he regretted that the final body count had been so low. "Instead of nine," he told the court, "I wish I could have been up here for 99." Furthermore, he declared, "I enjoyed what I was doing. I enjoyed shooting them. They're parasites and they're leeches, and they have no right to be alive. Somebody had to kill these people." He shot his victims repeatedly after death, Manny said, to further "punish" them for their crimes, and he had taken Polaroid snapshots of the corpses, afterward burning some in an alabaster ashtray. "I sent their souls to the eternal fires of damnation of hell," he testified, "for the misery they caused."

Pardo staunchly denied the state's claim that he, himself, was a mercenary drug dealer. The very idea was "ludicrous" and "ridiculous," he said. Prosecutor Waksman asked about the $50,000 Pardo had earned from selling two kilos of stolen cocaine, the sum recorded in his diary, but Manny insisted that he had kept only $2,000 for himself — the bare minimum required for purchasing guns and ammunition. After Pardo remarked that bullets cost him ten cents each, Waksman asked him whether it had cost him only $1.30 to kill two victims who were shot a total of 13 times. Pardo grinned as he replied, "That's a pretty good investment, isn't it?"

With Pardo's sanity at issue, both sides called psychologists to testify about his mental state. Syvil Marquit, speaking out for the defense, reported that Pardo was insane and had been at the time of the nine murders. Manny was competent for trial, Marquit said, and understood the physical consequence of his actions, "but he doesn't know right from wrong." Court-appointed psychologist Leonard

Haber, on the other hand, testified for the state that Pardo was "sane, but evil." Manny, for his part, agreed with the state, at least in regard to his sanity. As for psychologists, he told the court, "They're whores. Pay them enough money and they'll say anything."

Pardo's extreme racial views may have hurt him as much as the physical evidence of his guilt, when he appeared before a jury that included five blacks and at least two Jews. Metro Dade detectives listed the Nazi paraphernalia found in his home and described the swastika tattoo worn by one of his dogs, a big Doberman pinscher. Manny helped out with testimony that Adolf Hitler was a "great man," whose activities had inspired Pardo to read more than 500 books on Nazism. The panel deliberated for six hours on April 15, before convicting Pardo of nine murders and nine other felony counts, including robbery and use of a firearm in commission of a crime.

Court reconvened five days later, to consider Pardo's sentence. Attorney Guralnick and Manny's parents pleaded for leniency, citing his deranged mental state, while Prosecutor Waksman argued the reverse. "He was weird, weird, weird," Waksman said, "but he was not insane." At that, Pardo remained the star performer in his own private drama. "I am a soldier," he told the court. "I accomplished my mission, and I humbly ask you to give me the glory of ending my life and not to send me to spend the rest of my days in state prison. I'm begging you to allow me to have a glorious end." The jury complied, and Judge Phillip Knight accepted their recommendation, handing down one death sentence for each of Pardo's murders, plus a term of 15 years in prison on the noncapital charges.

His commitment to die notwithstanding, Pardo made no objection when his conviction and death sentence was appealed to the Florida Supreme Court. There, on March 6, 1990, public defender Calianne Lantz told the assembled justices that Pardo was insane when he committed his nine murders. Assistant Attorney General Ralph Barreira disagreed, describing Manny as a brute who simply liked to kill. The court agreed with Barreira, affirming Pardo's conviction and the "special circumstances" which allowed his execution under Florida state law. A year later, on May 13, 1991, the U.S. Supreme Court effectively upheld that decision, denying Pardo's plea for a writ of certiorari.

Pardo, meanwhile, had managed to attract at least a handful of admirers while his case was winding through the courts. One such, a self-described friend of the convicted killer, voiced his support in a letter to *The Orlando Sentinel Tribune*, published on April 22, 1990. It read in part:

> *Manny was never accused of corruption. He was let go for his overzealousness in pursuit of criminals — no matter who they knew or whose relative they were. And lest anyone get the idea that he just cruised around gunning people down, let me point out each of his victims was a thoroughly investigated, tried, convicted, and executed (by him) drug dealer whom Pardo had failed to get off the streets via the normal criminal justice system. Manny Pardo doesn't deserve condemnation, he deserves a commendation.*

In fact, as even cursory research would have shown, Manny had been fired in Sweetwater for "showing a lack of good judgment and a habit of lying" — specifically in defense of an accused drug dealer — but the details hardly mattered. He was awaiting execution at Starke, the state's maximum-security prison... but he was not entirely out of action, yet.

In March 1996, *The Miami Herald* revealed that Pardo, now christened the "Death Row Romeo," had been placing personal ads in tabloid newspapers, attracting lonely female pen pals who had mailed him thousands of dollars in return for hollow promises of love. The *Herald* reported that Manny had once accumulated some $3,530 in his prison canteen account, most of it sent to him by women, but prison officials declared that he had broken no rules, "although he may have broken several hearts." The lure was an ad that painted Manny in a near-heroic light. It read:

```
FLA. 116-156 CORRECTIONAL INSTITUTE INMATE.
Ex-cop Vietnam vet. Took law into own
hands and ended up on Death Row. He
needs letters from sensitive-under-
standing female, for real-honest rela-
tionship.
```

One who responded was Barbara Ford, a 46-year-old cleaning woman from Findlay, Ohio. Three weeks after she answered Pardo's ad, Ford received a letter from Manny, along with several news clips describing his police career in a favorable light. The letter told her, "I want one special lady in my life. I don't play emotional games cause I hate emotional games. I also hate liars and users." From that beginning, Pardo's correspondence — always addressed to "the love of my life" — swiftly degenerated into pathetic whining, invariably closing with mention of his need for "a few bucks a week to buy personal items like stamps, paper, shampoo, etc." One note described a tearful prison visit from his daughter, quoting her as saying, "Daddy, when I'm older and able to work, I will buy you a radio so you can listen to music and I will send you money from my weekly check so you can buy coffee, shampoo and your other needs."

In the meantime, Barbara Ford was happy to take up the slack, sending Pardo $430 from her yearly income of $7,500. Another "love of his life," mailing cash at the same time, was 54-year-old Betty Ihem, from Oklahoma, who began corresponding with Pardo ten months before he hooked Barbara Ford. By the time Ford entered the picture, Pardo and Ihem were addressing each other as husband and wife, Betty collecting 275 letters from her incarcerated lover, sending him $1,200 over time from the salary she earned as a part-time Wal-Mart employee.

The correspondence was finally too much for Pardo, and he tripped himself up with a clumsy mistake. On October 12, 1995, Betty Ihem received a letter meant for Barbara Ford. It read:

> *My Dearest Barb,*
> *Hi. I hope this letter finds you in the best of health.*
> *You are all I want and need. I am not a dream and if my*
> *love interests you, well then it's yours.*
> *I love you,*
>
> *Manny*

Predictably furious, Ihem sent the letter on to Barbara Ford, with her own explanatory note written on the back. Eight days later, Ford wrote to Pardo, addressing him as "Thief of Hearts" and enclosing photocopies of the money orders she had previously sent him.

> *You received the money under false pretenses [she wrote] which makes you a fake and not the "Man of Honor" which you professed to be. Needless to say, you are a liar and a hypocrite — the very things you said you hated in people. If you choose not to return the money, I will be your very worst nightmare and expose you for the hypocrite you truly are. I'm not a very patient person so I hope you respond to my request immediately. The choice is yours.*

Pardo replied on November 2, 1995, with all the arrogance of a condemned prisoner who knows he is effectively untouchable.

> *Barb,*
> *I hope you are in good health. I am reading your letter and am amazed you think your threats would affect me at all! You and your troubled life will also be exposed. In addition, my attorney will have a field day with you and*

*that will be your nightmare lawsuit for slander, etc. You are
a bitter and vindictive woman.*

*God bless,*

*Manny*

Ford took her case to Florida governor Lawton Chiles on November 18, asking, "What kind of people are you in Florida? You
have a guy on Death Row, and he still hurts people." Her reply
came from Judy Belcher at the Florida Department of Corrections,
on November 29, advising Ford that no law forbade prisoners from
placing personal ads or soliciting gifts from gullible pen pals. "On
the contrary," Belcher wrote, "Florida Statutes have ruled it illegal
to deny inmates that privilege because doing so would deny inmates
access to the outside world. Many inmates, both male and female,
have accumulated considerable amounts of money this way. They
are convicts and some are experts at 'conning' honest people out of
their hard earned dollars. Often, when we advise a person that an
inmate is not being honest, the person will still choose to believe the
inmate."

With that grudging seal of approval, Manny Pardo was free to
pursue his career as a swindler while he lived in his cage. Only the
final, inevitable date with "Old Sparky" would finally curtail his
correspondence with gullible women, and no final date of execution
has been set at this writing. With others who have killed repeatedly
across the Sunshine State, he takes his ease with pen in hand and
plays the waiting game.

# Peyer, Craig Alan

Craig Peyer was, from all appearances, a model cop. In 13 years
with the California Highway Patrol, he had enjoyed a spotless record, more or less, his cheerful gift of gab elevating him to a position
as the CHP's semi-official public spokesman on topics related to
highway safety. By the time it was revealed that Peyer's supervisors had ignored a series of complaints about his treatment of

young women on the job, it was too late. The "model cop" was already in jail, on charges of murdering a 20-year-old college student. Minnesota-born in 1950, Peyer was transplanted at the age of one year, when his family moved to San Diego, California. He graduated high school there in 1968, and took a few community college courses before joining the U.S. Air Force. Trained as a mechanic, he spent two years in Thailand at the height of the Vietnam war, repairing combat helicopters. True or not, Craig liked to tell his friends in later life that he had gone behind enemy lines with the elite Green Berets, but no combat experience was listed on his personnel record. Discharged in 1972, four months after marrying the sister of an Air Force buddy, Peyer tested high on his CHP entry exam in May 1973 and started his four months of training that July.

Something changed about Craig when he hit the streets, though. Deborah Peyer would later recall that "His head swelled. He became Mister Macho. The badge was a way to flirt." At home, Peyer's temper was so unpredictable and rotten that Deborah filed for divorce in July 1978. Peyer talked her out of it, but the domestic abuse continued, and they finally split in 1979. Craig remarried in May 1983, this time to the sister of a CHP colleague, but the union was short-lived, and she had filed for divorce by autumn. Third-time lucky, Peyer began a love affair with a married neighbor, prompting her to divorce her husband eight months later and marry Craig in July 1985.

Married or single, however, Peyer was still using his badge as a ticket to "flirt," his technique increasingly bizarre as time went by. He worked the night shift on a lonely stretch of Interstate 15, where he made a habit of stopping lone female drivers, using his patrol car's loudspeaker to order them off the main freeway, into dark, deserted side roads. From time to time, he stopped long-haired men by mistake, but Peyer always disposed of them quickly, writing the ticket and letting them go. With women, it was a different story, Peyer often detaining them for an hour or more, his spiel including everything from auto mechanics to the perils of driving alone after dark. He liked to ask personal questions — was the lady married?

did she have a boyfriend? — sometimes interjecting compliments about her eyes, hair, figure. As often as not, the women were let go with warnings, or written "fix-it tickets" for some trivial malfunction of their cars. Complaints were filed, but the CHP brass shrugged them off: once, when an angry mother complained about Peyer's forcing her daughter off the freeway, Sergeant John McDonald explained the move as a simple "escort" to "an area safely away from the high-speed freeway traffic," afterward commending Peyer for his "excellent tactics." As far as the CHP was concerned, Peyer's handling of young women was no problem.

At 7 a.m. on December 28, 1986, San Diego Police received an urgent missing-person report from the parents of 20-year-old Cara Knott. It was not first call about Cara: in fact, various police departments in the San Diego area had been dodging the reports all night, leaving Cara's relatives to conduct a hasty search themselves. Now, however, they had found her car abandoned on a lonely stretch of dirt called Mercy Road, off I-15. Her purse was in the car, but there was no sign of its occupant... and there were blood smears on the driver's door.

Belatedly, police rolled out, and one of them soon found the missing co-ed, sprawled on jagged rocks beneath an old abandoned highway bridge, nearby. According to the autopsy results, the only mercy found on Mercy Road that night lay in the fact that Cara had been strangled with a ligature, before her body was dropped 65 feet to the rocks below. The fall had cracked her skull and fractured her pelvis, snapping her collar bone and ten ribs, lacerating her liver and both lungs. At that, forensics experts soon determined that some of the blood drops on her boots did not belong to Cara: they were Type A, compared to the dead woman's Type O.

Cara Knott had last been seen alive on Saturday night, December 27, tending her sick boyfriend, Wayne Bautista, at his home. She had telephoned her parents before leaving Bautista's place, at 8:30 p.m., and told them she was going home. When she had not arrived two hours later, parents and siblings hit the road to search for her, Bautista joining in despite a 104° fever. In the process, they had telephoned no less than four police departments in the area, their calls dismissed each time with the advice that a 20-year-old woman "missing" overnight was not really missing at all. The cops had only changed their tune when Cara's Volkswagen was found — and by then, it was much too late.

The best they could do now, was collect evidence at the crime scene, beginning with photographs of tire tracks and footprints on the highway bridge. Three half-filled cans of beer, still cold, were found beneath the bridge, and some of them bore fingerprints. Additionally, half a dozen tiny "foreign" fibers were retrieved from Cara's clothing, but they had no value in the absence of a suspect whose wardrobe and belongings could be searched for matching threads.

Cara's murder hit the news on Monday morning, and one local TV station asked the highway patrol for a few pithy quotes regarding the perils of modern California freeways. The brass chose Craig Peyer for the interview, and he spent two hours tooling around in his squad car with a camera crew, cautioning prospective viewers, "Don't get into anyone else's car, because you're at their mercy. You could be raped if you're a woman — if you're a man, robbed — all the way down to where you're killed. People are safe with law enforcement officers." And how, he was asked, could drivers on a lonely road be sure it was a real-life cop who pulled them over? "Make sure they are in a black-and-white and have a badge on," Peyer advised.

San Diego police were already involved in one manhunt that winter, seeking the faceless serial killer who had murdered at least 30 women in the past two years, dumping their violated bodies in remote locations such as Mercy Road. The other victims had been hookers, though, some of them junkies, and Cara Knott clearly did not fit the mold. At the same time, however, there was another prowler on the local highways, and the CHP knew all about him. He was one of their own, and the complaints had been piling up for months. They had simply been ignored.

As recently as December 11, Kathy Deir had been driving along I-15 when a highway patrolman pulled her over with flashing lights, his amplified voice commanding her to pull off the freeway and follow him into the stygian darkness along Mercy Road. Her headlights were out of alignment, he told her, before launching into a history lecture on Southern California's freeway system. Before the 90-minute incident was over, Kathy had left her own car and entered the cruiser, letting the officer take her to visit an abandoned highway overpass. He kept his hands to himself and released her unharmed, but the whole thing was *strange*. Cheryl Johnson had been stopped for speeding, then received a fix-it ticket for driving on bald tires, but later examination in daylight revealed that her tires were all fine. One female motorist received a ticket, even after the flirtatious cop had complimented her on her "beautiful eyes." Yet another was surprised when the patrolman climbed into her car, yanking up and down on the parking brake handle while he harangued her on the critical need for safe brakes. The very night before Cara Knott's murder, December 26, Shelly Sacks had been sidetracked onto Mercy Road for a lecture from Officer Friendly. His behavior had been odd enough that she memorized his badge number — 8611 — for future reference.

Homicide detectives, meanwhile, were frustrated in their search for a suspect. Wayne Bautista was reluctantly cleared, and police could never find the "weird" hitchhiker reported by half a dozen motorists along I-15 the night Cara died. Meanwhile, calls were trickling in from various women about their strange encounters with Patrolman Craig Peyer on Mercy Road, and while none of the investigators wanted to believe a cop had committed the latest atrocity, every lead had to be checked in its turn. The capper came when a sheriff's deputy reported seeing Peyer with scratches on his face, the night of December 27.

Officially suspended from the CHP with pay on January 5, Peyer was on pins and needles when detectives searched his squad car two days later, recovering a length of non-issue plastic rope from the trunk, where it had been concealed beneath Peyer's spare tire. A day later, under questioning by San Diego detectives, Peyer defended himself as "a damn good officer." They asked about "those young honeys" he had "escorted" to Mercy Road, and Peyer confessed he was "a bullshitter," without admitting any misdeeds. As for Kathy Deir's claim that he had detained her for 90 minutes, Peyer said, it was all wrong; they had been together for "45 minutes tops." Concerning scratches on his face, Peyer said that he had tripped and fallen against a chain-link fence in the CHP parking lot. He denied stopping or even seeing Cara Knott, "as God is my witness," but homicide investigators made no secret of their skepticism. "We're coming after you," Peyer was told.

On January 16, Peyer was arrested and booked for Cara Knott's murder, spending six days in solitary confinement, under suicide watch, before he was arraigned before Judge Herbert Exarhos. Bond was initially set at $300,000, then bumped to $1 million when Deputy D.A. Joe Van Orshoven came back with a claim of new evidence. Unable to pay the new tab, Peyer was still in custody on May 28, when he was dismissed from the highway patrol.

His trial opened on January 4, 1988, before Judge Richard Huffman, with attorney Robert Grimes for the defense. Despite some problems with establishing the time of death, the state claimed Cara had been killed between 8:30 and 9 p.m., noting for the record that Peyer had written no tickets on the fatal night between 7:45 and 10 o'clock. A local gas station attendant testified that she had seen Peyer on the night in question, and that he "looked like he had been in a fight. I noticed claw marks on his face." San Diego policewoman Jill Ogilvie described Peyer quizzing her for details on the Knott investigation, specifically concerning blood samples and skin beneath the victim's fingernails. A couple whose car had broken down near Mercy Road that night recalled a CHP cruiser passing by, and seven young women testified to their roadside encounters with Peyer, one of them stopped twice in the space of ten days. Cheryl Johnson recalled that Peyer had told her, "Somebody could get raped or murdered down here, and nobody would ever know." Her plaintive reply: "At least I'm with you."

Scientific evidence closed out the state's case. Tire tracks from the highway bridge were the same size as tires on Peyer's cruiser, but no one had bothered to check out the treads. The blood smear on Cara's VW came back inconclusive, but the speckles on her boots matched Peyer's type, genetic markers narrowing the donors down to 1.3% of California's white population — with Peyer included. Gold fibers found on Cara's sweatshirt matched Peyer's uniform, while blue threads from her hands were identical with those from a CHP shoulder patch. Purple fibers retrieved from Peyer's boots and gun belt, meanwhile, were consistent with samples from Cara Knott's sweatpants.

Robert Grimes countered with testimony from brother patrolmen that Peyer was a straight-arrow cop who played by the book. He also suggested that Cara had not gone directly home from Wayne Bautista's house, producing a witness who saw a young woman and a white VW parked on the shoulder of I-15, arguing with three men around 11:30 p.m. on December 27 — after Craig Peyer had gone off-duty for the night. According to the witness, she had seen the young woman kicking one of the men, who "appeared to be Hispanic." Karen Peyer was the last defense witness, describing her idyllic home life with Craig, recalling the night his gun belt had brushed against a purple baby blanket, presumably picking up threads in the process. Closing arguments began on February 11, Cara Knott's 22nd birthday, and jurors began deliberations four days later, reporting themselves hopelessly deadlocked on February 25.

Prosecutor Paul Pfingst was placed in charge of Peyer's retrial, but before the case went back to court, a media leak revealed that Craig Peyer had failed an inadmissible polygraph exam in 1986. The revelation, on April 27, 1987, touched off a firestorm of accusations and counter-charges, but the source of the leak was never identified, and Peyer's attorney soon withdrew his motion for a change of venue. With the trial date approaching, Pfingst won some early victories, obtaining court orders that barred any reference to the "weird" phantom hitchhiker, along with hearsay testimony from persons who heard Peyer explain the bloody scratches on his face. If Craig had a story to tell, the court ruled, he could tell it himself, under oath. Pfingst also reviewed thousands of CHP traffic stops, more than tripling the number of women (and long-haired men) who had been stopped by Peyer on Mercy Road. New witnesses Scott and Traci Koenig had seen a CHP car stop a white VW along I-15 on the night of the murder, both cars disappearing onto Mercy Road, but they had not come forward in the first trial, thinking it would be "a slam-dunk case for the prosecution." Yet another witness also saw the white VW being stopped; a short time later, driving home, he saw a CHP cruiser speeding along I-15 with its headlights turned off.

Testimony in Peyer's second trial finally began on May 17, 1988, the state's 120 witnesses included 24 men and women who were stopped on Mercy Road by the defendant. One of the long-haired males recalled that Peyer wore "a surprised blank stare" on discovering that he had stopped a man, while the female motorists recounted Peyer's rambling, sometimes suggestive conversations. The defense called a former county pathologist to dispute the estimated time of Cara's death, along with a new witness who described a white VW parked near the murder scene, with a woman in the passenger's seat and a bearded "scruffy-looking" man behind the wheel. Karen Peyer closed the show once again, on June 10, and once again the defendant did not testify, attorney Grimes later calling it a decision "that will haunt me for the rest of my life."

Jurors deliberated six days before convicting Peyer of first-degree murder on June 23. Six weeks later, on August 3, Judge Huffman imposed a sentence of 25 years to life. He also took time to chastise the California Highway Patrol for ignoring the prior complaints against Peyer. "They led inexorably to this tragedy," he said, "as surely as the sun came up this morning." Craig Peyer, eligible for parole in the year 2004, remains philosophical in prison, still denying his guilt. "God must want me in here for a reason," he explains.

# Phillips, William Raymond

The son of a corrupt New York City police detective who ruled his home with an iron hand, William Phillips was born in the Big Apple on May 6, 1930. He spent the first six years of his life with his maternal grandmother, since the family home was "too crowded," and later regretted moving back in with his parents. "Completely terrified" of his quick-fisted father, Phillips left home again as a teenager, after a raging fistfight with his father sparked by William coming home late from a date.

Phillips joined the U.S. Air Force in 1950, but refused flight training and wound up in the Korean theater of war as an aircraft machinist. Following the cease-fire, he was stationed in Arizona, where he met his future wife in 1954, at a dance in Nogales. Discharged at age 24, Phillips returned to New York and applied for a job with the police department, doubtless encouraged by the fact that his father had earned an average of $1,000 per month in bribes throughout his career. An aggressive trainee, Phillips made three felony arrests while still in training, and upon graduation from the police academy he was assigned to the 19th Precinct in Manhattan. In his fourth year on the job, he was promoted to detective, and the extra money *really* started rolling in.

Phillips had quickly learned the difference between what New York's Finest called "meat eaters" — that is, the officers who energetically pursued bribes — and "grass eaters" who were satisfied to pick up any graft that came their way by chance. As a certified meat eater, Phillips developed a reputation for "selling" arrests at the drop of a C-note, wearing stylish clothes and driving a flashy sports car. In his fifth year as a detective, however, he ran afoul of the police commissioner's Confidential Investigating Unit — a.k.a. the "Fag Squad." His offense was tipping off an ex-policeman, now proprietor of a New York gay bar, that undercover cops were scouting his joint with an eye toward entrapping the customers. Word of Phillips's "betrayal" got back to the Fag Squad, and three weeks later, in August 1965, Phillips was busted to patrolman in the Harlem ghetto.

It was a double slap in the face, since Phillips made no secret of his ingrained racism. In later conversations with biographer Leonard Shecter, Phillips would describe himself as being "involved in a lot of head-breaking up there" during the Harlem race riots of 1964. In fact, he boasted that he "broke heads like coconuts. Fired shots, too." As for routine patrol in Harlem, Phillips remarked, "The whole fucking Harlem stinks. Every hallway smells of piss, garbage, smelly fucking people. I hated the fucking place."

Bill Phillips was resourceful, though, proud of his brains and skill with his fists, boastful that he had never found the need to use a blackjack when beating prisoners. In Harlem, he shot and killed a burglar named Elvin McCoy, who slashed at Phillips with a knife, and while the shooting raised a predictable outcry from the black community, McCoy's record — including 25 felony arrests and three prior police shootings — ruled out any serious thought of disciplinary action in the case. Phillips was soon back in plain clothes, sporting the detective's coveted gold shield, and "eating meat" with the best of them.

On Christmas Eve 1968, around 7:30 p.m., a ruddy-faced stranger entered the lobby of an apartment house on East 57th Street, telling doorman Duke Peterson to buzz him up to Apartment 11F. The tenant of 11F — Jimmy Smith, alias Goldberg — was a notorious pimp who ran girls from the building and hosted orgies in his flat without complaint from the landlord, booking some bets on the side and paying off police accordingly. While the stranger was waiting to go upstairs, Charles Gonzales arrived, also bound for 11F, and they were quickly joined by Sharon Stango, an 18-year-old prostitute from Smith's stable. Upstairs, Gonzales and Stango had sex in one of the bedrooms, emerging after they were done to find Jimmy Smith in a heated argument with the ruddy-faced man. Smith's visitor demanded money, in the amount of $1,000, and when Smith professed inability to pay, the stranger drew a .38 revolver, blasting Smith in the head. Sharon Stango screamed before the gunman turned on her and killed her with two shots at point-blank range. Gonzales was dropped by the next shot, but his wound was not fatal, the gunman mistakenly leaving him for dead.

The killing of a pimp and prostitute was low-priority in New York City, and the case remained unsolved until October 1971, when homicide detective John Justy sat down to watch the latest televised hearings of the Knapp Commission, appointed by Mayor John Lindsay to investigate widespread police corruption in the city. The witness of the day was William Phillips, describing his undercover work for the commission dating back to June 1971, when he began wearing a wire on his rounds of graft collection in the city. When asked how many detectives at his present posting, in the Sixth Division, were known to take bribes, Phillips replied, "Everyone, to my knowledge." One officer had skimmed $80,000 in drug money from a seizure of $137,000, walking out of the station house with the cash in a brown paper bag.

That kind of testimony was calculated to infuriate "loyal" officers who regarded any exposure of brutality or corruption as "betrayal" of the police "brotherhood," but John Justy was more interested in the witness's face. It struck him as familiar, though he did not know Bill Phillips personally, and he got the answer to the riddle when he checked his files, extracting a three-year-old composite sketch of the Smith-Stango murders. In short order, survivor Charles Gonzales confirmed the I.D. On March 20, 1972, Phillips was indicted on two counts of murder and one count of attempted murder, released on $50,000 bond into federal custody, as a witness in pending police prosecutions. At a preliminary hearing on June 14, Gonzales identified Phillips as his assailant, while eight other witnesses fingered him as the man who had demanded cash from Smith and threatened the pimp's life on December 23, the day before the shooting.

Phillips, for his part, dismissed the whole case as a frame-up, in retaliation for his work with the Knapp Commission. Defense attorney F. Lee Bailey, still two decades away from the O.J. Simpson case, was quick to buy the "frame" scenario, describing the prosecution's case as a sham "malevolently assembled" by corrupt police and district attorneys. The "real killer," Bailey claimed, was another unnamed pimp, perhaps an Italian, who had quarreled with Smith over rights to one of Smith's expensive whores.

The trial opened on June 28, 1972, prosecutors contending that Phillips killed Smith in a dispute over tardy payoffs, afterward shooting Stango and Gonzales in an effort to eliminate pesky witnesses. Gonzales was the key prosecution witness, backed up by several hookers who described Phillips as a notorious shakedown artist. Phillips, for his part, was caught in a lie on the witness stand: under oath, he denied any contact with Jimmy Smith since the fall of 1965, but prior testimony in a 1972 bribery trial placed them together, with Smith booking bets from Phillips through late 1968, within a few weeks of the murder. Bailey tried in vain to shake the prosecution witnesses, presenting an alibi for Smith in the form of a family Christmas Eve party, but relatives recalled that he arrived around 10 p.m., some two hours after the shootings on East 57th Street.

At that, it was enough to hang the jury, and a mistrial was declared on August 9, when the panel reported itself hopelessly deadlocked. Two years would elapse before the second trial, and Bailey dropped out of the case in the meantime, leaving Phillips in the hands of attorney Henry Rothblatt. The familiar cast of witnesses were on hand when retrial began on October 2, 1974, and this time the jurors were more easily convinced, convicting Phillips of all counts on November 21. Two months later, on January 28, 1975, the rogue detective was sentenced to a prison term of 25 years to life.

# Ponvenir Massacre: See Fox, J.M.

# Price, Cecil Ray

Mississippi historian James Silver once described the Magnolia State as a "closed society," ruled by racist whites who kept the black underclass in line with a virtual reign of terror, assisted by such groups as the White Citizens' Council and the Ku Klux Klan. That was certainly true of Neshoba County, where two known Klansmen held office as sheriff from 1960 through 1971, dispensing their own brand of "justice" even while they were under investigation for multiple murder. Deputy Cecil Price never wore the sheriff's badge, but he clearly aspired to the job, once tossing his hat in the ring. By that time, though, too much was known about his crimes, and even white Neshoba County voters could not stomach Price's kind of "law and order."

In 1964, Mississippi was the target of a massive voter registration drive conducted by a national coalition of civil rights groups. One of the group's advance men was Michael Schwerner, a New Yorker who rented quarters in Meridian, Mississippi, working overtime to recruit local blacks for the effort. As a Jew and "outside agitator," Schwerner was a natural target for Mississippi's militant White Knights of the KKK, a group which counted Neshoba County Sheriff Lawrence Rainey and Deputy Cecil Price among its ardent members. "Imperial Wizard" Sam Bowers ordered Schwerner's death, and Neshoba County, with its history of Klan-dominated law enforcement, was chosen as the safest killing ground.

By June 1964, the Klan had Schwerner under constant surveillance. When he left Mississippi for a training seminar in Ohio, on June 14, Klansmen were ready to take their first steps toward his murder. On the night of June 16, they raided the Mt. Zion Methodist Church near Philadelphia, Mississippi, beating several parishioners and burning the church to the ground. On June 21, Schwerner was back in the state and anxious to visit the scene of the fire. He drove from Meridian to Neshoba County, accompanied by northern volunteer Andrew Goodman and James Chaney, a black Mississippi native. After meeting with members of the Mt. Zion Church, the trio were stopped by Cecil Price on a trumped-up "speeding" charge and held in Neshoba County's jail until nightfall, while a Klan lynch mob gathered nearby. Finally released after paying a fine, Schwerner and company were stopped a second time by Price, outside of town, and delivered to the waiting Klansmen for execution. Schwerner's burned-out car was found on June 23, in a swamp on the local Choctaw reservation, but state authorities treated the disappearance as a hoax or publicity stunt, arranged by "communists" to blacken Mississippi's "good name."

It was August 4 before the missing bodies were found, and "inside" sources disagree on whether talkative Klansmen were bribed or beaten into pointing out the graves, beneath an earthen dam. Four months later, FBI agents arrested 21 Klansmen. Alleged members of the murder party were named as Cecil Price, Jimmy Lee Townsend, Horace Barnett (who later confessed), James Jordan (who also confessed), Jimmy Arledge, Travis Barnette, Billy Wayne Posey, Alton Roberts, Jerry Sharpe, and Jimmy Snowden. Charged with having knowledge of the plot were Sheriff Rainey, Patrolman Otha Burkes, Meridian Klan leader Frank Herndon, Neshoba County Klan leader Edgar Ray Killen, Olen Burrage (owner of the burial site), Herman Tucker (a contractor who built the dam), Oliver Warner Jr. (owner of a store where the killers bought gloves), James Harris, and Bernard Akin. Klansmen charged with misprision of a felony included Earl Akin (Bernard's son) and Tommy Horne. In the wake of his arrest, Deputy Price bragged that it took him an hour to reach work, because "I had to spend so much time shaking hands."

At a December 10 preliminary hearing, U.S. Commissioner Esther Carter threw out Doyle Barnetts's confession and dismissed all charges against the 21 suspects. The FBI rearrested 16 of the Klansmen, along with Philadelphia Patrolman Richard Willis, on January 16, but U.S. District Judge Harold Cox dismissed federal felony counts on February 25, ruling that the 17 defendants could only be tried on a misdemeanor charge of conspiracy to deny the right to be free from summary punishment. In June 1965, the U.S. Department of Justice announced plans to proceed with the case, but Judge Cox ordered dismissal of the new charges on grounds that the indicting grand jury had excluded blacks and women. A new grand jury indicted 18 Klansmen on civil rights charges in February 1967, adding Sam Bowers and E.G. Barnett (former and future sheriff of Neshoba County) to the list. Cut from the original list of defendants were Townsend, Warner, Otha Burkes, and James Jordan — the latter having filed a guilty plea and turned state's evidence against his fellow Kluxers.

Undeterred by his impending trial, Price ran for sheriff in Neshoba County that fall, losing out to fellow defendant E.G. Barnett. The federal conspiracy trial opened on October 9, with Meridian police sergeant Wallace Miller testifying that he was told in advance of the White Knights plot against Schwerner. Jurors initially deadlocked, but Judge Cox sent them back with instructions to continue their deliberations — the so-called "dynamite charge." When Price and Alton Roberts were overheard in the courthouse, threatening the jury with a dynamite charge of their own, a furious Judge Cox revoked their bond and warned all concerned against further "loose talk." Verdicts were returned on October 20, with seven Klansmen convicted. Bowers and Roberts were each sentenced to the ten-year maximum, Price and Posey to six years each, while Arledge, Snowden, and Horace Barnette drew three years apiece. Defendants Akin, Willis, Burrage, Harris, Herndon, Rainey, Tucker, and Travis Barnette were acquitted on all counts. Mistrials were declared in the cases of E.G. Barnett, Edgar Killen, and Jerry Sharpe, with charges dismissed against the trio in January 1973. The guilty verdicts were affirmed on appeal in July 1969, and the U.S. Supreme Court refused to hear the case in February 1970, thus clearing the way for the convicted Klansmen to begin serving their prison time.

Cecil Price served four years of his sentence, and was paroled in 1974, his felony conviction barring any further work in law enforcement. At last report, he was employed as a truck driver for an oil distributor, still living in Neshoba County. As for Sheriff Rainey, elected to office on his promise to "handle the niggers and outsiders," he was last seen working as a private security guard... ironically, under a black supervisor.

# Putnam, Mark Steven

**Mark Steven Putnam**
*Courtesy of*
*AP/Wide World Photos.*

Mark Putnam seemed to be the stereotypical "all-American boy." Born July 4, 1959, in Coventry, Connecticut, he grew up bright, strong, and handsome. A "B"-average student at the University of Tampa, where he majored in criminology, Putnam also led the school's soccer team to an NCAA Division II championship in 1982. Married to the daughter of a wealthy real estate developer, he was delighted by the birth of their first daughter. Finally, in October 1986, Putnam fulfilled a lifelong dream by graduating from the FBI Academy at Quantico, Virginia.

Rookie G-men are assigned at the Bureau's discretion, and Putnam's first posting sent him to the tiny two-man office in Pikeville, Kentucky, some 120 miles southeast of Lexington. His wife, now pregnant with their second child, hated the backwater district on sight, agitating for a transfer from day one, but Putnam threw himself into the new job with gusto, mindful of the fact that the surest way to impress his superiors and earn promotion was to compile an impressive arrest record.

He saw his golden opportunity in a series of local bank robberies. The prime suspect was a 32-year-old ex-convict who rented rooms in Pikeville from Ken and Susan Smith, a young divorced couple who still lived together, pursuing a life style steeped in drugs and petty crime. Putnam arranged a meeting with the Smiths, to solicit their cooperation in the case, and found himself instantly attracted to Susan. The feeling was mutual, and the coke-addicted eighth-grade dropout soon confided to her sister that she planned to make Putnam fall in love with her.

First, however, they established a professional relationship of sorts. Susan quickly accepted Putnam's offer of $5,000 for testimony against her boarder, remaining on the Bureau payroll even after he was duly convicted and packed off to jail in January 1988. Several weeks passed before Susan and Putnam began their love affair, coupling in his car and cheap motel rooms, but her frequent boasts of the affair were ignored by most who knew her, based on Susan's established penchant for lying. At one point, Susan confronted Putnam's wife, again without result. Finally, reasoning that a child would force Putnam to give up his marriage and settle with her, Susan stopped using contraceptives in December 1988.

By that time, Putnam had established himself as a rising star within the FBI, wrapping up another bank heist and closing down a local "chop shop," where stolen cars were stripped and modified for sale. By early 1989, he was already planning his next move, phasing Susan out as an informant, reporting alleged bomb threats against himself and his family. "For their safety," Putnam moved his wife and children out of Pikeville, convinced that he would follow them soon to a larger, more prestigious field office. In late March, he informed Susan Smith of his impending transfer to

Miami, and she countered with the news that she was pregnant. Putnam initially denied the child was his, but vaguely offered to "take care" of her. Resettled in Florida, he was bombarded with calls from Susan, threatening to go public with her pregnancy if Putnam ignored his obligations. Finally, he promised to discuss the problem with her when he returned to Pikeville, for testimony in the chop-shop case, in early June.

Susan Smith had been missing for nine days when her sister filed a police report, on June 16, 1989, and she was officially listed as missing three days later. Given her background and lifestyle, her absence from Pikeville was no great cause for concern to police, but relatives insisted on a full investigation. Ex-husband Ken Smith was quickly cleared by a polygraph test, and it was February 1990 before investigators from the Kentucky State Police asked Putnam to take a similar exam. His evasive response created further suspicion, and Kentucky authorities joined FBI agents in a joint investigation of their man, beginning on May 1. Interviewed at length on May 16, Putnam denied any link to Smith's disappearance, but a polygraph exam, administered two days later, indicated he was lying. On May 22, Putnam confessed to his wife, resigned from the Bureau, and ordered his lawyer to seek a plea bargain in Kentucky.

Over the next three weeks, a deal was negotiated in which Putnam agreed to confess Smith's murder and lead detectives to her body, in exchange for a maximum charge of first-degree manslaughter and a prearranged sentence of 16 years in prison, to be served in a federal lockup. The state's attorney in charge of the case later explained the bargain by noting that conviction, in the absence of a *corpus delicti*, was unlikely at best. Putnam's affidavit of June 4, 1990, included an admission of strangling Smith — then five months pregnant — when they met on June 8, 1989. According to his story, they were driving around Pikeville in a rented car when he offered to adopt Smith's baby and take it home to his wife, whereupon Susan had slapped him. "And in an act of extreme rage," he explained, "I reached across the car and grabbed her by the throat with both hands."

Later on June 4, Putnam led investigators to an old mining road, nine miles from Pikeville, where Smith's skeletal remains were found in a weed-choked ravine. Eight days later, Mark Putnam received his prearranged sentence, thus becoming the first — and only — FBI agent convicted of homicide. Under terms of the plea bargain and Kentucky law, he is eligible for parole in 1998.

# Raley, John

As town marshal of Warrenton, Georgia, during Reconstruction, John Raley was naturally expected to enforce the law, but that duty had several radically different definitions in those troubled years following the Civil War. In fact, Raley's oath as a lawman took third place to his political beliefs as a conservative Democrat and his racial bigotry as an active member of the Ku Klux Klan. Inevitably, such behavior brought him into conflict with Warren County's chief law enforcement officer, Sheriff John ("Chap") Norris, who — while no special friend of black freedmen — was despised by Democrats and Klansmen as a "radical" Republican.

The KKK began nightriding in Warren County during the summer of 1868 and killed its first victim that September. Shootings and whippings became routine in the backwoods surrounding Warrenton, and Sheriff Norris was unable to restrain the terrorists in an atmosphere where the majority of whites regarded blacks as lawbreakers by definition. Matters reached a crisis point in March 1869, through a personal feud between Dr. G.W. Darden, a prominent Republican, and Charles Wallace, who divided his time between service as a leader of the Klan and editor of the *Clipper*, a local Democratic newspaper. Wallace was well known as an ill-tempered street brawler, often wounded, who had killed at least one black in combat; he was also the acknowledged leader of a Klan mob that had shot and burned a crippled black youth outside Warrenton, afterward hanging the boy's mother from a nearby tree. That March, Dr. Darden heard that Wallace was gunning for him, and he decided to fight fire with fire. In lieu of calling Wallace out, however, Darden waited in his office with a shotgun, killing his adversary from ambush as Wallace passed by on the street.

Sheriff Norris was out of town when the shooting occurred, but Darden was duly arrested and lodged in the county jail. A mob of Klansmen soon formed in downtown Warrenton, and they were busy getting liquored up when the sheriff returned. Norris appealed to E.H. Pottle, an attorney and prominent Klansman, to help disperse the mob, but Pottle refused. Several Republicans initially agreed to guard the jail, but they promptly reconsidered after catching a glimpse of the mob, and Norris himself viewed discretion as the better part of valor, trusting iron doors to protect Dr. Darden while he made himself scarce.

Shortly after 8:00 o'clock that night, the assembled Kluxers donned black robes, in contrast to their normal white ones, and set off in search of the jail key. Marshal Raley later claimed that he was acting under duress when he searched the sheriff's home and came up empty. Undeterred, the mob next tried to batter down the jailhouse door and failed, finally ripping boards down from the wall of a nearby building and kindling a fire outside the front door of the jail. Inside, they found Darden locked in a cell, armed with a pistol, but the rolling cloud of smoke prompted the doctor to surrender his weapon. Klansmen wielding cold chisels broke through the second metal door and dragged their victim out, hustling him down the street to his medical office. There, he was allowed to write a letter to his family, after which the Klansmen forced him to drink a quart of whiskey. It was nearing 2 a.m. when they marched Darden to the edge of town, forced him to strip, then riddled him with bullets. His corpse was found after sunrise, fully dressed in clothes unmarked by bullets, and a pro-Klan coroner's jury professed itself unable to identify the "mysterious beings" responsible.

Things quickly went from bad to worse in Warren County, after that. State senator Joseph Adkins was assassinated by Klansmen on May 10, 1869, and Sheriff Norris himself fled the county after a near-miss attempt on his life. In his absence, Democrats declared his office vacant and appointed John Raley as sheriff, a choice which had the effect of declaring open season on blacks. When Norris finally returned, Raley and his supporters refused to recognize the sheriff's authority, prompting Norris to visit Atlanta and obtain a special commission from Governor Rufus Bullock. Back in Warrenton with a military escort, Norris jailed Raley and five other Klansmen pending trial for the Darden murder, but a local judge with no authority to hear the case released all six on writs of habeas corpus. The county grand jury declined to indict anyone for the lynching, and multiplying death threats finally drove Norris from the district for good, leaving Warren County "law" firmly in the hands of the KKK.

# Schaefer, Gerard John

**Gerard John Schaefer**
*Courtesy of Sondra London.*

Gerard Schaefer was born in Wisconsin on March 26, 1946, the oldest of three children in a family he later described as "turbulent and conflictual." Years later, interviewed by court-appointed psychiatrists, he would refer to himself as "an illegitimate child," the product of a hasty shotgun wedding. He described his father as a verbally abusive alcoholic, flagrantly adulterous and often absent from home on business trips or otherwise. By 1960, Schaefer's family had settled in Fort Lauderdale, Florida. He graduated high school there in 1964, and he was working on the first of several college degrees when his parents divorced three years later.

By that time, if we accept Schaefer's statements to psychiatrists, he was well on the way to troubles of his own. "From an early age," Dr. R.C. Eaton recorded in 1973, "[Schaefer] has had numerous sexual hang-ups." Experiments with bondage and sadomasochism began, by Schaefer's own estimate, around age twelve. "I'd tie myself up to a tree," he told Dr. Mordecai Haber, "and I'd get excited sexually and do something to hurt myself." Around the same time, he began to "masturbate and fantasize about hurting other people, women in particular." As if this weren't enough, Schaefer recalled, "I discovered women's underwear — panties. Sometimes I wore them. I wanted to hurt myself."

The violent self-loathing went back to his earliest childhood games. In those games, he told Dr. Haber, "I always got killed. I wanted to die. My father favored my sister, so I wanted to be a girl. I wanted to die. I was such a disappointment to my family, as a kid to my father — he loved my sister. I couldn't please my father, so in playing games I wanted to be killed."

Schaefer claimed to have visited a psychiatrist in 1966, seeking relief from his sexual deviance and homicidal fantasies, but therapy didn't help. If his later statements are credible, he kept on hearing voices "telling him to kill." That same year, he toured the South with Moral Rearmament, the cheery "Up With People" folks who sang that freedom isn't free. Schaefer thought about the priesthood as a calling, but he was turned away from St. John's Seminary, where, he recalled, "they said I didn't have enough faith." The rejection angered Schaefer so much that he quit the Catholic Church.

His next goal was a teaching job, through which he hoped to instill "American values" like "honesty, purity, unselfishness and love," but Schaefer was twice dropped from student-teaching programs for "trying to impose his own moral and political values on his students." The second time, supervisor Richard Goodhart recalls, "I told him when he left that he'd better never let me hear of his trying to get a job with any authority over other people, or I'd do anything I could to prevent it."

In 1968, Schaefer was married to Martha Fogg, but it didn't work out. Martha filed for divorce, claiming "extreme cruelty," in May 1970. Schaefer took a few weeks to recuperate in Europe and North Africa that summer, coming home with a new goal in life. If he couldn't be a priest or teacher, he would be a cop. He applied to several departments, and was rejected by the Broward County sheriff's office after failing a psychological test, but the small Wilton Manors Police Department hired him anyway. In March 1972, Schaefer earned a commendation for his role in a drug bust; one month later, on April 20, he was fired. Explanations vary: Chief Bernard Scott later said that Schaefer didn't have "an ounce of common sense," while FBI agent Robert Ressler, in his book *Whoever Fights Monsters*, reports that Schaefer was disciplined for running female traffic violators through the department's computer, obtaining personal information and later calling them for dates.

Whatever the cause of his firing, Schaefer needed a job. Near the end of June, he signed on with the Martin County Sheriff's Department, pulling up stakes and moving to Stuart, Florida. He had been on the job less than a month when he made a "dumb mistake" that would cost him his career and his freedom.

On July 21, 1972, Schaefer picked up two hitchhikers, 17-year-old Pamela Wells and 18-year-old Nancy Trotter, on the highway near a local beach. He told them (falsely) that hitchhiking was illegal in Martin County, then drove them back to a halfway house where they were staying. Schaefer offered to meet them next morning, off duty, and drive them to the beach himself. The girls agreed, but instead of taking them to the beach on July 22, Schaefer drove them to swampy Hutchinson Island, off State Road A1A. There, he started making sexual remarks, then drew a gun and told the girls he planned to sell them as "white slaves" to a foreign prostitution syndicate. Forcing them out of the car, he bound both girls and left them balanced on tree roots, with nooses around their necks, at risk of hanging if they slipped and fell. Schaefer left them then, promising to return shortly, but the girls escaped in his absence and reached the nearby highway, where they flagged down a passing police car. They had no problem identifying their assailant, since Schaefer had told them his name.

By that time, Schaefer had discovered their escape and telephoned Sheriff Richard Crowder. "I've done something very foolish," Schaefer told his boss. "You're going to be mad at me." He had "overdone his job," Schaefer said, trying to "scare" the girls out of hitchhiking in the future, for their own good. Fired on the spot, charged with false imprisonment and two counts of aggravated assault, Schaefer was released on $15,000 bond. At trial, in November 1972, he pled guilty on one assault charge, and the others were dropped. Judge D.C. Smith called Schaefer a "thoughtless fool" and sentenced him to a year in the county jail, to be followed by three years probation. The ex-deputy began serving his sentence on January 15, 1973.

The most shocking revelations were yet to come, however. Two other girls were missing from the neighborhood, and they would not be as lucky as Trotter and Wells. On September 27, 1972, while Schaefer was free on bond pending trial, 17-year-old Susan Place and 16-year-old Georgia Jessup had vanished from Fort Lauderdale. Susan's parents said the girls were last seen at her house, leaving with an older man named "Gerry Shepherd," on their way "to play guitar" at a nearby beach. They never came back, but Lucille Place had recorded Shepherd's license number, along with a description of his blue-green Datsun. It was March 25, 1973 before sluggish investigators traced the plate number back to Gerry

Schaefer, by which time he was already in jail for assaulting teenage girls.

Schaefer denied any contact with Place and Jessup, but the case began unraveling on April 1, 1973, when skeletal remains were found on Hutchinson Island by three men collecting aluminum cans. Four days later, the victims were identified from dental records. Susan Place had been shot in the jaw, detectives remarking that evidence from the crime scene indicated the two girls were "tied to a tree and butchered." On April 7, police searched the home of Schaefer's mother, where Gerard had personal items stored in a spare bedroom. Items recovered during the search included a stash of women's jewelry, 100-plus pages of writing and sketches depicting mutilation-murders of young women, newspaper clippings about two women missing since 1969, and pieces of I.D. belonging to vanished hitchhikers Collette Goodenough and Barbara Wilcox, both 19. The two girls had last been seen alive on January 8, a week before Schaefer went to jail in Martin County, and while their skeletal remains were found in early 1977, no cause of death could be determined, thus no charges were filed.

As for the news clips, one referred to the February 1969 disappearance of waitress Carmen Hallock, seemingly abducted from her home. Items of her jewelry were found in Schaefer's hoard, along with a gold-filled tooth identified by Hallock's dentist, but once again no charges were filed. The second missing woman, Leigh Bonadies, had been a neighbor of Schaefer's when she disappeared in September 1969. He had complained of her "taunting" him by undressing with her curtains open, and a piece of her jewelry was found among his belongings, but no charges were found when her skeletal remains were finally recovered in 1978. More jewelry linked Schaefer to the disappearance of 14-year-old Mary Briscolina, who vanished from Broward County with 13-year-old Elsie Farmer in October 1972. Their skeletons were found in early 1973, but once again, no cause of death could be determined, and no charges were filed.

The list of suspected victims would grow over time, but Schaefer faced charges in only two murders, indicted on May 18, 1973 for the slayings of Jessup and Place. Held without bond pending trial, he was convicted on two counts of first-degree murder in October 1973, drawing concurrent terms of life imprisonment. A long series of appeals, some 20 in all, were uniformly rejected by various courts.

Schaefer was nearly forgotten by 1990, when Sondra London, a former high-school girlfriend published a collection of his stories under the title *Killer Fiction*. More volumes followed, Schaefer insisting that his stories were art, police and prosecutors describing them as thinly veiled descriptions of actual crimes. In private letters to attorneys and acquaintances, Schaefer admitted as much, himself. Witness his reference to a story titled "Murder Demons," in a letter dated April 9, 1991: "What crimes am I supposed to confess? Farmer? Briscolina? What do you think ["Murder Demons"] is? Fiction? You want confessions but don't recognize them when I anoint [sic] you with them and we've just gotten [sic] started."

Other correspondence swiftly raised the body count. "As you know," he wrote on January 20, 1991, "I've always harped on [District Attorney Robert] Stone's list of 34. In 1973 I sat down and drew up a list of my own. As I recall, my list was just over 80." The next day, given time to reflect, he went on: "I'm not claiming a huge number... I would say it runs between 80 and 110. But over eight years and three continents... One whore drowned in her own vomit while watching me disembowel her girlfriend. I'm not sure that counts as a valid kill. Did the pregnant ones count as two kills? It can get confusing."

Years later, Schaefer's letters came back to haunt him, when he was described in various true-crime books as a prolific serial killer. His response, a series of lawsuits filed against various authors for libel, were uniformly dismissed by the courts. In one such case, Judge William Steckler officially branded Schaefer a "serial killer," finding him "undeniably linked" to numerous murders beyond the two for which he stood convicted. "He boasts of the private and public associations he has had based on the reports that he is a serial killer of world-class proportions," Steckler wrote, "and it is only arrogant perversity which propels him toward this and similarly meritless lawsuits in which he claims otherwise."

Schaefer's luck ran out on December 3, 1995, when another inmate barged into his cell, slashed Gerry's throat, and stabbed him in both eyes. Prison officials named the killer as inmate Vincent Rivera, serving life plus 20 years for two murders in Tampa, but no specific motive has been offered at this writing. It appears that Schaefer's reputation as a "rat" and troublemaker in the joint caught up with him at last.

And, with the threat of nuisance litigation buried, gun-shy law enforcement officers felt free to air their views on Schaefer. Bill Hagerty, ex-FBI agent who studied Schaefer in the early 1980s, said, "He was one of the sickest. If I had a list of the top five, which would include all of the serial killers I have interviewed throughout the country, he would definitely be in the top five." For Shirley Jessup, still mourning her daughter, Schaefer's murder was a case of justice overdue. "I'd like to send a present to the guy who killed him," she told reporters. "I've always believed he was going to get his. I just wish it would have been sooner than later."

## Seals, Andrew P.

Andrew Seals was 26 years old when he graduated from Philadelphia's College of Textiles and Science in 1991, but he craved a job with some excitement, applying for a post with the New Jersey State Police in 1995. That April, he graduated from the police academy and was assigned to the department's Absecon barracks, as a road-duty trooper, where he seems to have distinguished himself as a paragon of efficiency. Superintendent Carl Williams would later say that Seals "was admired by all the people he worked with, his fellow troopers, his supervisors. He was a model trooper."

By November 1985, "model trooper" Seals had found himself a mate, sharing quarters at the Robin Hood Apartments, in Voorhees

Township, with 25-year-old Kris Nicole Taylor. Kris was a social worker, employed in Philadelphia, and while she clearly loved Seals, the couple had some problems. Twice, Voorhees Township police were summoned by their neighbors, in response to loud arguments disturbing the peace from Apartment 308, but no charges were filed in either case. Authorities were adamant that no physical abuse was involved in the quarrels, no evidence of alcohol or drugs. In fact, things seemed to quiet down after Seals and Kris were married, on May 25, 1996. "The feedback we get from his co-workers," Superintendent Williams said two months later, "is their marriage was happy."

It was all the more astounding, then, when Seals and his wife were found dead at home on Sunday, July 7th, in the wake of an obvious murder-suicide. They had been dead several days, each killed with a single head shot from Andrew's 9mm service pistol, with Kris slain before Andrew turned the gun on himself. Residents of Voorhees Township, an upscale bedroom community of 24,500 residents, were stunned by the second murder-suicide within two weeks. (The first, ten days earlier, involved a Philadelphia attorney, shot five times by his mistress of decades, before she killed herself.)

And still, investigators from the state police could find no motive for the double slaying. There had been no reports of domestic discord since Andrew and Kris were married; if anything, quite the reverse. "They both were enthusiastic about the marriage," Superintendent Williams told reporters. "That's why we're befuddled." And so they remain, certain of *what* happened in Apartment 308, still hopelessly, helplessly, wondering *why*.

# Selman, John

An unsavory lawman with an estimated 20 kills to his credit, John Selman was born in 1839, dividing his youth between Texas and Arkansas. He later tried ranching in New Mexico, but always returned to his native Texas. It was there, in Fort Griffin, that he first met Wyatt Earp and Bat Masterson, enjoying their company and basking in the reflected glory of their frequently exaggerated exploits. At Fort Griffin, Selman became the deputy of Sheriff **John Larn**, himself a cattle rustler. One of Selman's early kills on the job was his "duel" with a deaf man named Hampden, shot six times in the back after he "ignored" Selman's call to stand still.

**John Selman**
*Courtesy of Denver Public Library, Western History Division.*

When Sheriff Larn retired from office, Selman joined him as a partner in a cattle ranch, building up a herd by stealing livestock from their neighbors. Selman escaped when vigilantes came to hang Larn, and went on to form a gang called Selman's Scouts, self-styled "regulators" who hired out their guns against organized rustlers. They were successful to a point, but there was a catch: once the rustlers had fled or were killed, Selman and company picked up where they left off, stealing thousands of cattle without competition. Pressure from the U.S. Army finally broke up the gang, and Selman moved to western Texas, where he organized a second gang. Arrested with his brother Tom in June 1880, Selman was spared by the lynch mob that claimed Tom's life. En route to Shackleford County for trial, Selman bribed his guards and escaped once again.

He ran all the way to Mexico, living by his wits along the border, sometimes venturing into New Mexico Territory, until 1888, when he learned that charges facing him in Texas had been dropped. Selman promptly struck off for El Paso, working various jobs around town and keeping his nose clean enough to get himself elected constable in 1892. Two years later — on April 5, 1894 — Selman met Deputy U.S. Marshal **Bass Outlaw**, retiring to Tillie Howard's brothel for some free amusement. A mean and trigger-happy drunk, Outlaw provoked a shooting incident which left Texas Ranger Joe McKidrict dead on the ground. Still unsatisfied, he kept shooting, hitting Selman twice in the leg before John returned fire and fatally wounded the renegade marshal.

It was probably as close as Selman ever came to a true stand-up fight in Hollywood's *High Noon* tradition. His most famous killing, three years later, was more typical of those that built his reputation as a backshooter and ruthless killer.

On August 19, 1895, gunman John Wesley Hardin was idling in an El Paso saloon, drinking quietly with friends, when Selman entered the joint, walked up behind him, and shot Hardin once in the back of the head. At the time, Hardin had a full pardon for all past events, and was not a fugitive from justice. Selman was charged with murder, but he won acquittal at trial on a plea of self-defense. His rationale: Hardin had seen him in a mirror hung behind the bar, and Selman feared for his life.

The acquittal left no obstacle to Selman staying on as constable, and he was still wearing the badge on April 1, 1896, when he got into an argument with fellow lawman George Scarborough. They took the quarrel outside, where Scarborough shot Selman dead. Ironically, Selman was unarmed, but it hardly mattered in El Paso, and the shooting was dismissed as "justifiable homicide."

# Smith, Stephen Richard

Stephen Smith was a study in contradictions, a gung-ho policeman who loved guns but seemingly hated authority — at least when he was called upon to follow regulations. In his three and a half years with the San Antonio Police Department, Smith was hit with seven complaints of excessive force, but the charges were usually disposed of with punishment which amounted to slaps on the wrist. In fact, he was something of a hero on the force, having killed an armed robber in 1982, but officially sanctioned violence was only the tip of the iceberg with Smith. In December 1982, a part-time handyman named Terrell Folsom was shot and killed by persons unknown, allegedly while breaking into a parked car, and Folsom's mother heard that Smith was bragging about the murder to friends. She informed police, but was unsatisfied with their response. "They swept it under the carpet," she said. "They covered it up, is what they did."

Smith was still on the street, meanwhile, patrolling a tough neighborhood and dispensing rough justice as he saw fit. Eugene Sibrian was trying to break up a fight between two of his sons, when Smith arrived to intervene. "He was angry, real angry," Sibrian recalled. "He came to me and said, 'I told you to get lost.' He walked from the porch to the fence and grabbed me from the shoulders and threw me against the fence." Sibrian filed a brutality complaint with the San Antonio P.D., and the family home soon came under sniper fire, a bullet striking Michael Sibrian in the head and leaving him partially paralyzed. Eugene suspected Smith, but he could never prove it to authorities.

Another local resident who earned Smith's wrath was Edward de la Garza, an employee of the San Antonio Power Company who fingered Smith's wife for sleeping on the job. A short time later, de la Garza's house was peppered with gunfire, and while no one was wounded, others were not so lucky. Adolfo Queyar was killed by a sniper bullet, during a party at his house, and Clarence Kane, Jr. — a bartender at Smith's favorite hangout — was fatally wounded while walking down a street on March 28, 1985.

A year later, in March 1986, Smith was indicted on charges of brutality stemming from the arrest of a shoplifting suspect on August 7, 1985. According to eyewitnesses, Smith had assaulted the 27-year-old subject without provocation, beating him to the ground, afterward brawling with bystanders who sought to intervene and help his victim. Suspended from duty in the wake of his indictment, Smith was furious at his superiors for their "lack of support," allegedly planning to retaliate against department brass with a campaign of violence.

By that time, suspicion was spreading of a vigilante lawman at large in the Lone Star State's tenth largest city. A headline in the *San Antonio Light* posed the question: IS 'KILLER COP' PATROLLING STREETS OF ALAMO CITY? Spokesmen for the department rejected any such theories, but they must have known something was wrong in their city. Deputy Police Chief Robert Heuck's home had been sprayed with gunfire in 1983, and a firebomb had damaged Chief Robert Hoyack's residence two years later. Anonymous letters had also been mailed to the press and various public officials, accusing department leaders of child molestation and other crimes.

On August 17, 1986, Smith quarreled bitterly with his wife, and she called on a mutual friend, Patrolman Farrell Tucker, for help. (Another cop with problems, Tucker had previously been caught lying to superiors about a shooting incident, and while a psychiatrist had recommended his removal from duty, Tucker remained on the street.) Tucker visited Smith's apartment, where he was informed — by Smith's wife — that Stephen was planning to kill Bexar County District Attorney Sam Millsap, along with several ranking members of the San Antonio P.D. Next morning, Tucker reported the conversation to his superiors, and a meeting with Smith was arranged, Tucker agreeing to wear a hidden microphone and record his friend's comments.

In fact, the recorder malfunctioned, but it hardly mattered. Smith and Tucker had barely begun to talk, in Smith's car, when Smith drew a pistol and disarmed his friend, threatening Tucker's life. Before he pulled the trigger, though, Tucker drew a backup gun and pumped five bullets into Smith, killing him instantly. Police initially doubted Tucker's story, despite a reenactment on videotape, noting that Smith's car had a manual shift, and he would have needed three hands to drive while aiming a pistol at Tucker. The San Antonio D.A. voiced suspicions of murder, alleging that Tucker had killed Smith to prevent himself from being charged with vigilante crimes, but no charges were filed in the case.

By that time, a search of Smith's home had turned up an arsenal of 18 pistols, six rifles, five shotguns, and at least 100,000 rounds of ammunition. Ballistics tests on one of the rifles — a semiautomatic AR-15 — positively linked the weapon to the sniper slayings of Clarence Kane and Adolfo Queyar. No link was ever demonstrated to the other unsolved crimes, but San Antonio police are confident that Smith's death closed the file on their local vigilante.

Stephen Smith, meanwhile, was laid to rest with full military honors, as a decorated veteran, while San Antonio's finest continued taking hits in the press. Mayor Henry Cisneros denied allegations that his police force was "totally out of control," but with William Gibson installed as the department's third chief in less than a year, grappling with one scandal after another, it was plain to see that San Antonio still had more problems in store.

## Stiles, Billie

An Arizona native, born sometime in the early 1870s, Billie Stiles was said to have killed his own father at age 12. The cause of their fatal dispute is unknown, but that kind of nerve helped build his reputation as a ruthless gunman. Drifting around the Southwest, he hired out as a deputy to various lawmen, winding up at last with Marshal **Burt Alvord** in Wilcox, Arizona. They hit it off at once, and were soon co-bosses of a train-robbing gang active around the turn of the century.

The illicit enterprise thrived until 1900, when the whole gang was arrested for a Southern Pacific holdup on September 9. In custody, Stiles alone admitted guilt in the robbery and was released on his offer to testify against the others. Once free, however, he returned to the jail after nightfall, wounded the guard on duty, and freed his confederates. The gang continued raiding until 1903, when

Alvord was captured again and served two years in prison, after which he vanished into obscurity.

**Billy Stiles**
*Courtesy of*
*Western History Collections,*
*University of Oklahoma Libraries.*

As for Stiles, he seemed to have made a clean getaway. In January 1908, a Nevada deputy sheriff named William Larkin shot and killed a wanted fugitive from justice. When Larkin rode back to the dead man's house, his victim's 12-year-old son produced a shotgun and blasted him dead from his saddle. Subsequent investigation showed that "Larkin" was, in fact, the elusive Billie Stiles, gunned down by a lad the same age as he, himself, had been when he shot his own father.

# Stoudenmire, Dallas

The prime example of a Western lawman who came to be feared and hated by the citizens he served, Dallas Stoudenmire was a native of Macon County, Alabama, born in 1845. Transplanted to Texas after the Civil War, he joined the Texas Rangers and soon established his reputation as a quick-triggered lawman who shot first and asked questions later — if at all.

**Dallas Stoudenmire**
*Courtesy of*
*Western History Collections,*
*University of Oklahoma Libraries.*

Stoudenmire was an ex-Ranger by 1881, when he was hired as the marshal of El Paso. A violent boomtown plagued with ineffective law enforcement, El Paso welcomed Stoudenmire at first, its citizens hopeful that a tough marshal would turn things around. It soon became apparent, though, that Dallas Stoudenmire's solution was sometimes worse than the original problem itself.

The new marshal's first official act was to fire Deputy Bill Johnson and demand the return of his keys to the El Paso jail. When Johnson balked, Stoudenmire roughed him up in public, nearly standing Johnson on his head to get the keys. Johnson lacked the nerve to challenge Stoudenmire directly, at the moment, but he started drinking that same afternoon, muttering darkly and brooding on thoughts of revenge, surrounded by friends who urged him to settle the score.

Meanwhile, on April 14, 1881, Marshal Stoudenmire had a chance to show off his marksmanship. Two locals, Gus Krempkau and George Campbell, were arguing downtown, when a third man,

John Hale, butted into the quarrel and shot Krempkau in the chest. Stoudenmire responded to the sound of gunfire, taking aim at Hale from across the street, but missed his first shot and killed an innocent bystander. The second shot was better, drilling Hale through the forehead and dropping him where he stood. George Campbell was frightened now, standing with pistol in hand, calling out to whomever would listen that he did not want to fight. Gus Krempkau, dying on the ground, squeezed off two shots at Campbell, striking his target in the hand and foot. Dazed and bleeding, Campbell stooped to recover the gun he had dropped, whereupon Stoudenmire wheeled on the wounded man and killed him, too.

It was quite a performance, even by El Paso standards, but it left Stoudenmire's quarrel with Bill Johnson unresolved. Three days after the gunfight, on April 17, Johnson waited for Stoudenmire in an alley, clutching a shotgun in one hand, a bottle of booze in the other. As Stoudenmire passed by, making his rounds with brother-in-law Doc Cummings, Johnson cut loose with both barrels, but his aim was so poor that he missed Cummings entirely, wounding Dallas only slightly, in one heel. Before Johnson could retreat, Stoudenmire and Cummings had their guns out, pumping him full of lead.

Larger trouble was brewing, meanwhile, in El Paso, between Stoudenmire and the wealthy Manning brothers — Frank, George, and James. Together, they dominated the gambling and liquor trades in El Paso, making them three of the richest, most influential men in town. They were also close friends of the late George Campbell, regarding his death at Stoudenmire's hands as cold-blooded murder.

In February 1882, with Dallas out of town on his honeymoon, Doc Cummings was left in charge of the El Paso marshal's office. Unfortunately, while he shared Stoudenmire's temper and taste for alcohol, Cummings lacked his brother-in-law's skill with a gun. Idling in a saloon one afternoon, Cummings provoked a quarrel with James Manning, accusing the brothers of sending Campbell and John Hale to assassinate Stoudenmire the previous April. Hot words led to violence, and Cummings was shot twice, with fatal results. A post-mortem examination revealed that his skull was also fractured, possibly by impact from a gun barrel.

The feud between Stoudenmire and the Manning clan soon turned El Paso into a veritable war zone, citizens complaining that a choice between their marshal and the Mannings was like "picking between two hells." The two sides signed a shaky truce in April 1882, but the cease-fire brought no improvement in Stoudenmire's demeanor or his drinking. He roamed the streets drunk at all hours, sometimes setting up targets at the scene of the 1881 triple killing, replaying the fight with live ammo. His behavior grew so erratic that the newspapers came out against him, and the town council demanded Stoudenmire's resignation on May 27. Officially unemployed two days later, he surprised all concerned by staying in El Paso, becoming a U.S. marshal on July 13.

Two months later, on September 18, Stoudenmire heard that the Mannings were gunning for him. He found George Manning in one of the family's saloons and challenged him to draw, both men blazing away from close range. Stoudenmire was hit in the arm and dropped his pistol, grappling barehanded with Manning, their brawl spilling into the street. Outside, the marshal drew a second gun and wounded George. Just then, Frank Manning arrived with pistol in hand and shattered Stoudenmire's skull with a single, well-placed bullet. George Manning, enraged, grabbed Stoudenmire's weapon and pistol-whipped the corpse until he was forcibly dragged away. The Manning brothers were subsequently cleared of all charges in court, on a plea of self-defense.

# Tellez, Ronald

At first glance, the murder looked like an open-and-shut gangland killing. The victim, George Mueller, was a millionaire vending-machine distributor operating in the Chicago suburb of Blue Island, Illinois, killed in his office on March 29, 1986, with three close-range gunshots to the head. Such crimes are rarely solved, in Chicago or elsewhere — but, then again, the hit men rarely confess on tape, and they are rarely active-duty policemen.

The Mueller slaying was old news by July 16, 1987, when Blue Island Patrolman Ronald Tellez, age 31, was arrested at work and charged with the murder. Held without bond at the same time were the victim's wife, 32-year-old Constantina ("Connie") Mueller, and her 48-year-old ex-husband, Joseph Henke. Prosecutors alleged that Mrs. Mueller had hired Tellez for $3,000 to kill her latest husband, whereupon she would inherit some 60 percent of the dead man's estate. Henke and Connie were living together at the time of their arrest, picked up by the police at Connie's fast-food restaurant in Frankfort, Illinois. From the state's viewpoint, Connie Mueller was "a woman who marries for money," having divorced Henke in September 1984, two months before she married George Mueller. As for Tellez, FBI agents had him on tape, bragging of the Mueller hit and other homicides, billing himself as a seasoned killer in conversations with a G-man posing as a Chicago mobster. His goal: a full-time job committing murders for the Mafia.

As described in court documents and media reports, the case had broken after federal agents cut a deal with Connie Mueller's father, Giovanni Branco. A reputed hoodlum from Las Vegas, Branco was doing time in a California prison on federal counterfeiting charges, having tried to purchase $5 million in funny money from undercover Secret Service agents, when the FBI approached him with a deal in mind. They would arrange his temporary release from prison, Branco was told, if he would assist them in solving the Mueller homicide. Branco would wear a hidden microphone, recording conversations with his daughter, Joe Henke, and Ronald Tellez, while an FBI agent ran interference, posing as a "made" member of the Chicago mob.

Branco agreed, and so the case was broken, after Tellez was recorded boasting of the Mueller hit and other contract slayings. One dated back to July 31, 1984, when tavern owner Harold Rowley had been killed in South Bend, Indiana — again, shot three times in the head. A .380-caliber pistol stolen from Rowley's home had been found in Tellez's car, after Ronald was arrested. Tellez told authorities he had purchased the gun from Rowley's stepson, Gary Kesson, but that was another problem. Kesson, it seemed, had vanished without a trace in 1985, shortly after naming Tellez as a beneficiary in his will. By late summer of 1987, police were also looking at another head-shot killing, this one in Tellez's native Texas, and the officer's own statements pointed to yet another slaying, this one in Franklin Park, Illinois, where Tellez bragged of killing a man on orders from "a president of a corporation," shooting his victim in a car while he was "guarded by three other individuals." Sgt. Rocco Fortino, tracking that case for Franklin Park P.D., acknowledged that four persons had been shot in a car, three of them surviving their wounds, while the dead man was known to be having an affair with the wife of a local businessman.

On July 22, Tellez, Connie Mueller, and Joe Henke were indicted for George Mueller's slaying by a Cook County grand jury. A month later, on August 28, Tellez tried to escape from the Chicago Criminal Courts Building, kicking a jailer repeatedly in the groin before he was overpowered in a nearby elevator. It was all very well for Tellez's defense attorney to describe the charges as resembling the plot from "a bad television show," complaining that tapes of the patrolman's comments were being withheld for dubious "enhancement" by the FBI, but the escape attempt spoke volumes about Tellez's state of mind.

Charges against Joe Henke were dismissed without explanation on April 15, 1988, suggesting that he had no actual part in the conspiracy to kill George Mueller. Tellez and Connie Mueller were left to face the music alone, while Mueller's children filed a federal lawsuit against Tellez and the city of Blue Island, charging the city with negligence in hiring a police officer of Ronald's violent tendencies.

Tellez's trial opened on November 8, 1989, his lawyers describing him as a "foolish" but "well-intentioned" officer who went undercover without official sanction in 1987, trying to solve the Mueller case as a favor to Connie. He had posed as a hit man in an effort to gain the confidence of those involved, his counsel said, and then was framed by Mueller's "secret, scheming" wife. Prosecutor James Reilly dismissed the frame-up story as a transparent sham, letting Tellez speak for himself on the FBI tapes. In one segment, Tellez described his favored head-shot technique by saying, "That man would be on the floor in a matter of seconds. Boom, with no hesitation." The FBI's "mobster" cautioned Tellez, "Do you understand that you are offering your services to hit people for the mob in Chicago?" To which Tellez replied: "I understand that, too. I have no qualms with that."

Giovanni Branco, paroled from prison after serving five years, in July 1989, appeared as a major witness for the state. His motive for cooperating with the feds, he testified, had been to protect his daughter and grandchildren from Tellez, whom Branco regarded as a dangerous psychotic. "He killed one," Branco said from the stand. "It ain't going to stop him from killing another one." Cross-examined on his motives by defense attorneys, Branco snapped, "I'm telling this jury that I was worried about this screwball killing my Connie or my grandchildren. To save my daughter, I'd cooperate with the devil."

Connie Mueller took the stand on November 13, admitting that she first met Ronald Tellez ten years earlier, when he had stopped her for speeding. To escape a traffic ticket, she agreed to have dinner with Tellez, and they wound up as "very good friends," having sex on occasion. In January 1986, she said, Tellez had volunteered to kill her husband after George had learned of her efforts to get a divorce and had beaten her bloody. Cross-examined by defense attorneys, she admitted wishing her husband dead, so that she could collect her inheritance, and she acknowledged giving Tellez something less than $1,000 for the job before she embarked with her children on a trip to Mexico. The murder had occurred while she was out of town.

Other prosecution witnesses were no more helpful to Tellez. An FBI expert described the murder slugs as "consistent" with a box of bullets found in Ronald's possession, and a longtime friend admitted on the stand that Tellez had paid him in 1988 to falsify various diary entries, indicating that he had helped Tellez with his spurious "undercover work" in 1986 and '87.

Tellez got a chance to speak for himself on November 15, breaking down in tears on the stand as he admitted forging diaries, claiming he was "broken" by the months he had spent in jail without bond. He further admitted discussing the Mueller hit with cellmates in jail, but it was all a front, he testified. "When you're down there on Death Row," he told the court, "you have to portray some kind of image." In fact, he maintained, he had launched his own unauthorized investigation of the murder after learning that George Mueller was "secretly married" to his good friend Connie Branco.

The performance was less than persuasive. Jurors deliberated for 90 minutes on November 16, before convicting Ronald Tellez of first-degree murder. The next day, at his sentencing hearing, former cellmates described his boasting of multiple murders, along with his plan to break out of jail by sawing through the metal bars on his window. Eleven jurors wanted to execute Tellez, but one stubborn holdout refused to agree, compelling the court to impose a sentence of life imprisonment without parole. In the aftermath of that decision, juror Lissa Cunneen described Tellez as "about the most venal little person I've seen in my life. He gave me the creeps." Jury foreman Dan Sopocy was even more outspoken: "The guy's scum. He should have died. The man is a piece of filth."

Connie Mueller, for her part, received a ten-year prison term in December 1989, for conspiring to have her husband killed. "No matter how bad you feel," said Judge Loretta Hall in passing sentence, "you could not possibly feel bad enough."

On April 29, 1992, Ronald Tellez was convicted of killing Harold Rowley in South Bend, back in 1984. Jurors deliberated eight hours before returning the guilty verdict, and Tellez drew a sentence of 50 years, to be served concurrently with his life term in Illinois. Eleven months later, on March 24, 1993, the Indiana Court of Appeals upheld his conviction.

# Thompson, Ben

**Ben Thompson**
*Courtesy of Texas State Library,
Archives & Information
Services Division.*

A pathological gunman with few redeeming qualities, Ben Thompson was English born, in 1842, but was raised in Austin, Texas. His first clash with the law, sometime before the Civil War, involved the fatal shooting of an unarmed black youth, and the fact that a white Texas jury sentenced him to prison for the killing is a measure of Thompson's low standing in the community. Released in time to join the Confederate army, Thompson was an undistinguished soldier, fighting as much with his fellow Rebels as he did with Union troops. Charged with a couple of killings while in uniform, he somehow escaped prosecution and was discharged after Lee's surrender at Appomatox.

Back in civilian life, he committed another murder in Austin, and was sent back to jail. Awaiting trial, he bribed two guards, who joined Thompson and five other escapees on an end run to Mexico, where they enlisted with the troops of Emperor Maximilian. Following Maximilian's execution in 1867, Thompson returned to

Texas, where he was promptly acquitted of the old murder charge, but spent two years in prison for another shooting. Pardoned in 1870, he became a gambler and eventually opened his own saloon-casino in Abilene, Kansas, in partnership with a friend named Phil Coe. It is reported that Thompson had a few near-miss confrontations with Marshal **James Butler Hickok**, but the arguments always stopped short of gunplay. It may have been just as well for the backshooting "Wild Bill," since Thompson had earned his reputation as a ruthless killer. "Others missed at times," Bat Masterson once said, "but Ben Thompson was as delicate and certain in action as a Swiss watch."

Thompson's saloon was best known for its sign, depicting a large bull with grossly exaggerated genitalia. Conservative residents dubbed it "the shame of Abilene" and urged Marshal Hickok to do something about it, but Thompson's lethal temper was a formidable deterrent. Waiting for Ben to leave town on business, Hickok picked a fight with Coe and killed him with a well-placed pistol shot. Discouraged from seeking revenge by the broken leg he had suffered in a wagon accident, Thompson soon sold out his holdings and left town.

He returned to Kansas in 1873, and was involved in several more killings. He also helped his psychotic brother, Billy, escape justice after killing Sheriff C.B. Whitney, at Ellsworth. The senseless shooting appalled Thompson. "My God, Billy," he said, "you've shot our best friend!"

"I don't give a damn!" crazy Billy replied. "I would've shot if it had been Jesus Christ."

Thompson kept on gambling and killing through the 1870s, briefly renting his gun to the Santa Fe Railroad in 1879, in the war to seize a right-of-way through Royal Gorge. Later that same year, he returned to Austin with money in pocket, opened a string of gambling dens, then ran for marshal. Defeated in his first attempt, he won the post in 1880, and his fearsome reputation produced a sharp drop in crime around the state capital. Granted, Thompson still liked to get drunk and shoot at street lamps, but he was popular — or feared — enough to win re-election in December 1881. The following year, Thompson shot and killed Jack Harris, an old adversary who ran the Vaudeville Variety Theatre in San Antonio. Murder charges in that case forced his resignation as marshal, but Thompson was acquitted on a plea of self-defense and returned to a victory parade organized by his friends in Austin.

Even without a badge, Thompson's bloody reputation kept many outlaws from dawdling in Austin, and his business prospered until March 1884, when **John Fisher**, a sheriff's deputy from Uvalde, rode into town on official business. On a whim, Thompson and Fisher decided to visit San Antonio — or, more specifically, the Vaudeville Variety Theatre. Thompson was predictably unwelcome in the club, but he and Fisher were shown to an upstairs box, where they were soon joined by proprietors Billy Simms and Joe Foster, along with bouncer Jacob Coy. Wits addled by liquor, Thompson taunted Simms and Foster about the death of their late partner, finally drawing his pistol and "playfully" shoving the barrel into Foster's mouth. Coy made a grab for the gun, and wild shooting erupted, joined by three *pistoleros* hiding in an adjacent box.

When the smoke cleared, Thompson was dead on the floor, with nine bullet wounds, while Fisher had soaked up thirteen slugs. The one shot Thompson fired had failed to find its mark, but it was all the killers needed to support their legal claim of self-defense, and they were promptly acquitted in court.

# Torsney, Richard H.

Police violence in minority communities has been a cause of civic trauma for decades in America, and no metropolis has seen more upheaval in this regard than New York City. One such case, on November 25, 1976, was the shooting of 15-year-old Randolph Evans in Brooklyn, by white patrolman Richard Torsney. Young Evans was unarmed, and two other policemen filed reports to the effect that Torsney had fired without provocation, prompting his arrest on November 26. Spokesmen for the Police Benevolent Association posted Torsney's bail, prompting several black officers to resign from the organization, but bond was revoked on November 30, after Torsney pled not guilty to a charge of second-degree murder.

Torsney's trial was delayed for a year in New York, finally convening on November 9, 1977. Faced with testimony from brother officers that he "seemed calm during and after the shooting," Torsney never denied the killing itself, preferring to take his chances with an insanity plea. His defense attorney claimed that the shooting sprang from a psychotic episode provoked by a rare form of epilepsy. In support of that claim, his sister and wife took the witness stand to describe frequent beatings that Torsney received from his father in childhood, presumably resulting in brain damage, and a psychiatrist described Torsney as being subject to unpredictable violent outbursts. Torsney himself described the shooting as "self-defense," but that claim itself became part of the insanity plea, psychologists describing the patrolman as a victim of involuntary "retrospective falsification." Prosecutors called their own psychiatrists to refute the claim, insisting that Torsney knew what he was doing when he pulled the trigger on Randolph Evans.

On November 30, Patrolman Torsney was found not guilty by reason of insanity, retained in custody pending designation of a mental hospital at which he would be confined for treatment. He wound up in Creedmoor State Hospital, a facility that often housed the criminally insane. A year after his acquittal, on November 14, 1978, New York state health officials recommended his release, stating that he had revealed no signs of mental illness while in custody. On December 21, at the request of the Brooklyn district attorney's office, the New York State Supreme Court stayed Torsney's release for two weeks. Justice Leonard Yoswein, for one, seemed to question the original acquittal, noting that available evidence suggested Torsney was not insane at the time he entered Creedmoor.

On February 5, 1979, the New York State Appellate Division ordered Richard Torsney held for individual psychiatric treatment, and New York's Mental Health Department instantly appealed.

Back in Brooklyn, Judge Bruce Wright of the criminal court denounced Torsney as "a killer and an enemy" of society. Finally, on July 9, 1979, a divided New York State appellate court ordered Torsney's release from custody. He was free of all charges, and those who claimed that he had gotten away with murder could only take consolation in the fact that his recent dismissal from the NYPD made Torsney ineligible for a $15,000 yearly medical-disability pension.

# Von Villas, Robert: See Ford, Richard

# Walker, J.P.

A morbid racist in the mold that has made Southern law enforcement a bad joke for decades, J.P. Walker was a Mississippi native, born in 1919. He joined the U.S. Army in June 1936, but deserted from Fort Benning, Georgia, on February 1, 1938. At that, his enlistment had been long enough for Walker to be convicted by court martial for neglecting proper prophylaxis during illicit sex, a charge that earned him one month at hard labor and a $12 fine. Two other convictions involved charges of being drunk and disorderly. Following his desertion, military police traced him back to his home town of Picayune, where he was arrested and held for his fourth military trial, and then dropped from the military with a "general" discharge on April 10, 1941. In the meantime, however, Walker had enlisted a second time, in New Orleans, using a phony name. On June 22, 1943, he was discharged a second time, on grounds of medical disability, presumably connected to a cyst on his tailbone. In fact, army psychiatrists had diagnosed him as being in a "constitutional psychotic state," with an "inadequate personality."

Back in Picayune, the hulking Walker — six foot one, 230 pounds and more — became a deputy with the Pearl River County sheriff's office, serving until 1956, when he lost the race for sheriff to W. Osborne Moody. His defeat was undoubtedly good for the county, since Walker was known to brutalize his prisoners, particularly blacks, and fellow officers had accused him of raping female inmates in the county jail. Still, he was expected to win the next campaign for sheriff, in August 1959, when a county ordinance barred Sheriff Osborne from succeeding himself. Despite his manifest character flaws, the pastor of Mississippi's largest Baptist church, in Picayune, saw fit to tell his congregation that "I've never known a finer man than J.P. He will be our next sheriff." Likewise, the state representative from Pear River County opined that Walker was "a solid citizen, one of the best."

In February 1959, Walker found an issue which, he was sure, could push him over the top in the August election. A local black man, Mack Charles Parker, had been jailed in Poplarville, the county seat, on charges of raping a white woman. Parker denied the charge, but racist sentiment was running high in Pearl River County, and Walker returned from Parker's arraignment to report that the "nigra" had been surly and unduly confident in court. Clearly, something had to be done for the honor of white Southern womanhood... and to bolster Walker's hope of nailing down a lucrative job in police work.

It may seem odd for a would-be sheriff to plan a murder as part of his campaign, but this was Mississippi in the 1950s, after all. Driving out to the tiny crossroads of Gumpond, six miles east of Poplarville, on April 22, 1959, Walker dropped in at the small Baptist church run by James Floren ("Preacher") Lee, a racist fanatic whose sermons were heavily weighted with right-wing politics and crackpot white-supremacy dogma. Following the "gospel message," Walker stayed behind to speak with Lee, his son Jeff, farmer L.C. Davis, and one Francis Barker, who worked for the county health department vaccinating dogs. The men were all friends of Walker, fellow members of the Masonic lodge in Pearl River County, and they shared his feeling that Mack Parker should be "taught a lesson" on behalf of white men everywhere. Lynching sounded like the ticket, and the would-be mob decided that Friday night, April 24, would be a good time to make their move. They agreed to meet at L.C.'s farm beforehand, bringing along reinforcements, and to plot their final moves from there.

The nocturnal meeting on Friday night drew 30 men in five cars, all anxious for a shot at Mack Parker. The mechanics of extracting him from jail were still a problem, and while Walker favored a frontal assault, hoping to burn through the doors with an acetylene torch from his auto-body shop, cooler heads decided to recruit an ally in the sheriff's office. Aging jailer Jewel Alford was consulted and agreed to join the mob, letting him into the courthouse with his keys. Once inside, they found keys to the upstairs cell block in Sheriff Osborne's office and went looking for Mack Parker.

Trusty Dwight Ladner later told investigators, "I had been told several times by Jewel Alford, the jailer, that if anybody came up there for Parker, I should point Parker out to them and make sure they got the right Negro." Ladner did as he was told that night, but even with masks on their faces, he was able to recognize Alford, Preacher Lee, and J.P. Walker. Mack Parker fought for his life as the three men entered his cell, but it was a lost cause. Beaten senseless and bound with rope, he was dragged downstairs, his head bouncing on the steps and leaving a ragged trail of blood behind. The abduction was so noisy, in fact, that nurses on the night shift at a hospital across the street were moved to call Sheriff Osborne at home, but Walker and company were long gone with their prisoner by the time Osborne arrived on the scene.

Parker was driven to the Bogalusa Bridge, spanning the Pearl River which forms Mississippi's eastern border with Louisiana. The mob had planned to castrate him and hang him from the metal superstructure of the bridge, but Parker had his second wind by the time they reached their destination, and he began struggling again as he was dragged from the car. Another beating followed, and two shots from a .38-caliber revolver were fired into his chest at point-blank range, killing him instantly. Their blood sport ruined for the night, the lynchers weighted his body with chains and dropped it into the river, where it quickly sank from view. They had reckoned without the current, however, and the corpse surfaced ten days later, two and a half miles downstream.

By that time, Mississippi's version of a murder investigation was underway. J.P. Walker was Sheriff Moody's prime suspect, having boasted of his plans to any drunken racist who would listen for the past few days. Governor James Coleman, considered a racial "moderate" by Mississippi standards, requested FBI assistance with the case on April 25, while Walker spent the morning hanging out with other spectators around the courthouse, hoping to learn details about the investigation. In fact, the identity of Parker's lynchers was no secret in Poplarville, and Walker himself was frequently named as the triggerman in muttered conversations around town.

FBI agents wasted no time in picking up on the gossip, and members of the lynching party soon had uninvited visitors on their doorsteps, flashing federal badges, asking pesky questions. Christopher ("Crip") Reyer was one of the first to spill his guts, describing the meeting at L.C. Davis's farm on Friday night, and Arthur Smith crumbled four days later, soon followed by Jewel Alford. None admitted direct knowledge of (or participation in) the murder, but the pieces were clearly falling into place. In the FBI scenario, local lawmen had made themselves scarce on Friday night, the 24th, because they were forewarned by members of the mob. Governor Coleman, for his part, replied with the observation that most Mississippi jails were unguarded at night.

J.P. Walker, for his part, stubbornly resisted interrogation by the feds. "They threatened me and talked to me like I was a nigger or a dog or something," he recalled. Worst of all, he was outraged at the thought of Uncle Sam "spending $100,000 [on the investigation] because of that nigger who wasn't worth two cents." In early June, Walker formally announced his candidacy for sheriff, issuing a declaration that he was "entering this race in good faith and with the utmost sincerity of purpose." It didn't help in the end, and he was edged out that August by Moody's hand-picked successor, Bill

Owen. When the final votes were counted, Walker had carried only his home town of Picayune.

Pearl County's grand jury met to consider the Parker case in November 1959, but no one was indicted for the lynching. That was no surprise in the Magnolia State, where the murderers of 14-year-old Emmett Till had been acquitted four years earlier, then turned around and sold their detailed confessions to *Look* magazine, but G-men staked their hopes on a federal grand jury, convened in January 1960. They had misjudged the depth of Mississippi racism, however, perhaps forgetting that even a federal grand jury would still be composed of lily-white locals. In the final event, J.P. Walker never even had to testify, one of fifteen scheduled witnesses whose appearances were canceled by the grand jury. A vote of "no bill" was returned, and the Parker case was effectively closed. One identified member of the lynch mob, Herman Schulz, went on to serve as a Pearl River County constable in the early 1960s before he finally left the state.

As for J.P. Walker, he finally saw his dream come true in 1963, when he was elected sheriff of Pearl River County by an admiring electorate. Unable to succeed himself in 1967, he ran his wife for office in the best George Wallace tradition, and was promptly appointed to serve as her deputy. Re-elected as sheriff in 1971, Walker caused a media sensation when his deputies planted marijuana on a visiting rock band, the American Indians, then arrested the musicians and forcibly shaved their heads. When TV journalists came from New Orleans to question Walker about the incident, he tried to run them over with his car. In 1976, the county abolished its rule against sheriffs succeeding themselves, but Walker's moment was past. Defeated by his brother-in-law in a last-ditch re-election bid, J.P. died a short time later, leaving only his legacy of bitterness and paranoia behind.

# Webb, Gregory Jon

As police chief of Lyons, Nebraska, 30 miles northwest of Omaha, Gregory Webb was a figure commanding substantial respect. A 36-year-old bachelor, he apparently enjoyed no shortage of female companionship, and chief among his ladyfriends was Anna Marie Anton, a 34-year-old neighbor who lived in the same apartment house with Webb. By December 1986, however, their relationship had fallen on hard times, Anton complaining about the attention Webb was paying to other young women in town.

On December 15, the quarrel came to a head, and Anton was killed by two gunshots to the abdomen. Chief Webb had already fled town by the time her corpse was discovered, and investigation led to his indictment on first-degree murder charges. Catching up to the fugitive cop was another matter, however, for Webb had run all the way to Central America. In March 1987, he returned to the United States and settled in Volusia County, Florida, working construction under a variety of pseudonyms that included "Mark Engelkens," "Gregory James Webber," and "Big Jim."

Webb had nearly stopped looking over his shoulder by February 1993, when his case was profiled by Robert Stack on the NBC television program *Unsolved Mysteries*. A neighbor in Holly Hill, Florida, recognized his photo on the tube and called police, who waited for Webb on February 23, arresting him when he appeared to pick up a crew of Daytona Beach construction workers. Returned to Nebraska for trial, Webb was held without bond, framing a defense based on alcohol-induced amnesia. Speaking for the record at a pretrial hearing, Webb told the court that he had awakened from a night of heavy drinking to find Anton dead on his floor, whereupon he had panicked and run for his life. He had no memory of killing her, and thus should not be charged with intentional murder. Defense attorney Michael Levy argued that there was no evidence of motive in the case, prosecutors responding that the murder resulted from an acrimonious "love triangle."

On March 3, 1994, Webb pled no contest to manslaughter in Anton's death; he also pled guilty to a charge of tampering with evidence, related to his attempted concealment of her body. Lawyer Levy said of Webb that "All he knows is he and Anton were drinking heavily the night of December 15 and [he] awoke to find her dead on the floor." Two months later, on May 5, Webb was sentenced to a maximum of 19 years in prison for his crimes.

# Bibliography

Asin, Stefanie. "Murder middleman gets death sentence." *Houston Chronicle*, July 11, 1996.

Bailey, Judy. "Accused cop's files show reprimands, suspension." *Atlanta Journal and Constitution*, March 20, 1993.

— — —. "Safe found in pond where accused officers fished." *Atlanta Journal and Constitution*, March 9, 1993.

— — —. "2 Riverdale officers charged in slaying of nude-club owner." *Atlanta Journal and Constitution*, March 2, 1993.

Bailey, Judy, and Rick Minter. "Atlanta, Fulton officers may be linked to burglary ring." *Atlanta Journal and Constitution*, March 4, 1993.

— — — and — — —. "Probationer, officers charged in killing." *Atlanta Journal and Constitution*, March 3, 1993.

Bardwell, S.K. "Gun discovery tied to victim's husband." *Houston Chronicle*, March 15, 1995.

Bardwell, S.K., and Jerry Urban. "Fratta charged with arranging wife's death." *Houston Chronicle*, April 22, 1995.

Bates, Warren. "Officer's arrest demanded." *Las Vegas Review-Journal*, January 16, 1997.

Benjamin, Caren. "Mortensen lawyer seeks new trial because of story on Brady." *Las Vegas Review-Journal*, June 18, 1997.

— — —. "Mortensen guilty." *Las Vegas Review-Journal*, May 15, 1997.

— — —. "Officer accused in killing denied bail." *Las Vegas Review-Journal*, January 1, 1997.

— — —. "Officer's bail at $500,000 in Las Vegas shooting." *Las Vegas Review-Journal*, January 16, 1997.

— — —. "Sentence: life without parole." *Las Vegas Review-Journal*, May 16, 1997.

Cantalupe, Joe, and Lisa Petrillo. *Badge of Betrayal*. New York: Avon, 1991.

Cartel, Michael. *Disguise of Sanity: Serial Mass Murderers*. Toluca Lake, CA: Pepperbox Books, 1985.

Charles, Alfred. "Davis jury lets U.S. seek death penalty." *Times-Picayune*, April 26, 1996.

— — —. "Frank didn't confess to killings, lawyer says." *Times-Picayune*, March 10, 1995.

— — —. "Officer's widow sues city, police; hiring of Frank cited in claim." *Times-Picayune*, March 3, 1996.

Codrescu, Andrei. "Terror Stalks the Big Easy." *Playboy*, March 1996.

Colquhoun, Laura. "Murderer sentenced in beating of guard." *Union Leader*, June 13, 1996.

Connelly, William Else. *Wild Bill and His Era*. New York: The Press of the Pioneers, 1933.

Coyle, Pamela. "Restaurant liable in triple murder, N.O. tells court; killer cop's rampage focus of suit." *Times-Picayune*, February 1, 1997.

Cutter, Henry. "Policemen charged in death of man." *Indianapolis Star*, November 28, 1995.

Del Vecchio, Rick, and Peter Fimrite, "5 found slain in Oakland." *San Francisco Chronicle*, April 15, 1992.

Del Vecchio, Rick, Michael Taylor, and Clarence Johnson. "Oakland cop admits killing wife, police say." *San Francisco Chronicle*, April 18, 1992.

Eagles, Charles. *Outside Agitator: Jon Daniels and the Civil Rights Movement in Alabama*. Chapel Hill: University of North Carolina Press, 1993.

Eckstein, Sandra. "Last 'bad cop' gets five-year term." *Atlanta Journal and Constitution*, July 28, 1995.

Elman, Robert. *Fired in Anger*. New York: Doubleday, 1968.

Erler, Bob, and John C. Souter. *The Catch Me Killer*. Wheaton, IL: Tyndale House, 1980.

Fimrite, Peter, and Clarence Johnson. "Cops baffled in strangulation of officer's wife." *San Francisco Chronicle*, April 16, 1992.

Flanagan, Tanya. "Charges considered in slaying." *Las Vegas Review-Journal*, January 7, 1997.

Frasier, David. *Murder Cases of the Twentieth Century*. Jefferson, NC: McFarland & Co., 1996.

Fritze, David. "The decline and fall of a policeman." *Arizona Republic*, September 10, 1995.

— — —. "Deputy held in killings took drugs, lab says." *Arizona Republic*, September 8, 1995.

— — —. "Yuma deputy's actions baffled family, friends." *Arizona Republic*, July 22, 1995.

Gibson, Eddie and Ray, with Randall Turner. *Blind Justice*. New York: St. Martin's Press, 1991.

Golab, Jan. *The Dark Side of the Force: A True Story of Corruption and Murder in the LAPD*. New York: Atlantic Monthly Press, 1993.

Gross, Jane. "Transit policeman is held in stabbing death of friend." *New York Times*, June 15, 1987.

Guy, Duncan. "Ex-colonel sentenced for apartheid crimes." *Indianapolis Star*, October 31, 1996.

Gwynne, S.C. "Cops and robbers; a shocking murder highlights the corruption among New Orleans' underpaid police." *Time*, March 20, 1995.

Halstuk, Martin. "Ex-cop due in court in killing." *San Francisco Chronicle*, January 11, 1993.

Herbert, Bob. "In America; killer cops." *New York Times*, September 15, 1995.

Herzog, Arthur. *The Woodchipper Murder*. New York: Henry Holt, 1989.

Hill, Holly. "Fugitive police chief held in 1986 killing." *Orlando Sentinel Tribune*, February 24, 1993.

Hoover, Ken. "Court upholds ex-cop's murder conviction." *San Francisco Chronicle*, November 22, 1996.

Humes, Edward. *Murderer with a Badge*. New York: Onyx, 1992.

Hunt, Maria. "A brother struggles over a cop's slaying of two other officers." *San Diego Union-Tribune*, July 17, 1996.

Jenkins, Phil. "State trooper arrested." United Press International, October 30, 1987.

Jensen, Lynne. "Accused killer a mystery to hometown neighbors; Frank seen as loner, failure." *Times-Picayune*, September 3, 1995.

Jones, Aphrodite. *The FBI Killer*. New York: Pinnacle, 1992.

Klein, Barry. "Killer of 9 gets his wish for a 'soldier's death'." *St. Petersburg Times*, April 21, 1988.

Lee, Henry. "Ex-cop sentenced for strangling wife." *San Francisco Chronicle*, October 26, 1995.

Liebrum, Jennifer. "Ex-officer charged in plot to kill wife." *Houston Chronicle*, June 3, 1995.

— — — . "Fratta hit with murder indictment." *Houston Chronicle*, June 29, 1995.

— — — . "Fratta trial turns lurid on first day." *Houston Chronicle*, April 10, 1996.

— — — . "Jury sentences Fratta to die for wife's killing." *Houston Chronicle*, April 24, 1996.

— — — . "Man who said he'd kill Fratta is sent to prison." *Houston Chronicle*, May 10, 1996.

— — — . "Testimony to begin in capital murder trial." *Houston Chronicle*, April 9, 1996.

Makeig, John. "Fratta holds dim view of women, expert says." *Houston Chronicle*, April 17, 1996.

— — — . "In punishment phase, mother of victim labels Fratta 'monster'." *Houston Chronicle*, April 20, 1996.

— — — . "Jury finds Fratta guilty of plotting wife's murder." *Houston Chronicle*, April 18, 1996.

Manzo, Mike. "Lawyer says Anderson abused his wife prior to murder." *Union Leader*, May 18, 1995.

Marks, Paula Mitchell. *And Die in the West* (Norman, OK: Oklahoma University Press, 1989).

Marshall, Scott. "3 former officers, 2 others indicted on murder charges." *Atlanta Journal and Constitution*, March 17, 1993.

Marshall, Scott, and Bill Montgomery. "Prosecutors: cop to plead guilty in killing of club owner." *Atlanta Journal and Constitution*, May 26, 1993.

Metz, Leon. *The Shooters*. El Paso: Mangan Books, 1975.

Minter, Rick. "Officer's wife talks of tragic events." *Atlanta Journal and Constitution*, April 1, 1993.

Minter, Rick, and Kathy Scruggs. "Police crime scandal." *Atlanta Journal and Constitution*, March 6, 1993.

Montgomery, Bill. "8 suspects charged in alleged metro police burglary ring go to trial today." *Atlanta Journal and Constitution*, June 1, 1993.

— — —. "Ex-officer admits murder; he'll get life for killing club owner." *Atlanta Journal and Constitution*, May 4, 1995.

— — —. "Ex-officer is sentenced to life in '93 slaying." *Atlanta Journal and Constitution*, July 13, 1995.

— — —. "Ex-officer pleads guilty in 1993 slaying." *Atlanta Journal and Constitution,* July 6, 1995.

— — —. "Mark Douglas McKenna trying to escape financial hardships." *Atlanta Journal and Constitution*, May 23, 1993.

Morehouse, Macon. "'Bad cop' trial looks at alibis of officers." *Atlanta Journal and Constitution*, June 15, 1994.

— — —. "Jury acquits 3 in Coweta 'bad cop' trial." *Atlanta Journal and Constitution*, June 16, 1994.

Myers, Linnet. "Bond denied in murder-for-hire case." *Chicago Tribune*, September 10, 1987.

Nauss, Donald. "Detroit officers guilty of murder in beating." *Los Angeles Times*, August 24, 1993.

Newton, Michael. *Hunting Humans*. Port Townsend, WA: Loompanics Unlimited, 1990.

— — —. *Serial Slaughter*. Port Townsend, WA: Loompanics Unlimited, 1992.

Newton, Michael, and Judy Ann Newton. *The Ku Klux Klan*. New York: Garland, 1991.

Nossiter, Adam. "New Orleans police scandals punctuated by woman's murder." *New York Times*, December 19, 1994.

O'Brien, John. "Too Many Bodies Spoiled the Honeymoon." *Startling Detective*, March 1997.

O'Connor, Matt. "Ex-Blue Island cop convicted in murder of Indiana bar owner." *Chicago Tribune*, April 29, 1992.

— — —. "Ex-Blue Island officer portrayed as hitman or fall guy in killing." *Chicago Tribune*, November 9, 1989.

— — —. "Ex-cop heard boasting of hit." *Chicago Tribune*, November, 10, 1989.

— — —. "Fellow inmate tells of killer's boasting." *Chicago Tribune*, November 18, 1989.

— — —. "Police officer admits faking entries in diary about slaying." *Chicago Tribune*, November 16, 1989.

— — —. "Rogue cop guilty in '86 murder." *Chicago Tribune*, November 17, 1989.

— — —. "Split jury spares life of ex-cop." *Chicago Tribune*, November 19, 1989.

— — —. "Wife gets 10-year prison term for hiring man to kill husband." *Chicago Tribune*, December 14, 1989.

— — —. "Wife says cop offered to kill mate." *Chicago Tribune*, November 14, 1989.

Oriole, Frank. "'Bad Lieutenants' — Southern Style." *True Police*, April 1994.

Patton, Natalie, and Tanya Flanagan. "Officer's arrest stuns sheriff." *Las Vegas Review-Journal*, December 31, 1996.

Perlstein, Michael. "Davis guilty of drug running." *Times-Picayune*, September 13, 1996.

— — —. "Ex-cop faces federal trial." *Times-Picayune*, April 8, 1996.

— — —. "Guilty: rogue NOPD officer, triggerman may face death for their roles in 'death squad.'" *Times-Picayune*, April 25, 1996.

— — —. "Jury gets Davis case after hearing tapes." *Times-Picayune*, April 23, 1996.

— — —. "Jury hands Hardy death." *Times-Picayune*, May 2, 1996.

— — —. "Killer officer delivers diatribe." *Times-Picayune*, November 7, 1996.

— — —. "Laughing cop is taped after woman's murder."
*Times-Picayune*, April 18, 1996.

— — —. "Officer had a history of complaints." *Times-Picayune*, December 7, 1994.

— — —. "Prosecutors: rogue cop ordered complainer killed."
*Times-Picayune*, April 16, 1996.

— — —. "U.S. to seek death penalty against rogue cop in killing." *Times-Picayune*, June 17, 1995.

— — —. "Witness: I drove getaway car after hit." *Times-Picayune*, April 17, 1996.

— — —. "Wrong man, Davis defense says of killing." *Times-
Picayune*, April 20, 1996.

Philbin, Walt. "Cop, teen indicted in slaying." *Times-Picayune*,
April 28, 1995.

Philbin, Walt, Lynne Jensen, and Mark Schleifstein. "But scheme
foiled by lone witness." *Times-Picayune*, March 6, 1995.

Ponzani, Michael. "Officer Jekyll — Mr. Hyde." *Detective Cases*,
February 1994.

Pristin, Terry. "Murder-suicide by trooper." *New York Times*, July
9, 1996.

Pult, Glenn. "Brady's background targeted." *Las Vegas Review-
Journal*, May 15, 1997.

— — —. "Mortensen at Brady traffic stop." *Las Vegas Review-
Journal*, May 16, 1997.

Pult, Glenn, and Joe Schoenmann. "LV police find relief with jury's
decision." *Las Vegas Review-Journal*, May 15, 1997.

Radner, Henry. "If the Handcuffs Fit..." *Detective Files*, March
1994.

Ritchie, Bruce. "Hunt says he remains confident in troopers."
United Press International, October 21, 1987.

Sanchez, Sandra. "Detroit cops in fatal beating fired." *USA Today*,
December 17, 1992.

Sanz, Cynthia, and Joseph Harmes. "A killer in blue." *Time*, October 2, 1995.

Schaaf, Barbara. *Shattered Hopes: A True Story of Marriage, the Mob, and Murder.* New York: Barricade Books, 1993.

Scruggs, Kathy. "Deals made 'with devils' in cop trial, defense says." *Atlanta Journal and Constitution*, June 24, 1993.

— — —. "Judge rips prosecutors in theft ring; robbery charges against 2 officers, civilian dropped." *Atlanta Journal and Constitution*, March 31, 1993.

— — —. "Officer: netted $30 in burglary ring." *Atlanta Journal and Constitution*, March 30, 1993.

— — —. "The police corruption case — Ex-officer described alleged ring's blunders." *Atlanta Journal and Constitution*, June 9, 1993.

— — —. "The police corruption case — Witness: needed $10,000." *Atlanta Journal and Constitution*, June 8, 1993.

— — —. "The police corruption trial — 'I [shot] him 9 times,' ex-officer says." *Atlanta Journal and Constitution*, June 18, 1993.

— — —. "The police corruption trial — Verdicts bolster other charges." *Atlanta Journal and Constitution*, June 29, 1993.

Scruggs, Kathy, and Scott Marshall. "Cop's sister says he confessed to killing." *Atlanta Journal and Constitution*, May 21, 1992.

Scruggs, Kathy, and Rick Minter. "Killing tied to suspected cop crime ring." *Atlanta Journal and Constitution*, March 12, 1993.

Shaffer, Mark. "Insanity, drugs at issue in Yuma trial." *Arizona Republic*, November 19, 1996.

— — —. "Insanity OK'd as defense in Yuma trial." *Arizona Republic*, November 19, 1996.

— — —. "Jury must find out 'why' in deaths." *Arizona Republic*, January 11, 1997.

— — —. "Murder defense hinges on 'involuntary' addiction." *Arizona Republic*, January 10, 1997.

— — —. "Undercover agent guilty of killings." *Arizona Republic*, January 14, 1997.

Sharkey, Joe. *Above Suspicion*. New York: Simon & Schuster, 1993.

Shecter, Leonard, and William Phillips. *On the Pad: The Underworld and Its Corrupt Police, Confessions of a Cop on the Take*. New York: G.P. Putnam's Sons, 1973.

Smead, Howard. *Blood Justice: The Lynching of Mack Charles Parker*. New York: Oxford University Press, 1986.

Smith, John L. "Former state trooper may have seen his last day in court." *Las Vegas Review-Journal,* May 15, 1996.

Sowers, Carol. "Deputy held in killing of 2 lawmen." *Arizona Republic*, July 6, 1995.

— — —. "Officers' last, desperate minutes: 'Please don't shoot me again.'" *Arizona Republic*, July 7, 1995.

Sowers, Carol, and Judy Villa. "Apparent killer of 2 stood tall in Marines." *Arizona Republic*, July 13, 1995.

Swindle, Howard. *Deliberate Indifference: A Story of Racial Injustice and Murder*. New York: Penguin Books, 1993.

Timnick, Lois. "Sergeant as suspect; police officer investigated in wife's slaying tells his side." *Los Angeles Times*, February 28, 1993.

Tracy, Paula. "Anderson: Killed wife. Anderson details murder in letter to daughter." *Union Leader*, January 17, 1996.

— — —. "Anderson pre-trial hearing focuses on body search." *Union Leader*, July 25, 1995.

— — —. "Defense challenges lack of warrant in Haverhill murder." *Union Leader*, July 19, 1995.

Trelease, Allen W. *White Terror*. New York: Harper & Row, 1971.

Varney, James. "Accused killer's outburst draws gag threat from judge; Frank demands a new attorney." *Times-Picayune*, September 6, 1995.

— — —. "Cop pleads innocent in triple murder." *Times-Picayune*, May 4, 1995.

— — —. "Ex-cop gets new attorney in murder trial." *Times-Picayune,* December 14, 1995.

— — —. "Ex-cop gets death in triple murder." *Times-Picayune*, October 21, 1995.

— — —. "Ex-officer admits shooting in tape played during trial." *Times-Picayune*, September 8, 1995.

— — —. "Families' pain fresh year after slayings; cop-turned-killer begins appeals." *Times-Picayune*, March 4, 1996.

— — —. "Frank's lawyers offer no defense; state's rebuttal won't be heard." *Times-Picayune*, September 10, 1995.

— — —. "Jurors doom Frank to death; deliberation took 45 minutes." *Times-Picayune*, September 13, 1995.

— — —. "Jury's decision: death for Lacaze." *Times-Picayune*, July 22, 1995.

— — —. "Killer shows no remorse." *Times-Picayune*, September 15, 1995.

— — —. "Lacaze guilty of killing; death sentence possible today." *Times-Picayune*, July 21, 1995.

— — —. "Police murder trial begins; lawyer cited for contempt." *Times-Picayune*, July 18, 1995.

Varney, James, and Christopher Cooper. "Lacaze execution set; judge rebukes Frank." *Times-Picayune*, September 16, 1995.

Varon, Joseph A. *A Matter of Judgment*. Hollywood, FL: Lifetime Books, 1994.

Villa, Judi. "Final '911': 'He's firing rounds! Hurry!'" *Arizona Republic*, July 15, 1995.

— — —. "Slain officers mourned." *Arizona Republic*, July 12, 1995.

Voelker, Bill. "Accomplice gets life in cop's murder plot." *Times-Picayune*, November 28, 1996.

— — —. "City drops family from countersuit; but restaurant still
defendant in slaying case." *Times-Picayune*, February 17, 1997.

— — —. "Claim against Vus is rejected; N.O. lawsuit out on technicality." *Times-Picayune*, February 19, 1997.

— — —. "Cop, 2 others plead innocent in killing." *Times-Picayune*, December 21, 1994.

— — —. "Ex-officer gets life for role in coke ring." *Times-Picayune*, December 19, 1996.

— — —. "Former police get jail in sting." *Times-Picayune*, October 10, 1996.

— — —. "Indictment: officer wanted to kill again." *Times-Picayune*, March 25, 1995.

— — —. "N.O. man indicted as accessory to murder." *Times-Picayune*, January 7, 1995.

Volkman, Ernest, and John Cummings. *Till Murder Do Us Part.* New York: Onyx, 1994.

Walsh, Jim. "Officer fell to drugs he fought, pals fear." *Arizona Republic*, July 9, 1995.

Worthington, Rogers. "Detroit tense as 2 police await brutality verdicts." *Chicago Tribune*, August 14, 1993.

— — —. "Police-beating trial puts spotlight on Detroit." *Chicago Tribune*, June 3, 1993.

# YOU WILL ALSO WANT TO READ:

☐ **34050 HUNTING HUMANS, An Encyclopedia of Modern Serial Killers,** *by Michael Newton.* More than 500 detailed case histories of serial killers from the 20th century. This disturbing book describes their lives and their exploits without any varnish or puffery — the chalking details speak for themselves. More than 60% of the killers described here have never been mentioned in a published book before. This huge book is an unforgettable chronicle of the world's most deranged homicidal maniacs. *1990, 8½ x 11, 353 pp, illustrated, hard cover.* $34.95.

☐ **58084 DIRTY TRICKS COPS USE, And Why They Use Them,** *by Bart Rommel.* If you think Rodney King had it rough, you ain't seen nothin; yet! Learn how vigilante cops plant evidence, ignore search and seizure laws, conduct illegal interrogations, torture and even execute people. The law is stacked in favor of the creeps, these cops say, and they're out to even the score. If you want to know how "justice" really works, get this shocking book! *1993, 5½ x 8½, 160 pp, soft cover.* $14.95.

☐ **34070 BAD GIRLS DO IT! An Encyclopedia of Female Murderers,** *by Michael Newton.* From the author of *Hunting Humans* comes the only book on female multiple murderers ever assembled. Over 180 Necrophilic Nurses, Baby Butchers, Black Widows and Angels of Death are chillingly catalogued in this grisly collection. Each blood-thirsty babe is described in detail, including childhood experiences, early crimes, how they killed and how they were caught. Based on ten years of research, *Bad Girls Do It!* proves that the urge to kill is an equal opportunity affliction. *1993, 8½ x 11, 205 pp, soft cover.* $16.95.

*Check out our Catalog ad on the next page.*

---

**Loompanics Unlimited**
**PO Box 1197**
**Port Townsend, WA 98368**

**KC7**

Please send me the books I have checked above. I have enclosed $_____ which includes $4.95 for shipping and handling of the first $20.00 ordered. Add an additional $1 shipping for each additional $20 ordered. Washington residents include 7.9% sales tax.

Name _____

Address _____

City/State/Zip _____

**VISA and MasterCard accepted. 1-800-380-2230 for credit card orders *only.***
**8am to 4pm, PST, Monday through Friday.**